THE MAKING OF
Major League

FADE IN:

TITLES APPEAR ON BLACK BACKGROUND

Titles END and we WIDEN to reveal that the black background is
actually the sludge-clogged surface of the Cuyahoga River. We
TILT UP from the river to reveal the city of CLEVELAND.

1   INT. THE INJUN DINER - DAY   1

Three men in Cleveland Indian baseball caps sit at the counter.
BOBBY JAMES, 22 year-old grad student, VIC BOLITO, 30 year-old
telephone worker, and JOHNNY WYNN, 45 year-old house painter.
THELMA GORDON, 65 year-old waitress, delivers their sandwiches.

                    THELMA
          Spring training starts the 12th.
          How do you think the Indians will
          do this year?

                    VIC
          They don't look too good.

The other two shake their heads in contemplation of this sorry
fact.

2   INT. MEN'S CLUB - DAY   2

A 45 year-old BUSINESS EXECUTIVE is talking to a fellow club
member over lunch.

                    BUSINESS EXECUTIVE
          They don't look particularly good,
          do they?

3   EXT. CLEVELAND DOCKS - DAY   3

Two LONGSHOREMEN are talking while they unload a freighter.

                    LONGSHOREMAN
          I'll tell ya. They don't look very
          fuckin' good.

4   EXT. CLEVELAND MUNICIPAL STADIUM - DAY   4

Down on the field, two KOREAN GROUNDSKEEPERS speak Korean as they
resod the outfield.

                    GROUNDSKEEPER
                  (in subtitles)
          They're shitty.

THE MAKING OF
Major League

A *Juuuust a Bit Inside* Look at the Classic Baseball Comedy

Jonathan Knight

GRAY & COMPANY, PUBLISHERS
CLEVELAND

Script and storyboard images courtesy of Morgan Creek Productions.

Gray & Company, Publishers
www.grayco.com

ISBN: 978-1-938441-64-6
Printed in the United States
1

In memory of Lou Brown, who inspired us all to give our critics a nice big shitburger to eat.

Contents

"Life imitates art far more than art imitates life."

—Oscar Wilde

SC. 101B CONT.

CONT. TO   REVEAL VAUGHN
& HIS NEW   GLASSES. HE DROPS
ROZEN BAG...

Foreword

BY CHARLIE SHEEN

Believe it or not, it's kind of hard for me to go to baseball games.

I'm a student of the game, and I love going to the ballpark. But that's been kind of a challenge for me since 1989, when *Major League* came out. Now when I'm at a game, everybody yells "Hey, Wild Thing!" at me as I'm walking to my seat. And if there's a pitcher in there getting lit up, they'll say, "Hey, Wild Thing, get in there!" It's all in fun, but it doesn't work like that. Baseball is the hardest sport to play well every day, and there's nowhere to hide on the baseball field. Or, for me at least, in the ballpark.

So it's difficult to go to a game unless I'm in some kind of box, but then I feel like a separatist. I want to watch the games down closer, but because I won't say "no" to a child, I'll spend the entire game looking down at my hands trying to sign these spherical, slippery baseballs that I've signed ten thousand of by now. Which is fine—you worry about the day they stop coming up to you.

It's a double-edged sword. I so want to be there, but I so don't want to be there.

Thank you, *Major League*.

In all seriousness, it's an honor to have been a part of that movie. I feel like I was part of something historic. Before I got into television, I'd done sixty-plus films, and I'm proud of six of them. And *Major League* is at the top of the list. I'm more proud of *Major League* than I am of *Platoon*, and we won Best Picture for that one.

And it's not just me. When I met Eric Davis, the first thing he said to me was that whenever he was on a road trip, he would watch *Major League* to pass the time. And when I met Joe Morgan, he said the same thing. Then I started to realize, "Oh my God—this is a backstage pass into Major League Baseball!"

Not long after the movie came out, I was in Atlanta and went to see the Reds play the Braves at the Launching Pad. I bought a cheap seat and was sort of wandering around and had "celebrit-ied" my way deep into the tunnels leading to the Reds' clubhouse. I'm kind of peeking through the door, and Tom Browning and Rob Dibble see me and say, "Wild Thing, get your fucking ass in here!" So I knew right then and there, this is as close as I can get without being in a uniform.

This is all because of *Major League*. Really, any baseball story I tell that I'm involved in is because of that movie. I could say, "Oh, it's because of what I did before or what I did after." Screw that. It's because of *Major League*.

David Ward really created a classic, and you can see its impact everywhere. I'm a little mystified by it. I mean, nobody came out of the bullpen to a theme song before that movie. Even today, guys are watching it all the time in big-league clubhouses, guys who weren't even born when it came out. It's nuts. People yelling, "Hey, Wild Thing!" at me when I go to a game is part of it, too. When Tim Robbins goes to a game, I don't think people are yelling, "Hey, Nuke LaLoosh!"

I wish we'd known the impact of what we were doing at the time so we could have savored it more in the moment. But we didn't. We were just having a good time.

Actually, I always saw it more as a legitimate baseball film than a baseball comedy. All the humor came out of how well we got to know these characters. You cared about them so much that when the guy is duct-taping the prop of the plane, you buy it because at that point you're in deep with these guys.

I also didn't see Rick Vaughn as a comedic role. It did have me laughing out loud, but I was in tears at certain points, the first time I read it. It had such poignancy and such heart without being sappy. So I played it straight. Then once I saw how the audience reacted, I felt like I was part of something special.

And I still do.

Preface and Acknowledgments

There was a period of my life when I watched *Major League* every single day.

No joke.

I'd come home from junior high school each afternoon, pop the movie into the VCR, and immerse myself in a delicious alternate reality in which baseball was hilarious and the Cleveland Indians were champions. It was the perfect movie at the perfect time. It enabled me and countless others to experience the ultimate day-dream of what would happen if the Tribe ever got its act together and snapped out of its three-decade slump.

As I watched and re-watched the film and the real-life Indians wallowed in fifth place year after year, *Major League* became more real in my imagination, the cinematic equivalent of talking to a volleyball while stranded on a desert island. In a strange way, I think of that fictional team as a real edition of the Indians, almost expecting to see the characters' names turn up in the franchise's all-time roster.

Weird? Absolutely. But to me, the division title captured at the end of *Major League* means as much as any of the others the real Indians won during their renaissance in the late '90s. Probably more.

Eventually getting to meet and work with the people who created the movie, then telling the story of how it was made, feels like an extension of that dream world. The experience turned out to be even more fulfilling than I had expected. In addition to having great conversations with fascinating people, I got to sift through behind-the-scenes photos, set blueprints, and storyboards dug out of file drawers, closets, and garages. I even got to examine various versions of the script, including the mythical first draft that had been scribbled out and patched together on notebook paper nearly as old as I was. Considering my background with the movie, it was kind of like holding the Declaration of Independence.

Needless to say, I appreciate the entire enterprise, but this book couldn't have happened without the help of a lot of fantastic people.

First, I have to thank writer/director David Ward and producer Chris Chesser, who embraced this project from the outset. Welcoming me into their homes and their lives, they patiently spent countless hours with me as we reconstructed the origin and development of the movie and dug up artifacts that helped bring details into clearer focus. Their enthusiasm and involvement legitimized the project right off the rip, and they helped me connect with a handful of others who provided insights that really made this a story worth telling. Thanks, guys, for making this so much fun and for making such a kick-ass movie in the first place.

At the outset, I never expected to be able to speak with each and every member of the primary cast, but damned if that's not exactly what happened, mostly because each of them shares a sense of genuine appreciation for the movie and still enjoys talking about it. I'm grateful to all of the actors who stepped away from their busy schedules to speak with me: Tom Berenger, Corbin Bernsen, Dennis Haysbert, Chelcie Ross, Rene Russo, Wesley Snipes, Margaret Whitton, and Bob Uecker. I also offer heartfelt thanks to Nancy Gammon for providing memories of her late husband James's experience playing the iconic Lou Brown.

Of course, the book wouldn't have been complete without the reflections of Wild Thing himself, Charlie Sheen, who graciously carved out some time in his Sharknado of a life and then gave me more than I could have hoped for, including a marvelous foreword. To borrow a phrase, you made my heart sing.

Just as helpful as those who appeared on screen were those who gave me insight into what was going on behind the scenes: Lisa Beasley, Julie Bergman-Sender, Bill Rea, Brian Sienko, Suzy Vanderbeek-Rea, and Steve Yeager. R.J. Stewart (who, as a Giants fan, actually enjoyed the '54 Series) helped lift the curtain on *Major League II.* The inspiring Maryhelen Zabas classed up the joint with her contributions, and I have to offer special thanks to the wonderful Julia Miller, who will always be my Wild Thing Girl.

The Cleveland Indians were on board with the book from the beginning, starting with the eternally helpful Bob DiBiasio, who provided invaluable reflections and assistance. Curtis Danburg, Kyle Emery, Jason Kidik, Dan Medlik, and Ryan Pritt all stepped up to the plate and came through with runners in scoring position.

Production company Morgan Creek also dug the idea of the book early on and regularly helped along the way. Co-founder Jim Robinson and his son Brian were gracious in providing their time and insights. And I must offer a special shout-out to Greg Mielcarz, who was incredibly helpful with some of the details, approvals, and general hootenanny that goes into the unglamorous underbelly of a book.

Speaking of which, I must offer my gratitude to David Gray, Rob Lucas, Jane Lassar, and Chris Andrikanich at Gray & Co. for believing in this idea, nurturing it, making it better, and then helping get it across the finish line.

Thanks to the Ferrara Candy Company for being cool about Super Bubble and to Canadian wunderkind Brian Wood for giving it his best shot. Jeff Ballard brought a glass of water to a man dying from thirst, and Steve Golebiowski tried like hell to do the same. John Crosby, Sharon Dwyer, Edmond Guidry, Ron Kellow, Mike Menchel, Deborah Miller, Samantha Rentz, Ken Spindler, and Steven Tabakin all played key roles in connecting me with the people who brought *Major League* to life, while David Huffman educated me about midnight movies and jumbo sandwiches.

Another hearty thank you goes out to a generation of fans who have made this movie a fellowship, defined by repeated lines and homages that have become like a not-so-secret handshake. It's a bond we share to this day that helps us get through the rough seasons and better appreciate the good ones.

I suppose I also need to thank my seventh-grade buddy Scott Finchum for recording *Major League* off TV for me a quarter-century ago—it turned out to be the VHS tape that launched a thousand ships. Although my boys are still a bit too young to enjoy *Major League*, Zachary and Jacob provide enough comedy to make my life as fun as the movie.

Finally, I have to thank my parents for being rock-solid role models and a pair of the finest human beings who've ever walked the face of the earth, but perhaps more important, for saying "pshaw" to the MPAA's rating system just this once and taking their 12-year-old son to see *Major League* on a muggy Saturday night in Beaufort, South Carolina, in the summer of '89. I love you guys.

And now, if you'll excuse me—Jobu needs a refill.

Prologue

Considering what it would ultimately lead to, it was a decidedly undramatic moment. But, as mundane as it was, the salvation of a despondent baseball franchise began with the ringing of an office telephone.

It was a typically cold and colorless winter day in Cleveland, Ohio, the kind that makes you almost physically ache for spring and genuinely wonder if baseball will ever be played again.

Fittingly, within the winding concourses and executive offices of rickety old Cleveland Municipal Stadium, whatever energy existed was fueled by the ballpark's gridiron tenants. The Browns had just completed a marvelous 1987 campaign that saw them reach the playoffs for a third straight year and once again come within a breath of the Super Bowl, making them undoubtedly both the talk of the town and the proverbial apple of Cleveland's eye.

By contrast, their housemates were the troubled siblings their parents rarely talked about. Like spring itself on this bitter winter day, the concept of the Cleveland Indians creating any kind of buzz like the Browns had generated in recent years seemed as remote as the Canadian shore across the frozen blackness of Lake Erie lying just outside the ballpark.

In this environment, Bob DiBiasio sat like a night watchman in an abandoned factory in his small office crammed just inside Gate A. A native of nearby Lakewood, he'd just returned to his hometown as director of public relations of his hometown team after a year in the same role with the Atlanta Braves. Now he was faced with the task of trying to promote a team that had just wrapped up its second 100-loss season in three years. Even without having to compete with their much more attractive orange-and-brown bunkmates, the Indians' task wasn't an easy one. In addition to posting the worst record in baseball in 1987, the Indians had also drawn fewer fans than any other team. Neither disturbing distinction marked the first time it had happened.

In the three-plus decades since the Indians' most recent postseason berth, Cleveland had gradually transformed from a gleaming baseball metropolis into an all-out football town. By the 1980s, the Browns simply owned Cleveland, while the Indians were a not-all-that-entertaining distraction that served little purpose other than to fill in the gap like window caulk between the NFL draft and the start of training camp. And of course, serve as a punch line for the rest of baseball.

IN ADDITION TO POSTING THE WORST RECORD IN BASEBALL IN 1987, THE INDIANS HAD ALSO DRAWN FEWER FANS THAN ANY OTHER TEAM.

DiBiasio, along with all the other marketing, PR, and ticket-sale staffers in the Indians' employ, was nobly fighting a losing battle. So when his phone jingled that winter day, he couldn't have known that the wheels of change were about to be set in motion.

The phone call was from Hank Peters, who asked DiBiasio to come down to his office. Peters, who'd taken over as the Indians' new president the previous November, had already quietly established himself as a front-office magician over the course of an impressive career in Oakland and Baltimore. Now entering his first full season as the head honcho in Cleveland, Peters was carefully laying the groundwork for the renaissance that was to come for the Indians franchise in the following decade. Little did Peters know that sitting on his desk at that moment was an unexpectedly vital piece of the upcoming revolution.

Meeting with the team president wasn't a unique experience for DiBiasio, who'd served as the Indians' PR director for seven years before his sabbatical in Atlanta. But as he made the short walk down the hallway, DiBiasio had no reason to expect that this meeting would be one of the turning points in the franchise's long history, nor that it would be the first step toward changing the public's perception of the franchise.

He stepped into Peters's office. Sitting behind the desk, Peters looked up to acknowledge him, then pointed casually to a thick stack of paper sitting on the desk between them.

"For some reason," Peters began, "our friends at Major League Baseball have agreed to allow a movie to be made with the Cleveland Indians as the subject."

It took DiBiasio a moment to process what he'd just heard.

The Indians?

These Indians?

His Indians?

In a movie?

The team, which had now gone 28 consecutive years without even sniffing a postseason appearance, and which was barely a topic of conversation in its own hometown, was suddenly being courted by Hollywood. Somebody out there, somebody who'd actually won an Oscar, DiBiasio would later learn, wanted to acknowledge the Cleveland Indians on film.

But just as DiBiasio began to wrap his head around the idea, what Peters said next nearly knocked him over.

"It's all yours. Have fun."

Peters instructed DiBiasio to review the script and mark anything in it that he found objectionable to ensure that "we keep the organization in the best light possible"—a truly challenging prospect under any conditions.

DiBiasio, stunned but still professional, stammered a reply. "Well, thank you, sir," he said. "I've never done this before." Neither had anyone else in the Indians organization. Other than the intensely forgettable *The Kid From Cleveland*, a 1949 morality tale about a troubled teenager "adopted" by real-life Cleveland players who cameoed as themselves, the team had never been featured in a major motion picture. There was no mystery why.

DiBiasio scooped up the stack of papers and hurried back to his office like a kid racing down the stairs on Christmas morning. He sat down and immediately whipped through the script. In a half hour, he'd finished it, and couldn't help but smile.

As he rearranged the pages into a neat stack, he again looked at the cover sheet, which had the title of this proposed cinematic enterprise centered neatly at the heart of the page:

Major League.

And beneath that, the name of the brave soul who was not only willing to use the Indians as the subject for a major motion picture, but was putting his career on the line to do it: David S. Ward.

1

Cracking the Show

As the clock ticked toward midnight on a cool spring Saturday night in 2013—just over 25 years since the day Bob DiBiasio first read the *Major League* script—the scene inside the Capitol Theatre on the near west side of Cleveland was a bit bizarre. Scurrying between the seats and carrying boxes of popcorn and snacks were similarly dressed patrons, each as excited as if it were Christmas Eve. They wore makeshift jerseys with names on the back that were neither their own nor those of actual big-league ballplayers, and their bellies were still full after devouring the special "It's Way Too High" melt offered by a neighboring restaurant for the occasion.

When the clock hands joined together, the theater darkened, and as the opening piano chords of Randy Newman's ballad "Burn On" tinkled through the speakers against a montage of downtown Cleveland, the crowd applauded and hooted, even though they'd seen these images dozens of times before.

Major League had reached a level (and time slot) of cult esteem reserved for such classics as *The Rocky Horror Picture Show* and was being played for an enthusiastic midnight audience, many of whom dressed up as their favorite characters, nearly a quarter-century after the film's release.

Not all movies graduate to Saturday-midnight-showing status. Even box-office blockbusters and critical darlings don't generally know the password into this proverbial cinematic speakeasy. It takes a true cult classic, the type of movie that nurtures a passionately dedicated base and subculture of fans who know each scene and each word by heart. *Major League* has become one.

Although not everyone is quite zealous enough to stay up until the witching hour for a viewing, many thousands of fans return to the film repeatedly and regularly. Maryhelen Zabas—previously known as Sister Mary Assumpta, and an iconic Indians fan who cameoed in the film—estimates she watches *Major League* at least once every three months. Like the prayers she committed to memory in her half-century in the church, she can recite every line of the film without hesitation. "Any time I need a good laugh," she says, "I watch it."

> **"OF ALL THE MOVIES I'VE DONE, THAT'S THE ONE MORE PEOPLE COME UP TO ME TO TALK ABOUT."**

She's certainly not alone in her repetitious viewing or rote memorization. In Key West filming a movie with Goldie Hawn, actor James Gammon (who portrayed Tribe manager Lou Brown on screen) was stunned when Hawn's 12-year-old daughter, future actress Kate Hudson, came up to him and began reciting his lines from *Major League*. "It happened continually," his wife Nancy says. "He'd be in the bank or the grocery store and people would come up to him. They'd know all of his lines." Other members of the cast have experienced the same phenomenon.

"Out of all the movies I've ever done," says Rene Russo, who catapulted from *Major League* into a fantastic Hollywood career, "that's the one that more people come up to me to talk about. It really is a cult classic. Not even cult, really. Everybody just *loves* that film."

The movie has become part of baseball's life cycle. As the snow begins to melt in late March (and, all too often, then begins to fall again), fans gather in rec rooms and basements and replay the movie in a cherished ritual that indicates a new baseball season is about to begin.

Like peanuts and Cracker Jacks, *Major League* has become intertwined with the fabric of baseball. With self-deprecation, strong comedic writing, classic performances, and repeated viewing, the film gradually entered the lexicon of the game. By the early 1990s, sportscasters, particularly ESPN's cadre of vivacious on-air desk jockeys, were borrowing terminology provided by Bob Uecker in *Major League* to describe actual game highlights, and the trend began to spread.

When you attend a major-league game anywhere in the country, you're bound to encounter *Major League* references and influences, even if they're so accepted you don't recognize them.

"Fans bring it into real life," explains Bob DiBiasio, who today is the Indians' vice president of sales and marketing. "It's the way they remember certain scenes and certain phrases from the movie. You'll be sitting at the ballpark and there'll be an outside pitch, and somebody sitting nearby will make the Uecker call: 'Juuuust a bit outside.' Somebody hits a long home run and you see guys in the bleachers saying, 'It's too high, it's too high.' It's morphed into people doing their own play-by-play. And there's such an age range—you've got people in their 50s doing it and kids doing it. You can't go through a game without hearing that kind of stuff. I feel like it's a part of us."

The film has spawned a cottage industry. Sprinkled among the inventory of the sidewalk concessioners outside Progressive Field on game day, you'll find dozens of different *Major League*-themed t-shirts and apparel. Once inside the ballpark, you'll see a handful of fans wearing replica jerseys mimicking the one worn by Charlie Sheen in his portrayal of "Wild Thing" Rick Vaughn, who became the most recognized character of the film.

"When you think about other baseball movies, is there any equivalent to somebody wearing a Vaughn jersey?" DiBiasio asks. "I don't think so."

While Vaughn's is the most commonly spotted, it's certainly not the only *Major League* jersey you'll see. There are jerseys for Pedro Cerrano, Willie Mays Hayes, and Jake Taylor. You'll even spot a few Roger Dorn jerseys floating around big-league ballparks if you pay attention.

Major League is both baseball's version of *Star Trek* and Cleveland's version of *The Wizard of Oz*. At its heart, it represents the hybrid of frustration, eternal optimism, and good humor that has defined baseball and its fans for more than a century.

A scene early in the movie encapsulates both the origin and the intention of the film. Dinged-up veteran catcher Jake Taylor has just received one last chance to resurrect his big-league career and, in street clothes, he strolls out to home plate in an empty Cleveland Stadium. Standing alone, soaking in his surroundings, he intones the voice of an imaginary announcer.

"Two down, bottom of the ninth, game is tied . . . "

He raises his arm and points to the center-field fence.

"Taylor calls his shot," he says casually, as if this were something he did each time he stepped into the batter's box. "There's the pitch . . ."

He swings his imaginary bat at the imaginary ball, and we hear the satisfying crack of solid contact mingled with the ghostly roar of imaginary fans watching the ball follow Taylor's projected path over the outfield wall.

He jogs triumphantly around the bases, pumping his fist. (He looks not unlike gimpy Kirk Gibson pumping his fist after his dramatic game-winning home run for the Dodgers in the 1988 World Series. Though of course on the day of this scene's filming, Gibson's celebration was two months in the *future*.) Taylor is offered congratulations by an invisible third-base coach and then is greeted by his jubilant, nonexistent teammates at home plate.

The exercise is as ordinary and understood as baseball itself, reflecting the dreams of youngsters who hope to one day make it reality as well as the nostalgic musings of adults on their unfulfilled—perhaps unrealistic—goals.

Although the scene sets up an ironic climax to the film, there's otherwise not much remarkable about it. It's overshadowed by funnier, more dynamic scenes that surround it. But in essence, the scene represents how and why this movie was made. Instead of acting out a baseball fantasy with an imaginary bat and ball, David Ward did it with a pencil and a pad of paper.

* * *

When you come right down to it, it was all the fault of Willie Mays.

The seed for one of the most memorable, most beloved sports movies ever made—and a piece of baseball cinema that wound up altering the game itself—was planted when Willie Mays made the most amazing play of his career and provided the game of baseball with one of its most iconic moments.

The 1954 World Series was supposed to be a coronation. The Cleveland Indians had spent the summer accomplishing two seemingly impossible feats: winning a record 111 games in a 154-game schedule and, perhaps more impressively, ending the New York Yankees' five-year dynasty as world champions. The Fall Classic, which began in the Polo Grounds against the outrageously overmatched New York Giants on a balmy late September afternoon, was essentially the anticlimax to a magnificent season.

Indeed, when Cleveland first baseman Vic Wertz launched a Don Little pitch into the dark recesses of the Polo Grounds' vast center field with the game tied and two on in the top of the eighth inning, it appeared the Indians had just secured a Game One victory. But anyone who knows baseball history knows what happened next. Mays, who was just beginning to show everyone how special he was, turned his back on the ball, sprinted to a part of the outfield seldom used in the course of a game, made an over-the-shoulder catch 460 feet from home plate for the out, then spun and whipped the ball back into the infield to thwart a rally.

Eight-year-old David Ward, his eyes glued to a minuscule black-and-white television screen back in Cleveland Heights, couldn't believe it. Even at his age, he knew this was a play that shouldn't—maybe even *couldn't*—have been made. Instead of winning the game as they'd done so many times this golden season, his Indians went on to lose, two innings later, on a chip-shot homer that traveled barely half as far as Vic Wertz's flyout.

Crazy as it sounds today, at the time, championships were not completely unexpected by Cleveland fans. The Indians had won a world title in 1948 and the Browns had captured three NFL championships in their first six years in the league.

This was the Cleveland that David Ward called home. Technically, he wasn't a native, having been born in Providence, Rhode Island, in the fall of 1945. But by Christmas of that year, his father, an airplane mechanic during the war, had moved the family to Cleveland to sell piston rings for TRW. In this town, in this era, it didn't take much to become a sports fan. Even at a young age, Ward could tell from his slender frame that he wasn't a natural football player, so he gravitated to baseball, and with his dad regularly able to score Indians tickets, Ward quickly adopted the Tribe as his own.

In turn, cavernous Cleveland Stadium became almost magical to him. Each time he neared the stadium and saw the giant metallic sign with grinning Chief Wahoo posted atop the outer wall, Ward's pulse would quicken.

"That was one of the first things you'd see walking to the turnstiles from the parking lot," he remembers. "God, that was great. I felt I was going to a sacred place where only the initiates were allowed. Like you'd actually gone to someplace that exists on a higher plane of reality. I'd just stand there with my mouth open and look at all of it, thinking, *This is where the gods play*."

The Indians' dominance in 1954 came as no surprise to the young Ward as his mania for the team hit its peak. He felt he was simply witnessing the natural progression of greatness. Surely this would be the first in a long line of Indians championship seasons he would experience.

Then Willie Mays dropped an anvil on Cleveland's head.

"I just couldn't comprehend it," Ward says. "As a kid you sort of looked to the adults around you to see how they process this. None of the adults I looked to knew how to process it, either."

Things only got worse. The Giants won another close game the following afternoon to put the Indians in a two-game hole. Nervousness began to spread around Cleveland like a low-grade fever. "I could just see it in my dad," Ward recalls. "I could see that creeping dread . . . the Cleveland disease." Rocked on their heels, the Indians faithful watched in horror as the Giants wrapped things up in Cleveland over the weekend, pummeling the Tribe in the next two games to complete a stunning four-game sweep.

Ward was still three weeks away from his ninth birthday, but he'd just received his first harsh lesson of adulthood: Things don't always turn out the way you want.

"I COULD JUST SEE IT IN MY DAD. I COULD SEE THAT CREEPING DREAD . . . THE CLEVELAND DISEASE."

"After that, it felt as if the baseball gods didn't want the Indians to win," he says. "When a guy hits arguably the longest ball in the history of the World Series and it's an out, that's when you know that being an Indians fan is a real mixed bag. It's been an uphill struggle ever since."

Although Ward would continue to follow the Indians on what turned out to be their long descent into oblivion, he did so from outside Cleveland. Just over a year after the World Series sweep, Ward's father moved the family again, this time to Kirkwood, Missouri, outside St. Louis. Ward adopted the Cardinals as his preferred National League team and envisioned the Cards and his beloved Tribe squaring off in an epic World Series.

And it was that kind of imagination that eventually paved the way toward David Ward's career.

•   •   •

He was supposed to be a doctor.

Like most parents of that generation, Ward's father saw a medical degree as the apex of the American dream, and always pressured his son to get grades good enough to get him into college and get him started on a solid career. After moving from

Cleveland to St. Louis, the Ward family then moved to northern California, and finally to Fullerton, just outside Los Angeles, where Ward graduated from Sunny Hills High School.

His grades were indeed good enough, and he enrolled at Pomona College in Claremont, California, then and now one of the finest liberal arts colleges in the nation. It didn't take Ward long to realize that he couldn't follow the path his father had planned for him. "I hit organic chemistry," he says, "and realized I wasn't going to make it through to being a doctor. It just wasn't for me."

He bounced among five different majors over the next three years, finally settling on government because it was the one for which he was closest to completing the credits he needed for graduation. He felt no real passion for the subject, though. So, in his senior year, when he was assigned to write an essay for a political theory class comparing Thomas Hobbes and Jean-Jacques Rousseau, he desperately tried to find a way to stave off the crippling boredom the assignment entailed. In an episode of slightly geeky 1960s counterculture rebellion, he wrote an essay comparing Rousseau to musician Bob Dylan and turned it in.

After class a few days later, his professor called him into his office. Ward cringed, thinking he was about to be berated and lectured for his lack of respect for the professor and his course. And that's how it started out. "First of all," the professor began, "your political theory is crap." Then the conversation—and David Ward's life—made a hairpin turn. "But," the professor continued, "your writing is really interesting. I was fascinated reading this essay. I don't get many like this. Have you ever thought of writing?"

In retrospect, he realized that the professor might have just been trying to get an uninspired student out of his class. Writing hadn't interested Ward before. He had been equally bored by an American literature course he'd taken.

"I'd never done any writing," he says. "I didn't go around making up stories or anything like that, and I was probably the least well-read person on the campus."

But the more he thought about it, he realized that even as a kid back in Cleveland, he'd always loved movies. From the day he came out of a theater swinging an imaginary sword after watching *Prince Valiant*, he had spent the rest of his childhood begging his dad to take him to the movies. And as it happened, the college class he remembered most fondly was a theater course he'd taken the previous year. Not long after, this convergence of realizations inspired Ward to gather some friends—one of whom was a photographer—and whip up an eight-minute movie just for the hell of it.

"It was the most fun thing I had done in college," Ward says.

With graduation on the horizon, he contemplated the craziest notion of his life: maybe he should go to film school. He applied to the University of Southern California's prestigious film school, in the middle of a golden era in which it produced George Lucas, Robert Zemeckis, John Carpenter, and Ron Howard. With nothing to show the school but his eight-minute lark of a film, an existential vignette about a guy meeting a girl in an airport, Ward applied anyway and was accepted.

His decision to attend film school wasn't well-received by his father, who told him if he wanted to take a misstep on his life's journey, he'd have to pay for it himself. Juggling classes between jobs as a security guard and an assistant editor at an educational film company where he'd put together dental films shot entirely inside people's mouths, Ward managed to make it through a year at USC before realizing he couldn't afford to continue. With USC out of scholarships, he went across town and enrolled at UCLA's film school, where tuition was about one-tenth that of USC's.

In his second year at UCLA, Ward started kicking around ideas for his thesis, which for most students meant making a longer film. Ward began writing a script, but it took on a life of its own, quickly exceeding the boundaries of what he could produce. Instead of making a movie, he decided his thesis would be a screenplay for a feature-length film. Over an eight-month period, Ward worked on his script—a screwball, counterculture comedy about a group of misfits trying to repair an airplane to fly to a deserted island in order to live life as they wanted, away from the pressures and pitfalls of modern society. He titled it *Steelyard Blues*.

After scribbling the words by hand on legal pads—a method that would continue throughout his career—Ward needed to package them into a clean, readable format. He took his tattered pages across the street from UCLA to the Venice Skill Center, where he made a deal to have the stenography students type them. He became friends with the man who ran the place, who eventually provided a cleanly typed screenplay. Ward thought it was good enough to shop around Hollywood, even though it was the first effort of a complete unknown. He got nowhere fast. But then, foreshadowing the type of witty, intelligent stories he would later tell over the course of his career, Ward got his first big break by accident. Or more specifically, *because* of an accident.

Out of the blue one day, his new buddy from the Venice Skill Center stopped by Ward's apartment with interesting news.

"Y'know what? Strange thing," he began. "You've been looking for an agent, right?"

Ward admitted he had and leaned forward with interest.

"My wife just had a fender bender with an agent a couple of weeks ago. He's a really nice guy. We settled it and actually had dinner the other night. Could I give him your script?"

And with that began a mesmerizing whirlwind that turned an unknown film-school student into an Oscar winner in fewer than 36 months.

The agent was Stu Miller, who loved *Steelyard Blues* and sent it to Tony Bill, a successful actor who'd just begun working as a producer. Bill also was enamored of Ward's script and shared it with his new partners, Michael and Julia Phillips, who were on the brink of becoming the dynamic duo of Hollywood producers. Then the ball really started rolling. They sent the script to actor Donald Sutherland, fresh from his breakthrough roles in the film version of *M*A*S*H* and *Kelly's Heroes*. Sutherland was eager to star in it. Jane Fonda, who was in a relationship with Sutherland at the time and was the up-and-coming star of *Barefoot in the Park* and *Klute*, in which she'd starred with Sutherland, also agreed to do it. Warner Brothers stepped in to finance the project, and in the proverbial blink of an eye, *Steelyard Blues* had gone from a stenography assignment to a major Hollywood production.

And just like that, David Ward had cracked the show.

But it didn't take long for reality to nibble at the edges of fantasy. The studio balked at Ward's casting suggestions, and the director seemed in over his head. Fonda refused to play certain parts of the script. Ward frantically rewrote scenes on the fly, but she still wouldn't cooperate, and her character—and the story—began to change dramatically.

Although this was his first time at the circus, Ward recognized the situation for what it was and quickly decided he had had enough, eventually walking away from the movie. Naturally, when it was released in January of 1973, he was disappointed by the final product. But there was a silver lining to *Steelyard Blues*'s dark cloud.

"It didn't hurt me that much because nobody saw it," Ward admits. "That's the only break we caught. If a film really bombed badly, especially back then, it didn't hurt you that much because nobody saw it and nobody even associated you with it. If a movie bombed, it just disappeared."

Steelyard Blues had come and gone in a puff of smoke. With it, Ward assumed, went his chances of succeeding in Hollywood. "I just thought I'd set a new world record for the shortest movie career in history," he says.

As it turned out, though, the opposite was true. David Ward, just turned 27, would soon be off to the races—both figuratively and literally.

•   •   •

You could say that David Ward pickpocketed an Academy Award.

Not that there was any thievery or chicanery involved; rather, Ward took a simple concept and turned it into a beloved legend. And nobody knew he was doing it.

Although *Steelyard Blues* certainly never received Oscar consideration, it inspired an idea that did. The script included a pickpocket scene, and, knowing nothing about how the practice worked, Ward began researching it. He learned about grifters and a shadowy subculture of street crime in which grifters were at the bottom of the food chain and confidence men were at the top. He was fascinated by their means, motives, and relative morality, particularly the way con men generally didn't use violence or technically steal anything, but leveraged people's greed to manipulate them into handing over their money. He thought it would make a great movie.

Ward conceived a tale of an elaborate ragtime plot cooked up by a young grifter who teams with an experienced con man to outsmart a powerful criminal with a fake racetrack gambling operation. When *Steelyard Blues* was purchased, Tony Bill asked Ward if he was working on anything else. Ward described his new idea, and Bill was fascinated. "Tell you what," he said. "Why don't you put together a little story and record it on a tape recorder and I'll take it up to Redford?"

"WHY DON'T YOU PUT TOGETHER A LITTLE STORY AND RECORD IT ON A TAPE RECORDER AND I'LL TAKE IT UP TO REDFORD?"

"Redford," of course, was 35-year-old Robert Redford, who'd just exploded into prominence with back-to-back hits *Barefoot in the Park* (with Ward's favorite leading lady, Jane Fonda) and *Butch Cassidy and the Sundance Kid*. Bill had already established a relationship with Redford, so when he played the cassette of Ward explaining the story, Redford loved the idea and asked that when the script was done, they bring it to him first. Ward completed the script in late 1972, Bill took it to Redford, and the rest is history.

"That film came together in about two weeks," Ward remembers. "It's never, ever happened like that since."

"That film" was *The Sting*, and once Redford was on board, things got real in a hurry. George Roy Hill signed on to direct and recruited matinee idol Paul Newman and venerable character actor Robert Shaw to star alongside Redford.

When it was released on Christmas Day 1973, it became a classic almost instantly. *The Sting* won seven Academy Awards, including Best Picture and Best Director, and, when Neil Simon opened the envelope for the winner for Best Original Screenplay, it was David Ward's name he announced. Ward floated onstage at the Dorothy Chandler Pavilion unable to quite believe what had happened.

"I didn't really understand it until I was backstage," he remembers. "Photographers were taking pictures, and there were all these famous people. Then it started to hit me that this was a pretty big deal."

The kid who'd never wanted to be a writer had reached the peak of his profession at the tender age of 28. He now had the financial and creative freedom to carefully select the scripts he wanted to write and take his time in developing them.

Yet as rewarding and thrilling as winning the Oscar was, it also became something of a burden. For the next several years, Ward felt that in order to meet expectations he had to deliver a script for another *big* movie. Eventually, though, the pressure eased. He turned his focus toward finding a smaller film—this time to both write and direct.

He scripted an adaptation of John Steinbeck's novel *Cannery Row*, a book he'd always loved, but this one didn't come together quickly, ultimately taking four years to make it to the screen. Along the way, the script landed on the desk of a young executive at brand-new Orion Pictures, Chris Chesser.

"I loved that script," Chesser says. "And that's how I met David." Although Chesser and Ward wouldn't work together on *Cannery Row*, the relationship they established would ultimately pay off.

Just prior to its release in February 1982, *Cannery Row* earned incredibly high preview-audience scores, and it appeared Ward had created another critical and commercial success. But on opening night, Ward walked into the cavernous Village Theater in

Westwood and counted 20 people in the seats. It was a depress-ing moment that ranked with the '54 Series and forecasted what was about to happen. *Cannery Row* made just $5 million—barely enough to crack the top 100 moneymaking films of the year and a figure that certainly wasn't going to encourage studios to hire Ward as a director. For him to keep up his promising career path, he needed to be very careful about selecting his next project.

"I'd had a big hit as a writer, but as a director I'd only done one movie, and it was a flop," he says. "I might get a second chance, but I wasn't going to get a third chance. The next movie I did had to work. So I started thinking about what kind of movie I'd like to do."

The concept came to him surprisingly quickly when he figured out a way to fuse two of his passions—storytelling and baseball—and use them to connect his future to his past.

Fresh from adapting John Steinbeck, David Ward decided to adapt the Cleveland Indians.

2

Fantasy Baseball

As far back as David and Goliath, something in the human psyche has naturally drawn us to underdog stories. No matter your status in life or how successful you might be, you can almost always see a part of yourself in the long-shot character who defies the odds. And even if you don't, you have an almost biological imperative to root for him.

Yet through the gritty 1970s and materialistic 1980s, Hollywood had largely foregone the simple magnetism of the underdog story for more realistic tales that better reflected the times. For every Rocky, there was a Dirty Harry, a Mad Max, and a Gordon Gecko. But, when a well-crafted underdog film emerged, it tended to find a devoted, if small, following.

Seeking a direction for the project that would make or break his directorial career, David Ward seized on the tried-and-true—and generally abandoned—concept of the underdog tale. And it didn't take long for him to choose the subject, for there was no greater underdog in the world than his beloved Cleveland Indians.

"The whole movie was born from David Ward growing up in Cleveland and wanting his Indians to make it to the playoffs," Corbin Bernsen observes. "That's all that movie is, which is great—it's nothing else. It's from a guy who grew up and said, 'If you can't get there, *I'm* going to get you there.' It's such a simple thing. It's so human. A little boy's desire to see his team win."

For almost three decades, while the little boy who had watched his baseball team win 111 games in 1954 had been growing up and then rising to prominence in Hollywood, his Indians had been plummeting into irrelevance. By the 1980s, they weren't simply a bad baseball team; they were a fire-and-brimstone object lesson straight out of the Old Testament. Yet, as bad as they were for as long as they were, the Indians were still loved. Not always with pride, not always with open arms, and not always by large crowds, but they were still undeniably part of Cleveland's social fabric.

Consider this back-and-forth dialogue—eventually cut from the script Ward was to write—between two die-hard Tribe fans who sit faithfully in the bleachers throughout the film (and, presumably, their entire lives):

> JOHNNY
> You read the *Plain Dealer* today? They said this is gonna be the worst Indians team we've had in years.

> THELMA
> Everybody laughs at the Indians now, but there were other times. Even won the Series in '48. Then Willie Mays made that catch on Vic Wertz in the '54 Series and Cleveland's never been the same since.

> JOHNNY
> As the Indians go, so goes Cleveland, huh?

> THELMA
> If we ever lost the Indians, Cleveland would die.

Actually, they came darn close.

When Ward began to mull over his movie idea, 1954 seemed like ancient Mesopotamia. The Indians hadn't made it to the postseason in nearly four decades. Sure, the Chicago Cubs had gone longer without making it to the World Series, but at least the Cubs were lovable losers. The Indians were just losers.

Win or lose (mostly lose), the Indians did it primarily in front of empty seats. Playing in baseball's largest ballpark only made it more conspicuous. Four times in a five-year period, between 1983 and 1987, the Indians drew the worst attendance in all of baseball, including three straight years in which their home attendance totaled less than 800,000—the threshold that would serve as a plot point in Ward's script. In fact, by the end of the 1980s, the Indians had failed to draw 800,000 for a season 16 times since their last trip to the World Series.

WARD DECIDED TO TAKE MATTERS INTO HIS OWN HANDS. SINCE THEY COULDN'T DO IT THEMSELVES, HE WOULD TURN THE INDIANS INTO WINNERS.

So the idea of the Indians being moved out of Cleveland wasn't just the figment of a screenwriter's active imagination. It had very nearly happened twice before. First in 1958, when they considered picking up stakes for Minneapolis. Then in a few frenzied weeks in autumn six years later, when they entertained the notion of moving to Seattle, then to Oakland, then to Dallas. The threats whipped up just enough public support, financial commitments, and ballpark improvements to keep the Indians in Cleveland, but the team remained insignificant both in the standings and at the ticket gate. The Indians were stuck in a massive sump of a ballpark, and the fans were stuck with a perennially lousy baseball experience in every conceivable way. It was a cash-poor franchise perpetually defined by disinterested owners, incompetent front offices, and at times comical on-field talent.

Put it all together and it was impossible not to quickly arrive at a conclusion as cold and hard as a Cleveland winter: The Indians were the most pathetic team in professional sports. By the 1980s, there was a better chance of seeing a man land on Neptune than seeing the Tribe in the World Series.

So Ward decided to take matters into his own hands. Since they couldn't do it themselves, he would turn the Indians into winners the same way he'd turned the glamorous Robert Redford into a grifter and the venerable Paul Newman into a down-and-out con man: through the magic of Hollywood.

• • •

The original idea was simple enough: What if the Cleveland Indians were in their usual dire straits and an owner came along and decided to move the team? A credible premise, but not unique enough to build a movie around. So Ward added some wrinkles.

For starters, the owner would be a woman, which—then as now—was both highly unusual and inherently intriguing. Then, to get around legalities that bound the team to the city (back in the days when such things mattered), she would hatch a nefarious plot, one based in reality and adapted from an ugly real-life scenario unfolding as Ward began to write the script.

In 1961, longtime franchise owner Calvin Griffith had moved his woebegone Washington Senators to Minneapolis, where they became the Twins. At first, it worked like a charm. After years of struggle and poor attendance in the nation's capital, the club enjoyed immediate success in its new home. It drew more than a million fans in each of its first 10 seasons in Minnesota, and the Twins became a frequent contender, winning a pair of division titles in addition to the American League pennant in 1965. But results leveled off, both on the field and at the ticket gates, in the 1970s as Minnesota's Metropolitan Stadium began to age. When plans materialized for a multipurpose domed stadium in downtown Minneapolis, city and state officials wanted the Twins to share the new facility with the NFL's Vikings.

During difficult negotiations, Griffith managed to score a coup with the addition of a suspiciously specific escape clause in his team's 30-year lease at the new stadium. If the Twins' home attendance did not average 1.4 million per season over a period of three consecutive years, the team could be released from its contract and thereby leave Minnesota.

When the Metrodome opened in 1982, the Twins were in the midst of their worst losing stretch since relocating from Washington. Griffith, among the last of the old guard of baseball owners, had adopted a penny-pinching philosophy of letting quality veteran players depart as free agents, rather than signing them to

expensive contracts, and replacing them with inexpensive, inexperienced rookies and has-beens. His dollar-stretching policies
trickled down to the players, who, rumor had it, had placed photos
of Griffith in the basins of clubhouse urinals.

Fans also turned hostile toward the embattled owner as the
Twins lost 102 games in their inaugural season in the Metrodome
and 92 in the next. Consequently, the Twins averaged fewer than
900,000 in home attendance in each of those two seasons. That
meant they would have to draw more than 2.5 million in 1984 to
push the three-year average up to the magic number. A member of
the Twins' own board of directors admitted it would take a miracle
to keep the team in Minnesota. Then, a month into the 1984
season, a group of investors from Tampa purchased 42 percent
of the franchise, and it seemed as though the moving trucks soon
would be backing up to the Metrodome's loading docks.

Griffith added fuel to the fire when he said he would try to
prevent the chamber of commerce from buying thousands of
tickets for cheap seats for upcoming games in order to artifi-
cially drive up attendance. To many Minnesota fans, things were
looking shady. It appeared as though Griffith had sneaked the
escape clause past desperate and naive city officials and then
manipulated his team's roster to ensure he'd be able to use it.
Whether he'd planned it all along or it was coincidental, the situation was ripe for Griffith to move the Twins to Florida for the
1986 season.

But just when all hope seemed lost for Minnesota baseball fans,
Griffith sold the Twins to Minneapolis banker Carl Pohlad, who
kept the team in the Twin Cities. (Pohlad eventually earned his
own reputation for being a cheap and out-of-touch owner, until his
death in 2009.) The Tampa group, thwarted in its attempt to land
a team, sold its minority stock to Pohlad, and that was the end of
the entire ugly episode.

Ward followed the situation closely and, even before it had
played out, saw that it would make a great hook for his story:
An owner with plans to move her team drives attendance low

enough to trigger an escape clause, in much the same way as it appeared Griffith was doing, bringing in a bunch of never-were, never-will-be ballplayers she knows can't win.

Ward now had an intriguing combination of two story concepts: the fiendish conspiracy and the rousing tale of the underdog.

What if he were to put together a bunch of guys who look like they have no shot, but somehow they come together to take Cleveland to the promised land?

That's a comedy if there ever was one.

•   •   •

Because the movie was supposed to be funny, it's fittingly ironic that the guy who would help David Ward's Cleveland Indians fantasy come true was a die-hard New York Yankees fan.

Chris Chesser did have a big soft spot for the Tribe. He had grown up in Tucson, Arizona, which had been the spring-training home of the Indians since 1947. Living less than a mile away from Hi Corbett Field, where the team played its exhibition games, Chesser would haunt the ballpark every March, soaking up as much big-league baseball as he could before it vanished from the desert landscape for another year.

Once the Cactus League season was over and the players and teams returned east, Chesser's only outlet for baseball was the game-of-the-week telecast, where he was introduced to and fell for the Yankees, particularly their All-American slugger Mickey Mantle. But having the Indians train in his back yard every year was the next best thing.

In a small alley just behind Hi Corbett's first-base dugout—interestingly, the spot used for the scene early in *Major League* in which the coaching staff watches the players arrive—Chesser would get autographs from the Indians' stars of the 1950s and 1960s like Rocky Colavito, Jimmy Piersall, and Tito Francona.

Chesser also was involved with the Indians off the field. His father, a doctor and an active member of the community, would attend dinners and civic events supporting the team, occasionally bringing his young son along to meet great players from the past, such as Joe "Flash" Gordon and Lou Boudreau.

The other big deal happening in Tucson at the time was movies, as Hollywood productions took advantage of Tucson's cactus-studded landscape and a small production facility called Old Tucson that would eventually become the site for more than 300 film and television projects. "My dad became the movie doctor," Chesser says. "He was always on call for anybody who might need attention. He'd take my older brother and me out to Old Tucson so we could watch them shoot."

Chesser's fascination with the movie business eventually pointed him to his career path. After earning a bachelor's degree from Dartmouth and an MBA from the American School of International Management, Chesser landed a job at Columbia Pictures in New York as an executive in international sales. Quickly realizing he'd rather be a part of making films than distributing them, Chesser returned west, swooping into Los Angeles without a clear plan of what to do next. Living in his car and changing clothes at gas stations, he used his Columbia ID to sneak onto sets and into the food lines to eat with the cast and crew as he hunted for a job in the film industry. Through persistence and a series of lucky breaks, he was hired as general manager of the American Film Institute, then spent the next several years bouncing between studios before branching out as an independent producer.

"I had two requirements," Chesser explains. "I wanted to work with writers who were really good, and I wanted to work with people I like. Nobody fit that bill better than David."

Casting his net, Chesser remembered the fantastic *Cannery Row* script he'd read five years earlier and gave Ward a call. When Ward told him about his idea for a baseball comedy about the Cleveland Indians, Chesser was all over it.

"I really loved the idea about the Indians because I'd always had a passion for them," he says. "Plus, the Yankees were going to be the bad guys, which I thought was fun because those were my guys."

Amazingly—considering what was to come—it didn't take long to generate interest. Chesser pitched the idea to his friend Martin Shafer, a big sports fan who had just been hired as an executive at Embassy Pictures. Shafer liked the idea and convinced Alan Horn, who was running Embassy at the time and would go on to serve as the president of Warner Brothers and chairman of Walt Disney Studios, to pay Ward and Chesser to develop the film.

The first hurdle was cleared. It appeared that Ward simply had to write the script, then Chesser would set up the production for Ward to direct, and that would be that.

But just as any Cleveland Indians fan would have known, things couldn't possibly be that easy.

EXTRAS . . .

"The Indians were the ultimate underdog team because nobody knew them," says Ward. "And, unless you were from Cleveland, nobody seemed to care. They were kind of invisible at the time. There was something comic yet lovable about them. I didn't know anybody who hated the Indians."

3

Making Losers Lovable

In so many ways, it was an ideal situation for a writer who was a baseball fan. David Ward would be paid to write his ultimate baseball fantasy, then climb behind a camera to turn it into a major motion picture. Even better, before the work began, he and Chris Chesser would embark on several research trips adding to the living-a-dream feel.

They traveled to Chesser's hometown to visit Hi Corbett Field and get a feel for the Indians' spring-training home. Back in Los Angeles, they visited Dodger Stadium and the Big A in Anaheim and hung out in clubhouses with Bobby Grich, Reggie Jackson, Pedro Guerrero, and Tommy Lasorda to soak up some of the game's genuine behind-the-scenes nuances.

"I just wanted to get a feel for the kind of camaraderie there is, what kind of practical jokes they pull. How their lockers express their personality," Ward says.

To get a bird's-eye view and experience the atmosphere surrounding an eccentric owner, Ward and Chesser flew to Chicago and took in a game from the Wrigley Field bleachers with Bill Veeck, who had recently retired after 40 years as a baseball owner (including three with the Indians, topped by 1948, their last world title).

Research was a blast, but soon the heavy lifting began. The movie that fans would one day mimic like macaws in a pet shop began to take shape first as handwritten text feverishly scribbled out on a series of legal pads. Ward generally wrote either first thing in the morning or late into the night. Editing involved literally cutting sections out and taping them in place elsewhere. The scrawl was then translated back into English by a typist gifted enough to be able to read Ward's frantic handwriting.

While Ward devised a story that would—fictionally—transform his beloved baseball team, the real Indians were enduring an utterly miserable 1983 season. With what few talented players they had demanding to be traded, the team lost 92 games, fired a manager midseason for the third time in seven years, and drew an average of slightly more than 9,000 fans per home game.

It was perhaps the bleakest time in the history of the franchise.

But little did Tribe fans know that out in southern California, a glimmer of hope was being scribbled, scratched out, cut apart, and taped back together. And it was beginning to take shape.

•   •   •

Elements of the movie were tweaked and changed throughout the process, but the basic elements—including Ward's original title, *Major League*—were there almost from the beginning.

Like *Citizen Kane*, the story begins with death. The owner of the Cleveland Indians has died, leaving the team to his wife, Rachel Phelps, a former Las Vegas showgirl who, as explained in the first draft of the script, "looks like a Fifth Avenue version of Carmen Miranda." After vaguely explaining her intentions to turn the long-suffering franchise around to front-office staffers, Phelps outlines her true intentions to general manager Charlie Donovan. She plans to put together a team so bad that attendance will drop to a point that will justify breaking the Indians' lease with the city and taking a lucrative offer to move the team to Miami. Hence, she invites a motley crew of has-beens and never-weres to spring training and taps minor-league lifer and tire-store employee Lou Brown as their manager.

One by one, the central characters are introduced. Jake Taylor is a 35-year-old catcher who'd been an All-Star with the Red Sox early in his career and enjoyed marginal success with the Indians in an earlier tenure. But like many long-term catchers, he began having problems with his knees and wound up playing in Mexico, where the Indians track him down and invite him to spring training.

Tall, ominous, dark-skinned Latino slugger Pedro Cerrano (originally named "Marano" in the early drafts of the script) appears to have all the intrinsic qualities to be a bona fide big-league player; the script describes him as looking like "a gunfighter coming into Dodge." Although he's able to consistently blast fastballs into the distant scenery, he's utterly lost when a curveball floats his way. For help, Cerrano turns to voodoo: his justification for defecting from his native Cuba.

Not invited, but showing up to camp anyway, is a brash young outfielder who has given himself a nickname, Willie "Mays" Hayes, because he "hits like Mays and runs like Hayes." His ruse is quickly discovered and he's removed from camp, then earns a shot after an impromptu demonstration of gazelle-like speed. Unfortunately, it's a skill that initially proves meaningless as Mays continually pops up pitch after pitch, rather than hitting the ball on the ground and using his speed to get on base. "You may run like Mays," Lou Brown gruffly proclaims, "but you hit like shit."

Not all the faces are new. Returning is high-priced third baseman Roger Dorn (originally named "Beck" but changed because Ward felt it sounded more like the name of a tough guy than a pretty boy), who was signed by the Indians as a free agent three years before but has yet to live up to his lofty salary. Although Dorn still hits well, his fielding is a liability, as is his toxic, self-centered attitude on and off the field.

Aging junkball pitcher Steve Harris (accidentally renamed "Eddie" later) is another mainstay clinging to his career with guile and cunning—and slyly putting illegal substances on the baseball.

Sitting high above the nonsense is broadcaster Harry Doyle, who, the script states, has "been with the Indians through thin and thinner" and "never walked past a bar in anger." Indeed, Jack Daniels proves to be a much more valuable partner in the booth than comically quiet color commentator Monty.

Finally, there's a good-looking, muscular, 19-year-old pitcher with a crazy haircut and a dangling earring, rarities in the relatively buttoned-down landscape of 1980s baseball. However, not only is Rick Vaughn no longer playing organized baseball, he has landed in jail for auto theft. Vaughn arrives at camp straight from the clink with his possessions in a trash bag, having hitched a ride on a motorcycle. Not only does his appearance justify his "Wild Thing" nickname, but so does his on-field prowess: His pitches explode toward home plate with tremendous velocity—and zero control. Vaughn's bold appearance instantly draws the ire of Dorn, who wastes no time in antagonizing the rookie.

Spring training starts predictably. In spite of manager Brown's old-school incentives—mandatory push-ups and sit-ups for silly mistakes—the team is dreadful, as each player's Achilles' heel becomes more obvious. But with little competition, each of the central characters makes the club and the team returns to Cleveland.

The season begins with a humiliating opening-day loss to the defending-champion New York Yankees as Vaughn loads the bases with walks on 12 straight pitches in his big-league debut, then serves up a grand-slam home run to pompous slugger Clu Haywood.

Rachel Phelps's plan works like a charm as the Tribe wallows through the first two months of the season. Along the way, Jake Taylor rediscovers old flame Lynn Wells (renamed "Westland" in the script, although "Wells" is listed as her last name in the end credits). He tries to reconnect, only to repeatedly be told that she's moved on. Lynn, now a librarian, is in a committed relationship with a stable, intelligent, and complete douchebag attorney. To her, Jake is a little boy who won't grow up.

As the season unfolds, the Indians begin to show signs of maturity, further irritating Rachel Phelps. In response, she ramps up her

Machiavellian measures, designed not only to save money, but to make the team play even worse. From the army-barracks, bunk-bed atmosphere of spring training to a ramshackle apartment building for the players colloquially referred to in the script as "The Turk," she downgrades the team's transportation to a World War II–era prop plane and then a rickety revival-tent tour bus.

Through it all, the Indians continue to improve, including Taylor, who takes Lynn's criticisms to heart and begins acquainting himself with the literary classics she had always encouraged him to read, albeit in a comic-book format. His efforts pay off in a nostalgic one-night hookup with Lynn, but she remains unconvinced that Taylor has really grown up.

Meanwhile, Vaughn turns a corner when his control issues (pitching, not anger) are diagnosed as a simple vision problem. Donning thick black glasses, he finds his niche and begins to emerge as a promising pitcher, although he's still not quite ready for the Yankees and Haywood, who lights him up again in a game in New York.

With the team hovering near .500 in August, GM Charlie Donovan finally comes clean and lets Brown in on Phelps's dastardly plot. Brown, in turn, tells the disbelieving players that their sole purpose has been to comprise a miserable team to serve Phelps's needs. Angered and motivated, they agree that the only thing to do is, as Taylor puts it, to "win the whole fuckin' thing."

And with that, the Indians catch fire. With each player overcoming his weakness, the pieces come together and the team begins to rocket up the standings, becoming a national sensation and converting the long-suffering, cynical Cleveland fans from doubters to believers. The Tribe catches the Yankees on the final day of the season, setting up a one-game playoff for the division title, much to Rachel Phelps's dismay—or delight (more on that later).

In front of a capacity home crowd, the upstart Indians finally stand up to their longtime rivals, with each main character playing at his full potential to propel the Tribe to victory. Dorn excels defensively. Hayes legs out a ground ball for a single, then steals a key base with the game on the line. Cerrano abandons his voodoo and hits a game-tying homer. Vaughn comes out of the bullpen to strike out Haywood on three power pitches. And finally, Taylor—demonstrating his newfound maturity and capacity for self-sacrifice—lays down a bunt in a high-profile macho situation to score the winning run. This ragtag mishmash of castoffs has finally made the Indians champions, and Cleveland rejoices.

After six months of writing, editing, and rewriting, Ward sat back with satisfaction. His baseball fairy tale was complete.

•   •   •

For as much as the plot propels the story forward, the characters would ultimately make or break the movie.

In *Major League*, each primary player has a key problem (on or off the field) that needs to be solved, and over the course of the story—in line with the underdog theme—he overcomes his weakness. Resolution of the character arcs provided the steak, but Ward needed to add the sizzle.

The real Indians had been fielding bad players for decades, but few of them exhibited much color or personality, befitting the team's bland, lifeless on-field performances in its mausoleum of a ballpark. (One of the exceptions was John Lowenstein, an infielder in the 1970s who boasted that instead of a fan club, he had an "Apathy Club.") Ward's Indians instead would be peppered with dynamic, hilarious, and yet often remarkably accurate composites of actual professional ballplayers.

Even before the characters became real on the screen, their verisimilitude leapt from the script. "Each of the players was based on a collection of different guys," notes Indians' longtime public relations director Bob DiBiasio. "Nobody was based on anybody specifically. It wasn't that this guy is portraying 'X', but that this guy is portraying that group of 'Xs'. And because they did it that way, different age groups could identify with different characters."

Undoubtedly, Ward's most creative—and memorable—

character was Rick Vaughn. As outlandish as he might have seemed, he was based on a real-life pitcher who, even in his prime, looked like a middle-aged insurance adjuster.

In the late 1950s and early 1960s, Ryne Duren foreshadowed a type of ballplayer that was far from common in his era: a hard-throwing relief pitcher who struggled with control, making him, if not entirely respected, then universally feared by opposing batters. He emerged from a tiny Wisconsin town like an urban legend, carrying with him tales of how in high school he'd broken a batter's ribs with a pitch and, when playing second base, had been instructed to throw the ball underhanded to first—as a safety measure.

But there was enough talent to counterbalance the erraticism. Duren broke into the bigs in 1954 and quickly became an integral part of the great New York Yankees teams of the late '50s. Feeding his reputation (and showmanship), Duren would often intentionally toss at least one warm-up pitch over his catcher's head and high up onto the screen behind home plate, just to give the incoming hitter something to think about before he dug into the batter's box.

AS OUTLANDISH AS HE MIGHT HAVE SEEMED, HE WAS BASED ON A REAL-LIFE PITCHER WHO LOOKED LIKE A MIDDLE-AGED INSURANCE ADJUSTER.

In addition to his nearly 100 mph-fastball, what made Duren memorable were the thick, Coke-bottle eyeglasses he wore to correct his hilariously miserable vision, reported to be 70/20 in his right eye and 200/20 in his left. His specs—also a rarity in pro sports in the 1950s—perpetuated the myth that he couldn't control his pitches because he couldn't quite see where they were going, and it was whispered around batting cages that he became a pitcher because he couldn't see well enough to play in the outfield.

Despite hop-scotching among seven big-league teams in his 10-year career, Duren was successful, averaging more than one strikeout per inning. In addition, although the "save" statistic wouldn't be implemented until 1969, Duren would have led the league with 20 saves in 1958, and he tallied a minuscule 1.88 ERA in 41 appearances the year before. He pitched well in a pair of World Series with the Yankees and earned three trips to the All-Star Game.

Duren's control problems carried over off the field, though, as alcoholism crippled both his career and his marriage. He once got soused after a game, climbed a bridge, and shouted at the moon. Another time, he parked his car on a set of railroad tracks, daring an oncoming train to hit him. After his career ended, he spent three months in a mental hospital and was in and out of rehab during the next several years before he finally got his life on track. Duren spent the rest of his life speaking about the dangers of alcoholism and promoting counseling. Although he hadn't played in nearly a half century at the time of his death in 2011, the *New York Times* obituary headline summed up his career succinctly and accurately: "Ryne Duren, 81, Pitcher; Made Batters Nervous."

Although Duren was the primary template for Wild Thing, Ward also sprinkled in a little influence from another similarly eccentric closer from the unpredictable 1970s. Nicknamed "The Mad Hungarian," Al Hrabosky was a long-haired wild man with a trademark Fu Manchu mustache who became well-known for stomping around the mound like a caged tiger between pitches. But in spite of his antics, he was one of baseball's most dependable relief pitchers, leading the National League with 22 saves in 1975 as a member of the St. Louis Cardinals.

The irony in these composites is that the Rick Vaughn character isn't a relief pitcher; he becomes an ace starting pitcher as the story plays out. But reflecting the impact of the signature scene of the script, Wild Thing personifies the colorful, crazy closer, a role that would evolve in the years to come.

"I just wanted Wild Thing to be a rebel," Ward says, "a kid who's been in prison, who represents rebellious youth. Basically the last guy most organizations would ever let on their team."

Most of the other characters were more general composites. For instance, almost every team at every level of the game has a

Jake Taylor, a weary veteran catcher trying desperately to keep his career going. "He's not Johnny Bench, but he'd been a good player and he was looking for one last day in the sun," says Ward. "He'd had his career, but thinks he's got one more good year left in him."

Pedro Cerrano, the intimidating slugger who turns to voodoo for help with his struggles with the curveball, evolved from the superstitions and idiosyncrasies of many players. For example, the Alou brothers—Felipe, Jesus, and Matty—who rose from the then-untapped baseball kingdom of the Dominican Republic to stardom in the 1960s, drew attention with their quirky approaches to the game, such as not stepping on the foul lines.

Cerrano's devotion to his bat, which includes lighting candles and offering sacrifices to entice the bat to serve his purposes, is essentially the converse of Hall of Famer Orlando Cepeda's beliefs. He was convinced that each bat was capable of delivering only one hit, so he'd stop using a bat once he got a hit with it, going through dozens in a season.

And then, of course, there's the voodoo.

"At some point, there was a rumor about the Alou brothers that because they were from the Dominican Republic, they practiced voodoo down there," Ward says. "It was all racist hooey, but the idea was interesting. I thought I could have a guy come from Cuba, just when people were starting to become aware of how good the Cuban players were. So what if a guy comes from Cuba, he's got his head shaved, he's a badass motherfucker, and he practices voodoo?"

Yet Ward admits Cerrano's religion is nothing like the real deal.

"The voodoo he practices has nothing to do with real voodoo," Ward says. "I didn't want him sticking pins in things. I wanted him to have a little voodoo character that could appease the voodoo gods."

Which brought him to what—after Wild Thing—might have been the most memorable character created for the story . . . even though he wasn't technically a character. He has no lines, he doesn't move, he's made of clay, and he has straw hair. He's only about a foot tall, but seems larger than life, particularly since the intimidating Cerrano did everything in his power to make him happy. We know him by a name so simple, it's almost elemental: Jobu.

In an attempt to resolve his trouble with the curve, Cerrano places a small figurine of Jobu (spelled "Jo-Buu" in the early versions of the script) in his locker and offers it shots of rum (originally gin) and lit cigars so that Jobu will take the fear of Uncle Charlie away from Cerrano's bats.

That raises the question that has persevered for years: Exactly what *is* Jobu?

"JOBU IS LIKE THE KING OF THE VOODOO DOLLS. YOU DON'T STICK PINS IN HIM; YOU APPEASE HIM."

Ward wove a potential answer into the script in the form of a Jake Taylor one-liner, later removed: "Maybe he's the pagan saint of baseball." But that's not quite right, just as Jobu is not quite real within voodoo. "Jobu is not a god," Ward explains. "Jobu is a voodoo icon, but not in the way we use the term 'icon' today. He's like the voodoo equivalent of a statue of the Virgin Mary. In voodoo, there's a whole thing about using dolls and having them represent things. Jobu is like the king of the voodoo dolls. You don't stick pins in him; you appease him."

But Jobu wasn't the only character who saw himself as a deity. Ward's starting third baseman also fit that bill. By the 1980s, the enthusiastic and—let's be honest—mostly mythical "Let's play two" mentality had been essentially exterminated from baseball. Fans had long been disabused of the illusion of big-league ballplayers as innocent, boyish, Norman Rockwell characters. With free agency now the norm, money had moved to center stage. Everybody knew what everybody else was being paid, and for many (perhaps most) players, the next season was far less important than the next contract.

"Free agency was really hitting its peak, and guys were getting big contracts," Ward notes. "This is when fans were first getting disillusioned with free agents and prima donna players in general. I just took it to another whole level of excess."

Roger Dorn became Ward's poster boy for this new age of ball-players in it primarily (if not solely) for the money. With his fancy car, expensive golf clubs, and focus on his stock portfolio, Dorn became perhaps the most believable, recognizable member of Ward's Indians to a nation of cynical 1980s baseball fans.

While Dorn was a broadly familiar composite, the character who would come to be known as Eddie Harris was clearly based on a single source. He was a thinly veiled depiction of Gaylord Perry, who'd made a Hall of Fame career out of both coating the ball with illegal substances and making batters think he had when he hadn't. Pitching until he was 45, Perry won a Cy Young Award with the Indians in 1972, making Harris even more believable.

Also grounded in the new reality of the game was the lightning speed of Willie Mays Hayes, reflecting the new generation of speedsters who began to dominate baseball in the 1980s—specifically, spectacular showman Rickey Henderson. Even the character's name directly reflects it: "Hayes" after 1960s Olympic champion sprinter and Dallas Cowboys wide receiver Bob Hayes. (Plus "Mays," of course, for the man who tipped the first domino in this entire story back in the fall of '54.)

The nonplayers also had real-life counterparts. Manager Lou Brown is the classic no-nonsense, throwback manager who had largely faded away by the 1980s. Good-hearted mensch Charlie Donovan personifies the handful of weary, handcuffed general managers who can do nothing more than follow the frenzied whims of their owners, who by the 1980s had become much more public figures than the silent monarchs of previous eras.

Hard as it is to believe now after what has been immortalized as an inspired bit of casting, Ward didn't write the role of Harry Doyle to mirror any specific baseball broadcaster. If anything, Doyle was a more compromised, effervescent version of Herb Score, who was the dignified radio voice of the Indians for 33 years and witnessed some of the worst baseball ever played, season after season. "I thought it would be funny to have the broadcaster so beaten down after all these years that he's basically drinking during the games," Ward says.

Rachel Phelps, in contrast, had two very specific inspirations. Originally she was envisioned as a combination of George Steinbrenner, the perpetually meddlesome owner of the New York Yankees, and Georgia Frontiere, a one-time performer who'd inherited the Los Angeles Rams after her husband, Carroll Rosenbloom, died in 1979. Later, parallels would be drawn to Marge Schott, who had purchased the Cincinnati Reds in the mid-1980s and became infamous for racial, anti-Semitic, and pro-Hitler remarks that ultimately led to her twice being suspended from daily operations. Schott also had a canine sidekick, a massive St. Bernard named "Schottzie," mirrored by Phelps's handbag-sized Pekinese, Cha-Cha. "She's a woman who has her own agenda," Ward says. "She doesn't really care about the team as much as she cares about what the team can do for her."

What this team of characters did for the story was quite apparent: They provided vibrancy, personality, and—most of all—comedy.

Ward completed the script just as the 1984 baseball season was about to begin, and he felt good about it. Under pressure to revive his career, he'd created a crackerjack little story with some of the most memorable characters ever to grace a sports film.

But it would be five years before anybody knew it.

EXTRAS . . .

Trimmed from the opening scene of the movie, in which Rachel Phelps meets with team executives, is dialogue revealing that Charlie Donovan had been the team's manager the previous year and that Phelps suddenly promotes him to general manager. This explains his later comment, "If I'm the GM, who's going to be the manager?"

•

Actor Charles Cyphers, who plays Donovan, had previously played the sheriff of the town that masked killer Michael Myers descends upon in the original *Halloween*.

4

"Tootsie," Vietnam, and Wild Thing

A common thread runs through the histories of many successful movies: At one point or another, nobody in Hollywood wanted to make them.

No matter how valid the studios' objections about these beloved films might have seemed at the time, they always seem preposterous in retrospect. Such was the case with *Major League*, which hit turbulence immediately after David Ward finished writing it.

When Ward and Chris Chesser delivered the completed script to Martin Shafer in early 1984 and Shafer took it to his comrades at Embassy Pictures, their response caught Ward and Chesser completely off-guard. The Embassy executives thought it was funny, but felt the story was simply too fantastic for the audience to believe. It didn't matter that the characters were based on real people or that the premise was ripped directly from the headlines of the sports pages.

"We tried to tell them about Calvin Griffith and that whole thing, but they just said 'no,'" Ward says.

So *Major League* fell into the film industry purgatory known as "turnaround," a term used when a studio develops a project, then decides it doesn't want to make the movie. For *Major League* to see the light of day, another studio would have to buy the rights at a price set by Embassy and reimburse the funds spent on development, with interest. In baseball terms, it was like stepping into the batter's box with a 0-and-2 count.

But Ward and Chesser still believed in the idea and were committed to making the movie. They set up meeting after meeting with other studios around town, pitching the idea for this baseball comedy conceived by an Academy Award–winning writer. But they kept hearing the same response: "Nobody goes to baseball movies."

Although *The Natural* became a critical and commercial hit just as Ward and Chesser began shopping *Major League*, it seemed to be the exception that proved the rule. It was the highest-grossing baseball film since the original *Bad News Bears* in 1976. But even in the aftermath of Roy Hobbs and Wonderboy, studio executives were convinced that if people wanted to see baseball, they'd simply watch a baseball game by going to the park or taking advantage of the increasing popularity of televised baseball.

The Natural did well at the box office yet did little to change Hollywood's perception. In fact, until 1988—which proved to represent a long-overdue sea change for the genre—only three baseball movies had been released theatrically by major studios in the decade (and that's using the term "baseball movie" liberally). With demand down and the expectation for return on investment decidedly low, studios were hesitant to green-light a baseball picture, particularly one that would also deviate from the sentimental, nostalgia-heavy formula that had worked for *The Natural*.

"Baseball movies just weren't being made," Ward says. "We tried to tell them we weren't going to have two hours of people playing baseball; we were going to do a film about the guys who play on the team and what a bunch of lovable losers they were. And when we did show baseball, it wasn't going to be the kind of baseball you're used to seeing."

It made no difference. The industry mentality had set like concrete, and over the next three years, *Major League* wallowed in turnaround like a promising minor-league player who just couldn't make it to the bigs.

It took the intervention of a comedy legend to light the fire that got *Major League* into production. And he didn't even know that's what he was doing.

• • •

Bill Murray had already had a hell of a decade.

After wrapping up an outstanding three-year run on *Saturday Night Live*, he kicked off a long, successful film career with three hit comedies in a four-year stretch: *Caddyshack*, *Stripes*, and *Ghostbusters*.

Now he was about to save *Major League* from oblivion. Not directly, of course, and, as it happens, completely by accident. But if you trace the series of events that eventually led to *Major League* seeing the light of day, you wind up at Bill Murray and a connection he'd made with a small role in 1982's *Tootsie*, directed by the esteemed Sydney Pollack.

Five years later, Murray had an idea for a comedy in which he'd play an average, blue-collar American who, through a series of happenstances, discovers he's the heir to the throne and becomes the king of England. He pitched the idea to Pollack, who had become a good friend and a huge fan since their work on *Tootsie*. Pollack liked the idea and wanted to direct the movie with Murray as the lead. He just needed a writer. Pollack, who'd recently won an Academy Award for directing *Out of Africa*, had known David Ward for years and thought he'd be the perfect guy for the project.

Ward was working on an adaptation of the novel *The Milagro Beanfield War* in 1987 when he got the call from Pollack inviting him to a meeting at the offices of Mirage, his production company in Burbank. Ward agreed to meet with Pollack, but, with *Major League* still on his mind, he planned to go in with a secret agenda. After he got off the phone with Pollack, Ward called Chesser and asked him to come to the meeting, too. "I think he wants to talk about something else," Ward explained, "but let's tell him about

Major League." Chesser agreed. He knew Pollack from his days at Columbia Pictures when he helped develop *Absence of Malice*, which Pollack directed.

At the meeting, Pollack outlined Murray's king of England idea, and Ward agreed to write the script. (It would eventually become *King Ralph*.) Then he pivoted to his baseball movie that had been in turnaround for three years.

Pollack was intrigued, even though he'd never been to a baseball game in his life. When he later read the script, he loved it instantly and thought it would make a great movie. Mirage purchased the rights from Embassy, and Pollack agreed to serve as the executive producer, along with Mirage's co-founder, Mark Rosenberg, who, ironically, had passed on the movie when he was the head of production at Warner Brothers.

And with that, it was a whole new ballgame.

With the prestigious Pollack on board, *Major League* suddenly had a newfound gravitas that ensured more eyes would see it and more doors would open. The script began to make the rounds at the prominent Creative Artists Agency, where both Pollack and Ward were clients. It was eventually passed to Joe Roth, an ambitious producer who'd just co-founded a new production company called Morgan Creek with Jim Robinson, an automobile import executive from Baltimore.

Specializing in both development and bridge financing between production companies and studios, Morgan Creek was in the middle of developing its first feature. *Young Guns*, a sexy action-western, would be released the following summer and earn $45 million from a modest $11 million budget. Both Roth and Robinson saw similar potential in *Major League*, and Morgan Creek stepped in to finance it.

After nearly four years, *Major League* was once again on the cusp of production. But one piece of the puzzle still was needed. Two, actually—both fresh from Vietnam.

•　　•　　•

By the 1980s, the misery and controversy of the Vietnam War had cooled enough that Hollywood felt it was safe to tread back into the quagmire for story material. When that proved successful, it went back for more.

Perhaps the best of this ever-growing genre was Oliver Stone's gritty, intense *Platoon*, which exploded into theaters like a mortar shell in 1986, winning both the Golden Globe and the Oscar for Best Picture. A big part of the movie's success was a pair of breakthrough performances by two rising actors playing the film's primary characters: the young, untested soldier and his battle-scarred sergeant.

Tom Berenger had labored for years through a handful of small television and film roles before earning notoriety for his role in the ensemble comedy/drama *The Big Chill* in 1983. His portrayal of grizzled Sgt. Barnes in *Platoon* earned an Academy Award nomination for Best Actor and established him as a leading man.

Similarly, 20-year-old Charlie Sheen was a relative unknown when he landed his role in *Platoon* as wide-eyed recruit Chris Taylor. At the time, he was better known as the son of Martin Sheen and the younger brother of "Brat Pack" charter member Emilio Estevez. *Platoon* catapulted him to an entirely new level. Another critically praised dramatic role followed in Stone's *Wall Street* the following year, then Sheen tapped into the younger demographic as part of the bad-boy ensemble cast of Morgan Creek's *Young Guns*.

BERENGER AND SHEEN HAD LEAPT FROM VIRTUAL ANONYMITY TO BECOME TWO OF THE HOTTEST NAMES IN HOLLYWOOD—CERTAINLY A PAIR YOU COULD BANK YOUR MOVIE ON.

In only a few years, both Berenger and Sheen had leapt from virtual anonymity to become two of the hottest names in Hollywood—certainly a pair you could bank your movie on—and that's exactly what Morgan Creek was thinking.

Before other casting decisions for *Major League* had been discussed, Joe Roth came up with the idea of re-teaming Berenger and Sheen in lead roles that in some ways reprised the characters they played in *Platoon*: Berenger as veteran catcher Jake Taylor and Sheen as rookie pitcher Rick Vaughn. Ward and Chesser also saw the benefit, although neither actor had much experience in comedy.

The good news was that both actors did have experience playing baseball. Berenger had played in Little League, and Sheen had been a star in high school. Better still, Roth had gotten to know Sheen through *Young Guns*, and knew that he was a huge baseball fan. He figured Sheen might be interested.

He had no idea.

•   •   •

Midway through the *Major League* script, Rick Vaughn and Jake Taylor are hanging out in a bar discussing Wild Thing's newfound infamy as a record-breaking erratic pitcher.

"I thought you had to do somethin' good to be a celebrity," Vaughn says.

"Not if you do it colorfully," Taylor replies sagely.

Indeed, considering Charlie Sheen's public life up to—and especially after—*Major League*, this snippet of dialogue seems particularly apt. In the history of film, there might not have been a truer connection between an actor and the character he played, to the point that Charlie Sheen and Wild Thing no longer are separate entities.

Born Carlos Irwin Estevez in New York City in 1965, Sheen took an early interest in the acting career of his father, Martin Sheen, eventually taking his dad's stage surname as his own. At age nine, Charlie appeared in a bit part in one of his father's films and traveled to the Philippines with his parents when Martin got his breakthrough role in *Apocalypse Now*, also appearing as an extra in that film.

By the time he was a teenager, Sheen was the quintessential bad boy. After years of poor attendance, he was expelled from Santa Monica High School just before graduation, ending a sterling career as a pitcher and shortstop on the varsity baseball team.

While the legend of his baseball skills may have been embellished over the years, there are genuine indications that Sheen could indeed have had a career in baseball. For as undisciplined as he was in other aspects of his life, he showed a real dedication to the game, attending the Mickey Owen Baseball School in Missouri for four summers and impressing several coaches there. The consensus was that he could have earned a Division I college scholarship, and Sheen said the University of Kansas offered one to him. "I was scouted as a shortstop, and it was all about my arm and my speed," he says. "But I couldn't hit a slider, I couldn't hit a curveball. Unless it was dead red and I knew it was coming, I couldn't hit it."

There are mixed opinions on whether he could have made it to the big leagues, especially considering what was going on in his life. A little more than a year after he had been kicked out of high school, his girlfriend became pregnant, and he became a father at 19. He was also in trouble with the law at an early age, being arrested at age 15 for using stolen credit cards for a variety of purchases, including hiring a prostitute, and for smoking marijuana in his car. By the time he had reached his 20s, Charlie Sheen was already a magnet for trouble. Considering what was to come, this was perhaps the most innocent period of his life.

Despite his rocky adolescence, Sheen was committed to following in the footsteps of his father and older brother by becoming an actor. He landed his first real role in *Red Dawn* in 1984, then picked up a few small film and TV parts, showing genuine talent in modest roles in *Lucas* and *Ferris Bueller's Day Off* before *Platoon* launched his career. A year later, *Wall Street* expanded his visibility and gave him the chance to work alongside his father, who co-starred with Charlie and Michael Douglas. Then, after *Young Guns*, Sheen got his first baseball role, albeit a subdued one, as Chicago White Sox outfielder Happy Felsch in the critically acclaimed but box-office-challenged *Eight Men Out*. It was just a nibble, but it was enough for Sheen to want more.

Knowing his lifelong passion for the game, Joe Roth hoped Sheen would consider doing *Major League*. From the moment his agent passed him the script, Sheen wasn't just interested; he was enamored.

He recalls: "I was going to a film premiere, and because I knew I had this meeting with David Ward the next day, I sat in a limo in my tux and would not get out until I finished this script because it was that good. So I missed the red carpet and pissed off a lot of people. But I showed up to the meeting with David and told him all about my baseball background and that I was born to play this role. And I told him basically to not change a word."

Ready to jump on board, Sheen called Berenger to get his take.

"Tom, are you doing this?" he asked.

"It looks great to me," Berenger replied. "It's a great comedy, too. Why not? It looks like it would be a lot of fun. How about you? You played baseball."

"Oh yeah," Sheen said emphatically. "I just wanted to make sure you were in on this, too."

"Yeah," Berenger said. "I'm on board."

"OK, OK," Sheen replied, his voice betraying his excitement. "Good."

And with that, all that remained was the i-dotting and t-crossing.

It was an ideal situation for Ward and company. Not only would Berenger and Sheen provide star power and solid acting chops; they also brought the gravitas and subtle reminder of a highly respected war film, which perhaps helped *Major League* in another way. When production of the film was announced a few months later, *Plain Dealer* columnist Bill Livingston found another perspective: "There are those who will say a tour of duty in Vietnam is the proper psychological preparation for being an Indians fan."

Ward flew to Berenger's home in Beaufort, South Carolina, to talk about the movie.

"Berenger was probably at the height of his career," Ward says.

"I had directed one movie that nobody had seen. So I think it was as much him wanting to vet me as me wanting to vet him."

The meeting went well, and Ward was encouraged by Berenger's enthusiasm for the role.

"I thought [Jake Taylor] was kind of sweet and endearing," Berenger reflects. "He reminded me a little bit of Burt Reynolds. He's sort of a good-time Charlie, but he's obviously a leader, too. He's made some dumb personal decisions, and he's a little bit of a boy. But is that all bad? Teddy Roosevelt's wife said he was always a boy, but he was also a man."

As would become custom throughout the casting process, Ward brought his baseball glove with him to the meeting with Berenger, and eventually the two went outside for a game of catch. What Ward saw troubled him. While Sheen had the polished, completely believable delivery of a major-league pitcher, Berenger's throwing motion was noticeably awkward and nothing like that of a seasoned big-league catcher.

"He could catch the ball and he could hit the ball, but he couldn't throw that well," Ward recalls. After a moment of panic, Ward realized the problem had an easy solution. Because Berenger would be playing a catcher, the majority of the times Jake Taylor would be seen throwing the baseball, he'd be wearing a catcher's mask. And with a catcher's mask on, you couldn't tell if it was or wasn't Berenger behind it. Finding someone to fill the physical part of the role would be a problem for another day. For now, Ward had his catcher and fictional team captain.

Once the contracts were signed and they were able to coordinate a schedule around Sheen's suddenly slim availability, the stars aligned, literally and figuratively. "That's what got the green light," Ward says. "As soon as we got them and could fit Charlie in, we could make the movie."

After years of no movement, *Major League* suddenly sprinted into development with the quick rhythm of a Tinker-to-Evers-to-Chance double play.

•   •   •

There was one more hurdle to clear, and it was perhaps the most important: Major League Baseball had to give the film the thumbs-up.

"That was a hugely nervous point," Ward says. "With all of the bad language in the script, we thought if they're really image conscious, they might have a big problem." And if Major League Baseball did have a problem with either the language or the premise of an owner deliberately sabotaging her team, the project would be painted into a corner.

"At the end of the day, we couldn't do it without their approval," Chesser agrees. "It would have been a complete deal-breaker."

Equally important, if the league approved but stipulated that the primary ballclub be fictional, that would have been the ballgame. For Ward, the entire story was predicated on using the Cleveland Indians. "For them to be the Decatur Buffaloes or something just wouldn't work," Ward says. "It had to be the Cleveland Indians."

"FOR THEM TO BE THE DECATUR BUFFALOES OR SOMETHING JUST WOULDN'T WORK. IT HAD TO BE THE CLEVELAND INDIANS."

They were so desperate for approval, there were actually discussions of whether they should send a doctored script omitting some of the spicier language. Ultimately, they sent the actual script and hoped for the best.

To their surprise—and in stark contrast to how these deals would change in years to come—there were no problems. Ironically, the aversion in Hollywood to baseball films that had long crippled the development of *Major League* suddenly became beneficial at a crucial moment.

"I think they were a little bit thrilled," Chesser says of Major League Baseball's response. "Nobody was approaching them about doing movies. So they just said 'OK' and we made it up as we went along."

Reflecting the simpler time, the script had been shown to MLB commissioner Peter Ueberroth, who provided a few suggestions to clarify some of the baseball details and requested minor changes. But by and large, *Major League* sailed through without resistance.

Improvising a deal that would become a template for baseball films in the years to come, Morgan Creek paid a flat $100,000 fee for permission to use team names and uniforms, and Major League Baseball approved the script.

"It would be hugely different today," Chesser says. "If we were to bring them that script today, I don't think they'd say 'yes.' They've got a whole division that deals with script approvals. I think it's a lot like when you're working with an animal on the set and you need somebody from the humane society there. They want to see a rough cut of your movie to make sure that you didn't sneak something in there that wasn't good for Major League Baseball."

The script was also sent to the Indians for review, where it was casually passed from team president Hank Peters to public relations director Bob DiBiasio on a fateful winter day at the stadium. DiBiasio was excited by the idea of his long-suffering Indians being made winners on the screen, but had to be certain his club wouldn't be portrayed in a bad light—or at least one worse than reality. After speaking with Ward and Chesser and helping them with some research, DiBiasio knew he had nothing to worry about. "I knew these guys cared about the Indians," he says. "That was an underlying comfort throughout the entire process. That made you feel good about embracing the project and helping in any way."

Conversely, the Yankees, who also could have thrown up a roadblock, were neither embracing nor helpful. Before Chesser could even broach the topic of making the Yankees the villains in the film, he had to get through formidable Fort Steinbrenner.

"I was having a helluva time just talking to anybody about anything," says Chesser, who, remember, was a lifelong Yankees fan. "They were really pissing me off. When I finally did get through, they were a little bit pissy. Actually, I don't think I even waited for their official response about whether it was OK to make them the bad guys. In truth, I think they kind of liked it because it aggrandized them in a curious sort of way: *If we're big enough to be the bad guys, then we're the New York Yankees.* And I really didn't worry about it because Major League Baseball had already approved the script."

With the league's permission granted and the lead actors on board, the project suddenly showed genuine potential. Accordingly, Morgan Creek decided to produce it in-house, rather than handing it over to a studio. They'd pay to make the film; once it was completed, the company would deliver it for release to Paramount, with whom Morgan Creek had a distribution deal.

And just like that, David Ward's baseball fantasy was finally about to become reality.

5

My Kinda Team

After years of jumping through development hoops, it now boiled down to streetball basics: They had to get a team together.

With Tom Berenger and Charlie Sheen on board, *Major League* already had its two stars, but it needed talented supporting actors to round out the lineup. When the casting process began in the spring of 1988, David Ward was open to all possibilities—except for one role. Since writing the first draft of the script five years earlier, Ward had had in mind a specific actor to portray the leader of this wacky bunch. To him, James Gammon always was manager Lou Brown.

Gammon was in his late 40s, but seemed ageless. His hardened face, thick mustache, and gravelly voice had made him ideal for roles in westerns, which he'd sprinkled through his twenty-year career. He was continually active in the theater, making his mark in several Sam Shepard plays and co-founding the MET Theater in Los Angeles in 1973. Gammon also got a lot of TV work, including a recurring role on *The Waltons*. He broke into films in the 1980s, including small roles in *Silverado* and *Ironweed*, and had also worked on Ward's last project, *The Milagro Beanfield War*, again donning a dusty cowboy hat and riding a horse.

"I just always liked his work," Ward says. "He always had that western feel, a man of authority, the strong, silent type. And he had that great voice. The character wasn't based on any particular manager, but on those gruff, ultimately very wise managers from the old days of baseball.''

Still, because Gammon was somewhat unknown, the idea of asking Billy Crystal to make a cameo appearance as a bench coach was discussed to add star power to the dugout. That was eventually ruled out, allowing Gammon elbow room to create one of the more memorable performances in the film. With Gammon and the other casting decisions that would follow, Ward had a strange sort of freedom.

"We weren't looking for stars," he says. "First of all, we couldn't afford them, and second, we already had Berenger and Sheen. So it wasn't about having an all-star cast; it was about finding people who could really embody the characters and be funny."

For the players Gammon would oversee, there were two principal qualifications: They had to be solid actors, and they had to be believable as ballplayers, not just by looking good in the faux clubhouse, but by looking right on the field.

This process proved to be trickier than you'd think. "If you ask an actor if he can do something, believe me, he can do it," Chesser says. Thus, the casting sessions became part line read, part tryout. "We'd both have our gloves with us," Ward says. "One of us would read with the actors and the other would go out and play catch with people we thought were potential actors for the film, just to see if they actually could play baseball. You can tell by playing catch with somebody if they look like they can play the game."

This process quickly whittled down the field of prospects. Ward was amazed at how far actors were willing to go to get a part. "I had a guy tell me he'd played triple-A ball for the Cardinals," Ward says. "I thought, *This is great*. Then we go out to play catch, and he couldn't throw the ball 15 feet. He literally had no clue. He had been told by his agent to tell me he'd played triple-A ball for the Cardinals."

Of all the actors cast as the principal players, only one had no baseball experience. On the plus side, he was also the only member of the cast who had worked with Michael Jackson.

Born in the Bronx, Wesley Snipes had attended New York's High School for the Performing Arts, where he'd parlayed his athleticism, studying dance, fencing, and martial arts. Building his resume on the stage, he quickly landed his first two film roles in sports movies. He debuted as a high school football player in *Wildcats*, then played a boxer in an obscure film titled *Streets of Gold*, directed by Joe Roth, who'd go on to launch Morgan Creek the following year. When discussions for the role of Willie Mays Hayes came up, Roth remembered Snipes and recommended him. He didn't know whether Snipes could play baseball, but he knew he could act and thought he'd be a good fit, visualizing what *The Plain Dealer* would conclude nearly a year later: that Snipes had "the looks of Arsenio Hall and the quickness of Eddie Murphy."

They sent the script to Snipes, who'd just appeared alongside the King of Pop as a gang member in the celebrated "Bad" music video directed by Martin Scorsese. Snipes recorded a Willie Mays Hayes scene on a

"I DIDN'T HAVE ANYTHING ELSE TO WEAR, SO I FLEW TO CALIFORNIA IN AN AVIATOR FLIGHT SUIT AND MY BOXING SHOES."

black-and-white videotape and sent it back. Ward and Chesser were impressed and had him fly out to Los Angeles for what in essence was less an audition than a tryout.

"I was in Florida visiting my great grandmother and got a call to come to California for the audition," Snipes says. "I'd just finished *Streets of Gold*, so I was in the habit of wearing boxing shorts and a type of boxing shoes. I didn't have anything else to wear, so I flew to California in an aviator flight suit and my boxing shoes."

When he arrived at Rancho Park, across the street from the 20th Century Fox studios, he instantly realized he was out of his element. "The first thing they said was, 'We're going to go over here to this baseball field,'" Snipes says. "I said, 'OK, so where's the audition going to be?' And they said, 'On the field.' And I thought, *Not gonna get this job.*"

Other than an appearance in a high school production of *Damn*

Yankees, Snipes had had no experience with baseball, unlike the other actors he was up against for the role. "They had all of these actors sitting in the bleachers, and these guys are dressed in full baseball uniforms," he recalls. "They had their gloves and their cleats, and I'm out there in an aviator flight suit and boxing shoes."

Snipes's only hope was to hang on until he could hit the base paths and demonstrate his athleticism. "The problem is, I had these boxing shoes on, and they had no traction," he says. "So every time I started running the bases, I wound up in center field. The rest of these guys were laughing their asses off, thinking, *Who is this dude?* By the time I got back to home plate, they were thinking, *We're not worried about him.* I started laughing myself. I thought, *Well, this was fun. I enjoyed the plane ride from Florida to California.*"

But despite his dubious on-field performance, Snipes had already made his mark. After a short line-reading that followed the tryout, Ward knew Snipes was his Willie Mays Hayes. "I decided to take a chance on Wesley even though he didn't have a lot of base-ball experience," Ward says. "He just had that Willie Mays Hayes attitude. He's funny and cocky and likable all at the same time. You could tell Wes had star quality."

To his surprise, Snipes was offered the job that afternoon. Although he was probably the slowest runner of all of the actors cast in the movie and his awkward throwing motion was a telltale sign of his baseball inexperience, he looked like a natural athlete. Plus, he turned out to be a quick learner, making his novice status as a ballplayer moot.

While Snipes was the baseball newbie who looked like an athlete, the least-athletic-looking actor of the primary cast actually had logged substantial experience on the diamond. Chelcie Ross was 45 when he read for the part of aging pitcher "Steve" Harris, and he certainly didn't look like a typical professional baseball player. But because that was the hook of the character—a junkball pitcher surviving on guile rather than prowess—Ross was an ideal fit. And as it happened, he'd played more baseball than most of the more polished-looking cast members.

A self-described Air Force brat, Ross had lived all over the country, playing sports at every stop, sometimes playing baseball with his older brother all day, every day throughout the summer. He was a pitcher in Pony League and high school and even played one year of college ball at Southwest Texas State Teachers College (now Texas State University). Fueled by his lifelong interest in baseball, Ross loved the *Major League* script and desperately wanted the role. He understood the character and saw similarities between Harris and many of the forthright-yet-slightly-vulgar coaches he'd had in his youth.

"I'd never had an opportunity to do a baseball film," Ross says. "That was something I thought I could do. I loved the script. It sounds contradictory, but it just had so many baseball clichés and baseball truths." In some ways, it was similar to a movie he had worked on three years before: the nostalgic but genuine high school basketball picture *Hoosiers*, which had quickly found its own niche among sports films.

Long-time Chicago-based casting director Jane Alderman brought in Ross (and several other Chicago-based actors) to read for *Major League*. Already building a career as a voiceover artist and appearing in hundreds of commercials, Ross was convinced his distinct Texas accent was what earned him a callback. "I think it resonated with what they were looking for," he says.

After Ross read with Ward again at the callback, Chesser took Ross out to the parking lot for a game of catch. They threw long enough for Chesser to see Ross knew what he was doing, then Chesser asked if Ross could throw something other than a fastball.

"I said I used to throw a curve," Ross remembers. "He asked to see it, so I threw a big lollipop, thank-you-ma'am curve up there— this big roundhouse that anybody in any softball league could hammer. But apparently it was enough, combined with my acting and my accent, to get me the role."

Ross's curveball would be forever preserved in the final cut of the film. In the spring-training scene in which Pedro Cerrano sees a curve for the first time, the camera is perched just over Ross's shoulder and captures Cerrano whiffing miserably at the pitch. Although it wouldn't have made anyone forget Sandy Koufax, the Chelcie Ross curveball had a little mustard. "Sad to say, that is in fact me, and is actually my yakker," the ever-humble Ross admits. "It didn't curve so much as it curled. I should have called it a 'curl ball.'"

Finding a guy who could be so fooled by the Chelcie Ross curveball was another tall order. Pedro Cerrano needed to be both incredibly intimidating and comically vulnerable, both on the field with his hitting struggles and in the clubhouse with his superstitions. Ward needed an actor who could simultaneously be Darth Vader and Linus naively waiting for the Great Pumpkin.

"I'd seen a bunch of people, then this big guy came into the room," Ward remembers. "He started to read in a deep voice, and I thought he'd make a great Cerrano."

That deep voice, which would one day become instantly recognizable, belonged to then-unknown, six-foot-four, 230-pound Dennis Haysbert. Although he had never appeared in a movie, he had found a lot of work in television throughout the previous 10 years, appearing in more than 30 shows, including *Dallas*, *Magnum P.I.*, and *The A-Team*.

A friend had told him that a baseball movie was looking for somebody to play a Cuban ballplayer. Haysbert remembers going to his agents and asking whether they'd heard about it. "They said, 'Well, yeah. But they're looking for a Latin ballplayer.' And I said, 'C'mon guys—you're going to go there? There are black Latins.' And they said, 'Oh, yeah. You're right.'"

Though Haysbert wasn't Hispanic, he had the look Ward needed for Cerrano, and he developed a unique quasi-Caribbean accent for the character. He also had the necessary athleticism. A defensive lineman on his high school football team, Haysbert had played quite a bit of recreational league and Babe Ruth baseball over the years, and his first TV role was as a high school basketball player.

Perhaps because he was a bit intimidated by the man who

would be Cerrano, Ward didn't initially mention to Haysbert that he'd have to shave his head for the role. Once he was cast, Ward broke the news.

"Wait a minute," Haysbert said after a moment of realization. "You mean I have to shave my head entirely?"

"Yes," Ward replied.

Haysbert considered it again. "I have to shave off all of my hair?"

Ward smiled wryly. "Yup," he said. "That's what I meant by 'shave your head.'"

"Why do I have to shave my head?" Haysbert asked, almost in desperation.

"Dennis," Ward replied, "it's because you're going to look really menacing with your head shaved."

So menacing, in fact, that Haysbert would become Charlie Sheen's unspoken bodyguard, walking alongside him whenever the cast had to maneuver through a crowd. But the surprise Haysbert felt in that

"WAIT A MINUTE. YOU MEAN I HAVE TO SHAVE MY HEAD ENTIRELY?"

moment of revelation was shared by fans of the movie who later didn't immediately recognize him in other roles. With his distinctive voice, though, it didn't take long for them to connect the dots.

And even though the role required an entirely new look, to Haysbert, the opportunity to play the character was worth it. "I just loved this guy," he says. "He was serious about his game, and I especially liked the fact that the man had faith. And his arc was that he was going to go beyond that faith and get back to the man and start to have faith in himself. The character was just written very, very well. Really, he was the basis for a lead type of character."

And in that spirit, Haysbert modeled the role on the larger-than-life personality of then-Dodgers superstar Pedro Guerrero.

Filling the roles of the ballplayers came fairly easily, but casting the two primary female roles proved more complicated.

There were a handful of contenders for the role of Jake Taylor's former flame Lynn Westland, including Sheila Kelly and Bruce

Springsteen's first wife, Julianne Phillips, but Ward was leaning toward an unlikely choice he'd read for the lead role in *Cannery Row* seven years earlier.

Discovered by an agent at a Rolling Stones concert, Rene Russo had been a successful model, having graced multiple covers of *Cosmopolitan* and *Vogue* in the 1970s as well as appearing in numerous fashion and makeup ads. As her modeling career began to fade, her agent pushed her into acting. "I didn't want to act because I'd modeled forever and was sick of being in front of the camera," Russo says. "He had to drag my ass every step of the way. I went into acting not by choice, but because I needed a job."

It took time for her skills to develop, but from the beginning, her potential was obvious. "When I read her that first time for *Cannery Row*, she was very raw," Ward says. "She hadn't done hardly any acting, and she was very shy. But you could tell she had a quality about her that was very attractive. She wasn't just physically attractive; you just liked her. You sort of took her to your heart. She had a lovely emotional range, but she didn't have any of it under control yet."

When casting the role of Lynn for *Major League*, Ward remembered Russo and called her agent to ask her to come in and read. When Russo heard about it, she initially declined: "I said, 'no way.' I told them I'd be playing a swimmer and I couldn't swim—totally as a way to get out of it. When I look back, I was scared to death and was just trying to escape."

Eventually Russo did read for the role of Lynn, and Ward saw the same qualities he'd noticed seven years earlier. "She sort of stood in a corner and read the lines, but she had much more ability now," Ward says. "Even though she didn't give the best reading, she had the best quality about her. She's just the kind of girl you would be attracted to. There was something about her that I thought would be great with Berenger—that she was a bit more sophisticated and was someone with intelligence. And that would make it harder for him to win her back."

"I honestly don't know why he took a chance with me," Russo

says. "This was a big role that he threw my way, and I hadn't done anything to speak of. A lot of people wouldn't take a chance on a newcomer, especially a model. So I really lucked out. I really didn't know what I was walking into or anything about the business. I'm surprised he got his way with casting me, honestly. I'm surprised the studio said OK."

Indeed, Ward knew it was a risk hiring a green actor for a major role, and he had to talk both Morgan Creek and Paramount into allowing him to cast her. But he was sure Russo would come through. He also knew he'd be in trouble if she didn't, recalling the disaster that followed casting Raquel Welch as the female lead in *Cannery Row*. After two miserable weeks, Ward knew Welch wasn't working out, and the decision was made to let her go and eventually bring Debra Winger in to play the role.

Interestingly, a similar kind of recasting happened with the Rachel Phelps role in *Major League*, albeit before the cameras began rolling.

They thought they'd found their villain when Chesser offered it to Dyan Cannon, whom he'd met in his days at the American Film Institute and who was best known for her Academy Award–nominated performances in *Bob & Carol & Ted & Alice* and *Heaven Can Wait*. Then, just after Paramount had agreed to distribute the film, and only two weeks before shooting was to start, Chesser got a phone call from Joe Roth. Unaware that the part had been offered to Cannon, Paramount had a suggestion for the role, and Roth knew better than to get into a pissing match with the distributing studio.

The actress suggested for the part of Rachel Phelps was Margaret Whitton, who'd impressed Paramount executives the year before in the Michael J. Fox corporate comedy *The Secret of My Success*. It had been a breakthrough role for Whitton, who'd established herself on the New York stage before climbing the ranks in small roles in film and television in the 1980s. Paramount saw her as an up-and-comer and thought she'd make a great Rachel Phelps.

Chesser carefully talked Cannon out of the role right after talking her into it, and the issue was resolved.

It turned out to be a brilliant casting move. Whitton latched onto the character from the beginning, painting a full emotional portrait. Whitton remembers: "When you really think about the backstory of Rachel, she was probably from an economically deprived area and didn't have much. So she became a showgirl, met this man, and fell in love with him. And he dies and leaves her in a lurch in terms of how she's going to make her way in the world. So she's kind of like a Barbara Stanwyck character—she's got to be smart and savvy and figure it out because nobody's going to help her out. She's playing the cards that she's dealt."

With filming about to begin, Paramount had one more suggestion. The studio was excited about the potential of rejoining Berenger and Sheen, but—primarily because of the risk they were taking by casting newcomer Russo as the romantic lead—they asked that one more recognizable actor be cast in a lead role. Paramount didn't have a specific actor in mind this time, so Ward and company were able to provide their own solution.

Throughout the casting process, they hadn't been able to settle on the right Roger Dorn. At one point, the idea of getting singer Huey Lewis to play the role was floated, but he was touring and unavailable. Several actors had read, and the producers had a few in mind, primarily Wings Hauser and Chris Mulkey. But before they could make a decision and extend an offer, another candidate emerged at the last minute, right out of the plush offices of a fictional Los Angeles law firm.

Like Sheen and Berenger, Corbin Bernsen had leapt into celebrity status in 1986, albeit via a completely different vehicle. While *Platoon*'s grit and stark reality made it a hit at the box office, Steven Bochco's slick and stylish primetime drama *L.A. Law* had premiered that fall and quickly became the hottest show on television. Bernsen, cast as womanizing divorce attorney Arnie Becker, earned Emmy nominations in both of the show's first two seasons and joined Harry Hamlin and Jimmy Smits at the heart of a terrific ensemble cast that would help *L.A. Law* anchor NBC's Thursday-night lineup for the next eight years.

With his quick rise to fame, Bernsen suddenly went from struggling actor to a hot prospect for film work. He was cast in a pair of movies following *L.A. Law*'s first season, then landed a role alongside Anne Bancroft in *Bert Rigby, You're a Fool* after its second. In the middle of production, Bernsen got a call from his manager telling him about a great script he had received for a baseball movie with Tom Berenger and Charlie Sheen. Bernsen was intrigued by the premise, and completely enamored with the script after he had read it.

Bernsen saw similarities between Roger Dorn and Arnie Becker, but was able to pinpoint the primary difference between the two. "They were both guys with something missing," he says. "Arnie Becker was a guy who has everything, but I read between the lines and saw this poor son-of-a-bitch who's got everything, but got nothing. He's got no soul. The minute he shuts his office door, he pounds his head on the desk. Roger Dorn had some of that, but he was caught up in his own thing. I don't know if he closed the door and felt empty, but he was able to play through it all. He bought his own bullshit."

With shooting on *Major League* about to begin and Bernsen in the middle of filming *Bert Rigby*, he figured he'd be unavailable to accept the role. But because Bernsen was a natural fit for Roger Dorn and recognizable enough to appease Paramount's request for a third star, Ward was willing to adapt. He'd heard that Bernsen regularly played in celebrity baseball games alongside fellow actors, but there wasn't going to be time to have Bernsen prove his skills barely a week before shooting was to start.

"I told him that he just had to trust me that I could play baseball," Bernsen says. "I was confident enough in myself that I could—at least in a movie—make it look good."

Like several other actors cast in the film, Bernsen had the experience to make it believable. He'd played through Little League and high school and had even entertained the idea of playing after enrolling at Humboldt State University. At least until 18-year-old Bernsen, whose blond hair fell almost to his shoulders, met with the athletic director about joining the baseball team.

"He said, 'First thing: that hair goes,'" Bernsen recalls. "This is 1972, so everybody's growing their hair and getting high and hanging out and getting laid. And I thought, *My baseball career is now officially over. There are more important things, and I want to have sex.*"

Yet another major role was filled just before production began.

As summer approached, the character of Harry Doyle had yet to be cast. It was a decision that came with its own challenges.

Although he would prove to be one of the most memorable characters in the film, Doyle was essentially detached from the rest of the characters, so his scenes would be filmed independently. Whoever played the role had to be able to own each and every scene he was in.

In mid-June, Chesser was in Chicago with John Travolta wrapping up production on *The Tender* (eventually retitled *Eyes of an Angel*), and the two went to a White Sox game at old Comiskey Park as the guests of club owners Jerry Reisdorf and Eddie Einhorn. As it turned out, the Sox were playing the Milwaukee Brewers that night, and someone mentioned that Bob Uecker was the Brewers' play-by-play radio announcer.

In that moment, lightning flashed in Chris Chesser's mind as he pictured Harry Doyle. *Of course . . . Bob Uecker!*

Even then, Uecker was something of a household name. He had been an obscure backup catcher with the Milwaukee Braves and St. Louis Cardinals in the 1960s ("I played 13 years of pro ball," he wrote in his autobiography, "and remember all but the last six clearly") but made his mark on the game after his playing career was over. Ironically, the career .200 hitter became as much a part of modern baseball as the jockstrap, eventually adopting the tongue-in-cheek yet fitting nickname, "Mr. Baseball."

Known as a clown during his playing days—perhaps best remembered for catching fly balls with a tuba prior to the first game of the 1964 World Series—his legendary sense of humor made a mark on fellow players and fans alike. He began broadcasting Milwaukee Brewers games shortly after his playing career ended, and became famous for his quick wit and self-deprecating humor.

After landing a spot as a national broadcaster with ABC, and through a series of appearances on *The Tonight Show* with Johnny Carson, Uecker became a bona fide celebrity in the 1980s when he began appearing in television commercials for Miller Lite beer. In the spots, which were often more entertaining than the program they sponsored, he adopted the role of a big-time former ballplayer who is ignored and disrespected.

Uecker's work in the commercials and his role as a sportswriter on the ABC sitcom *Mr. Belvedere* later in the decade made him the perfect choice as the radio voice of the fictional Indians.

In retrospect, Ward concedes that he might have unconsciously written the role of Harry Doyle with Uecker in mind, although at the time he had no idea that Uecker was a real announcer. "I'd seen him in the beer commercials," Ward says, adding: "I can't say that I wrote it specifically for him, but Doyle was always a Uecker-esque kind of guy."

That night at Comiskey, Chesser asked to meet Uecker between innings and was taken to the press box for a quick introduction. They shook hands, and Chesser mentioned that he was developing a baseball movie with David Ward. He asked Uecker whether he would be interested in the role of the beleaguered announcer. "He gave me this 'Yeah, maybe,' kind of thing, but it was clear he was interested," Chesser says.

Uecker explains: "I could see myself as Harry Doyle. I just didn't know what the schedule was or how much time it would take, so I didn't know when I was going to be able to shoot."

Discussions began, and schedules were compared. Two weeks later, when the Brewers came to Anaheim for a three-game series with the Angels, Chesser closed the deal with Uecker by the pool at the team's hotel.

And with that, *Major League*'s starting lineup was complete.

•   •   •

Although James Gammon had been cast as the manager, the team still needed a coach.

Ward and Chesser had been careful in selecting actors with baseball skills, but most of them were raw and needed smoothing out. To help suspend the disbelief, they needed someone who would be credited as the "technical adviser," but in reality would be the "coach" of the entire production.

"We knew we needed a baseball player," Ward says, "not only to put everybody through their paces and get them baseball-sharp, but to get them in shape so they weren't pulling hamstrings and hurting themselves, thus not being able to shoot for days on end."

Ward also wanted someone who had experience as a catcher to serve as a stand-in, quasi-stunt double for Tom Berenger, and who could both alleviate the concerns about the actor's throwing motion and prevent his wearing down from spending too much time crouched behind the plate.

Ward got back in touch with Tommy Lasorda, whom he'd gotten to know while researching story concepts a few years earlier. Lasorda recommended that Ward get in touch with Steve Yeager, the nephew of renowned pilot Chuck Yeager, who had been a big-league catcher for 15 years. Known for his defense behind the plate and a rocket arm, the personable Yeager had helped propel the Dodgers to four pennants and was named co-MVP of the 1981 World Series.

"I got a phone call from the Dodgers saying there's a gentleman trying to get ahold of me by the name of David Ward," Yeager recalls. "I called David back and set up a lunch for the two of us and Chris Chesser. David said, 'This is what I'm doing, what do you think? Do you want to come on board?' And I said, 'Let's do it.'"

Yeager's task was formidable. He'd have to whip the actors into shape, work with them during filming to make sure they were following correct baseball techniques and protocol, and hit and throw countless baseballs to specific spots and people during filming.

Also, despite having no acting experience, Yeager would also play two different characters in the movie. First, he would serve as Berenger's stand-in, primarily to deliver the bullet throws necessary to make Jake Taylor look like an all-star catcher. He was also inserted into the cast as Duke Temple, the Tribe's batting coach. "I just thought he was a natural in the sense that he was a ballplayer and he was comfortable on camera," Ward says. "Why get an actor when you've got a guy right here?"

For Yeager, playing Duke Temple was like rolling off a log. "I can hit the ground running in a baseball uniform, no doubt about it," Yeager says. "It was easy to look and play the part because I *am* the part."

In another ironic bit of casting, the man tapped to play Rick Vaughn's nemesis was a much closer facsimile to Wild Thing in real life. When looking for someone for the minute role of the intimidating Yankee relief pitcher at the film's climax, the *Major League* team brought in former Milwaukee Brewers pitcher Pete Vuckovich, who had retired two years earlier and was now a color commentator for Brewers telecasts.

He was a natural choice, having built a successful major-league career as a massive, intimidating force on the mound in the early 1980s. Vuckovich led the American League in victories in 1981 and won the Cy Young Award the following year, gaining notoriety for his frantic movements on the mound. Known for living large off the field as well, Vuckovich admitted he'd sometimes pitch hung over, throwing up behind the mound after finishing his warmups.

Still sporting the Fu Manchu mustache of his playing days, Vuckovich had just the right look—so much so that after their meeting, Ward recast him in the slightly larger role of Clu Haywood, the antagonizing Yankee slugger who lights up Vaughn twice before they meet in the ninth inning of the final game. Vuckovich then referred former Brewers pitcher Willie Mueller to play Duke Simpson, the imposing Yankee closer.

Jane Alderman cast a wide net for most of the other smaller roles and found several great fits, including another diamond in the rough for the quick but memorable role of a foul-mouthed construction worker: Neil Flynn, who just over a decade later would become one of the most recognizable comic performers on television, as the antagonistic janitor on the hit show *Scrubs*.

But perhaps the most important secondary roles were the ones that didn't require dialogue. While the primary actors were being groomed to look like ballplayers, they would still be in the minority on the field. Extras were needed for the game sequences, and not just ordinary actors but actual ballplayers to maintain and support the verisimilitude carefully constructed through casting. Once the locations were settled, open calls for local talent were announced and a mass tryout was organized. More than 1,200 guys showed up—several of whom had either played in college or the minor leagues—and around 50 were selected for nonspeaking roles, primarily to round out the dugouts and on-field lineups for the Indians and Yankees.

Ward was careful to make sure none of the extras' character names matched those of real-life big-league ballplayers to avoid offense. As an inside joke that's barely noticeable in the final film, one extra even donned a jersey with "Ward" stitched on the back—which only seemed appropriate, considering the daydream-like basis of the entire enterprise.

•   •   •

For all of the time and energy spent on reading and reviewing actors, perhaps the most important casting decision was not for a person or character at all. Ward and company had to decide what location would stand in for Cleveland.

It had become evident very early on that shooting the movie in Cleveland wasn't going to be possible. The primary obstacle, as it usually is for any film production, was money. Because Cleveland was a strong union town, setting up a production there and paying union scale would have cost an estimated million dollars more—roughly 10 percent of *Major League*'s modest budget. Even without the higher costs, the film couldn't have been shot in Cleveland for the same primary reason the Indians couldn't win there: the ballpark.

Cleveland Municipal Stadium's design blocked a large quantity of sunlight from reaching the field. Long shadows crisscrossing through the massive horseshoe structure would have limited the number of daytime shooting hours, and considering the amount of time and film *Major League* would require, they'd need every minute they could get. The Indians' housemates created another logistical problem. With filming scheduled to begin in July and last into September, production would overlap with the beginning of the Cleveland Browns' 1988 football season. Not only would the stadium's availability be shortened, but yard markers would be painted on the field and would be noticeable on film.

THE FILM COULDN'T HAVE BEEN SHOT IN CLEVELAND FOR THE SAME PRIMARY REASON THE INDIANS COULDN'T WIN THERE: THE BALLPARK.

"It was going to look stupid if we were shooting baseball and there were football lines on the field," Ward says. "We couldn't do that. So even if we had been able to negotiate the union situation, we couldn't have shot in Cleveland because we were too late in the year." Plus, just as the Indians had learned—the hard way—during the previous three decades, cavernous Cleveland Stadium was going to be hard to fill. It would even be hard just to make it appear full on film.

They needed another Cleveland Stadium. And because the choice of the city to film in would hinge on the choice of the ballpark, they also needed another Cleveland. Ward and Chesser considered Buffalo's War Memorial Stadium, which had been used in *The Natural* and was now unoccupied, scheduled for demolition later that year. But Ward felt it didn't look quite right, and it would have cost too much to make it double for Cleveland Stadium. After some location scouting, the producers settled on Milwaukee's County Stadium, which was slightly more than half of the size of Cleveland's and had been designed and built in the early 1950s by the same architectural firm.

The *Major League* team contacted the owner of the Brewers—a then-unknown car dealer named Bud Selig—who graciously agreed to cooperate. The city of Milwaukee was eager to help, too.

Although the city hadn't been the site of a major film production since the comedy *Gaily, Gaily* was shot there in 1968, it had gotten a taste of celebrity in the 1970s when the hit television shows *Happy Days* and *Laverne and Shirley* were set (but not filmed) there. For *Major League*, county officials offered the use of facilities for constructing sets. That, combined with the variety of rust-belt locations in and around town, made Milwaukee a suitable stand-in for Cleveland.

Now, with the roster filled out and the home ballpark open for business, it was time to play ball.

EXTRAS . . .

The four faithful fans who follow the Indians throughout the season from the bleachers appear only briefly in the movie, yet David Ward sketched out their character details and backgrounds in the script. Bobby Jones is a 22-year-old grad student. Vic Bolito is a 35-year-old telephone worker. Johnny Wynn is a 45-year-old house painter. Thelma Gordon, who serves them coffee in the "Injun Diner" in their first scene, is a 65-year-old waitress. You can also see Thelma knitting in the bleachers in her early scenes. Described in the early drafts of the script as the "Madame Defarge of Cleveland," she's knitting a blanket with the scores of all the Indians games stitched into it. The finished blanket hangs from a railing in front of the group during the playoff game.

•

Cleveland columnist cameo (sort of): Bill Livingston of *The Plain Dealer* didn't actually appear in the movie, but his photo and column are visible on the newspaper shown in the opening moments, announcing the death of the India ns owner. His imaginary column was titled "Can Vegas beauty turn Tribe around?"

6

Breaking Training

After five years imprisoned in the Siberia of turnaround, *Major League* had finally been liberated. The cast had been assembled, the production schedule was locked in (including pinpointing a five-week subset of the 10-week shoot for which Charlie Sheen was available), and a release date was set for spring 1989.

Now all that could screw things up were the real-life Cleveland Indians. And in the weeks leading up to the start of filming, they toyed with the possibility of doing just that.

Coming off a 101-loss season, the 1988 Indians got off to one of the finest starts in franchise history, winning 11 of their first 13 games and then standing at 30-16 going into Memorial Day weekend, just a game and a half out of first place in the American League East. Home attendance increased more than 30 percent, and *Sports Illustrated* put together a four-page feature on the Tribe's resurgence. If the Indians were somehow able to capture a division title—or even just finish an exciting, competitive season—it could undermine the appeal of a movie based on the Tribe's eternal incompetence.

A conflicted David Ward watched nervously as his beloved team completed a three-game sweep of powerful Toronto to pull within a half-game of first place in early June—just days before the *Major League* cameras began to roll. "I was of two minds," he says.

"It would be great if the Indians won, but it would sort of make our movie obsolete. I didn't know what to think, so I actually just stopped following them."

In fact, the good start would help the movie as Ward and his small army prepared to load the cameras for the first time.

Finding enough extras to make Milwaukee's County Stadium look packed would be challenging enough in the weeks to come; filling Cleveland Stadium was even more daunting. Filming establishing shots of the exterior of the real Cleveland Stadium was one thing, but Ward wanted an epic shot of a jam-packed ballpark to insert just before the film's climactic playoff game. Even with their strong start, the Indians were still averaging slightly more than 17,000 per home game, meaning that on any given night, odds were the mammoth ballpark would be at least three-quarters empty.

"IT WOULD BE GREAT IF THE INDIANS WON, BUT IT WOULD SORT OF MAKE OUR MOVIE OBSOLETE."

Rather than abandoning the idea or trying elaborate special effects, Ward took advantage of an annual Indians tradition that was endearing at the time, but now seems almost laughable. From 1986 to 1991, Marathon Oil offered a special promotion in northeast Ohio in which fans would receive two tickets to a designated Indians game with a fill-up at a Marathon station. Usually scheduled for a Friday night in June and followed by a fireworks show, "Marathon Oil Night" (as it informally came to be known) was always a highlight of the schedule, joining the home opener as the only two games of the season at which a massive crowd could be expected.

Fueled by the team's fast start, 1988's Marathon Oil Night provided the promotion's best turnout ever. On the cool, breezy evening of June 10, the Indians, who were holding steady in second place, hosted the third-place Detroit Tigers. More than 71,000 fans filed into Cleveland Stadium that night—roughly 40,000 holding promotional tickets, unaware that in addition to witnessing a good game and fireworks, they were about to be immortalized on film.

It was the Indians' largest home crowd in eight years, and exactly what Ward needed.

A helicopter was commandeered for the first shot of the production, an aerial clip of the mammoth ballpark filled almost to the brim. But Ward, who had a fear of flying, declined to climb on board, so Chris Chesser strapped in along with cinematographer Reynaldo Villalobos to make sure everything worked. And it had to, because they'd only get one chance.

The shot was going to be inserted as a setup for the final game before it began, therefore the field had to be completely clear. So the *Major League* team made an unusual arrangement with the Indians: They asked both the umpiring crew and the Tigers if one of the usual 90-second breaks between innings could be stretched to three-and-a-half minutes when the helicopter flew over to allow more time to get the shot. At the designated moment, the umpires left the field and the players remained in the dugout for an extra two minutes while the helicopter hovered overhead. "I can't remember if we even announced to the crowd that's what we were doing," PR director Bob DiBiasio said. "I don't think you could get that done today."

They did get it done, despite the logistical challenges, and the moving shot coming in off the lake and over the lit-up, nearly full stadium fits the final movie like a velvet glove. The Indians lost that night, but the game served a more lasting, memorable purpose.

*   *   *

When the film and its subject matter were officially announced to the public 12 days later, it was big news in the two places that would be most affected.

Major League instantly became one of the most exciting things ever to happen to Milwaukee, and the announcement made the front page of the *Milwaukee Sentinel.* In Cleveland, however, the news was buried inside the lifestyle section, and the reaction was decidedly mixed. On one hand, many felt it would be exciting to see their oft-neglected ballclub on the silver screen. On the other, there was a sense that this might be a prank. Although it was made clear that David Ward was a native son who loved the Indians— implying that he could be trusted—it was still a sensitive subject. It was one thing for Clevelanders to joke about the Indians, but they weren't exactly comfortable with the idea of Hollywood using them for laughs. Rather than embracing the idea of the film, Cleveland stiffened a bit as a protective, almost parental instinct subtly kicked in.

There was also skepticism about the Brew City being used in place of Cleveland. "Milwaukee, according to Hollywood, looks more like Cleveland than Cleveland does," wrote *Plain Dealer* columnist Bill Livingston. "I don't know about you, but when Lenny and Squiggy and Carmine and Mr. DiFazio show up at a tryout camp in the movie, I think I smell a rat."

But Ward and company explained they also planned to come to Cleveland to film exterior shots of the stadium and downtown areas. "We really want it to look like Cleveland," Ward told *The Plain Dealer* just before filming began. "There's a side of Cleveland the country doesn't see. The media has portrayed it as a rust-belt city, but there are all kinds of beautiful things here."

DiBiasio, for one, knew those weren't just empty words. "We knew Chris and David and knew they weren't going to shoot it on some sound stage in New Mexico or something," he says. "They were going to come to the city streets and go out of their way to make sure it had authenticity."

To capture some of that authenticity, a second-unit crew swept back into Cleveland to kick off the Fourth of July weekend. Leading the crew was seasoned production manager Irby Smith, brought in by Morgan Creek a few months earlier to assist with the movie. The trip to Cleveland was just one of many responsibilities for Smith, who would play a much larger role over the course of production and eventually wound up with a producer credit.

With Smith heading up the mission, a crew roamed through Cleveland Stadium during a Friday night Tribe game with hand-held cameras to capture actual game and crowd footage that would be blended into the film's final game sequence, albeit from a distance so as not to betray the reality.

Although it wasn't Marathon Oil Night, the crew had again selected an evening with a fireworks promotion, this one drawing more than 40,000 to watch the Tribe, which was still hanging around high enough in the standings to make everybody involved with the film nervous.

Unlike the crew's first trip to the ballpark three weeks earlier, this one wasn't under the radar. Their arrival was splashed through the media. "Remember," a *Plain Dealer* article dramatically declared that Friday, "the way you look tonight at the game may be preserved forever on film." And in the spirit of full disclosure (and legal permission), fans entering the ballpark that night were greeted by production assistants holding signs stating that by entering the stadium, the fans were providing their consent to be photographed and included in the film.

To maintain the buzz of the initial announcement of the film, Tom Berenger and Charlie Sheen were brought along, and, wearing caps and personalized Indians jerseys, they threw out ceremonial first pitches. Sheen, using a glove borrowed from Indians second baseman Julio Franco, looked particularly sharp with his pitch, hinting what the movie would hold. Earlier, Sheen mingled in the dugout, chatting with outfielder Mel Hall, who later said that Sheen offered advice on starting a Hollywood career after Hall was done with baseball.

Unfortunately, *Major League* delivered no magic for the Indians that night, as they were pounded by the last-place Seattle Mariners. Since news of the film first broke in Cleveland one week earlier, the real-life Indians had now lost six straight—almost as if, on cue, they were attempting to preserve the premise of the film.

•   •   •

As background footage and establishing shots were gathered in those frenzied few weeks before principal photography began, David Ward's Indians went to boot camp.

Borrowing Oliver Stone's idea to send his primary cast through simulated military training prior to the start of shooting on *Platoon*, Ward and Chesser set up a two-week mini-camp for most of the primary actors just before shooting began: one week in Los Angeles and another in Tucson, where the spring-training sequences would be filmed. Steve Yeager ran the show, hitting countless grounders and fly balls and putting actors through their paces at the plate and on the base paths—not only to get them into shape, but to show Ward what they could and couldn't do.

"These guys worked as hard as they could possibly work," Yeager says. "It's easy to coach somebody who wants to learn. They made my job a lot easier because of their attitude going in. And they took enough pride in their profession to say, 'If I'm going to do this, I'm going to look the part and play the part.' They didn't want to embarrass themselves."

Yeager's professionalism and experience inspired the actors. "I just didn't want to disappoint Yeager," Dennis Haysbert remembers. "We really played for him."

"I didn't know who Steve Yeager was, so I didn't really understand the magnitude of the man I was working with," Wesley Snipes says. "It wasn't until we got on the field and he started throwing at me that everything became crystal clear. I was way out of my league."

Ward also got an early sense of Yeager's legitimacy when they started a casual game of catch. "I threw him the ball, then my script supervisor came up to me and asked a question, and I turned my head," Ward says. "Usually when I'm playing catch with somebody, I can carry on a conversation with someone else and glance back as the ball is coming. The ball came back so fast that I just heard it go whizzing past my head. I wondered, *What was that?* And I looked at Steve and realized, *Fuck—that was the baseball!* Steve had such an arm, and his idea of catch was that you whipped it back and forth."

In addition to introducing the director to the realism he brought to the set, Yeager had already gotten an early start with the headliners. He'd spent two weeks with Sheen and Berenger at Pepperdine University near Los Angeles honing their skills, then another three weeks near Berenger's home in Beaufort. A friend of Berenger's was the head of maintenance for the local school district, and he gave them keys to one of the high school baseball diamonds that was screened off and isolated by pine and palmetto trees, offering some privacy for their practice. They also rounded up a handful of local guys who'd once played baseball to form a small scrimmage team.

They trekked to nearby Hilton Head to the only batting cage in the area and hit baseballs for hours on end, and visited the triple-A team in Savannah for Sheen to pitch batting practice and Berenger to catch some of the pitchers. Through those five weeks of training, Yeager worked on fine-tuning both actors' technique. He was impressed with their natural ability and commitment.

"I BEAT HIM UP SO BAD: BLOCKING BALLS, THROWING, AND FOOTWORK. I FELT SORRY FOR HIM."

"Charlie was a helluva athlete," Yeager said. "It was just a matter of getting his arm in shape." His goal was to prep Sheen as if he were a relief pitcher—he could pitch for three or four straight days, then get a day off.

From the outset, Sheen's skills were evident. "Of the first 10 pitches he threw me, nine were on the edge of the strike zone," Berenger said. "He had great control. On his good days, I think he was throwing his fastball about 88 miles per hour."

According to Yeager, "The bigger project was Tom because he had never caught a day in his life. I just treated him like a young kid who had never caught before. I put the gear on him, gave him one of my old gloves to use, and I beat him up so bad: blocking balls, throwing, and footwork. I felt sorry for him. But he came out there and religiously did everything you could possibly do, and didn't complain."

"Yeager was a great, great coach and a great teacher," Berenger says. "He was incredibly patient and absolutely wonderful about all the tiny details. He was really good with me, especially considering I had never played catcher and had a lot to learn."

Nonetheless, Berenger's experience as an actor was already paying off. One of the reasons he'd suggested shifting their training to South Carolina was to help them adjust to the dense humidity they'd encounter later that summer in the Midwest. Because the weather would turn out to be even worse in Milwaukee than anyone could have predicted, the Palmetto State primer proved particularly valuable.

But before they were introduced to one of the hottest midwestern summers on record, they'd begin filming in the dry heat capital of the United States, the Arizona desert.

• • •

Even before cameras began rolling, a quick reminder of the difference between movie ballplayers and actual ballplayers popped up with some mild drama over haircuts.

What turned out to be one of the trademark details of the Wild Thing character was described only vaguely in the script as "a radical haircut with a pigtail." But by the first week of shooting, Ward had a clearer vision. Once everyone had arrived in Tucson, Sheen sat down in a barber's chair in the hairdressing trailer and Ward and the stylist discussed the style they wanted. Ward liked the idea of a lightning-bolt pattern just above the neck on one side. Thinking his instructions were clear, Ward left and the stylist went to work. When Sheen emerged a few minutes later, Ward saw to his surprise that the lightning bolt had been trimmed onto both sides of the neck.

"I was afraid it would look like less of a rebel gesture and more like a conventional haircut if it was both sides," Ward says. "It was more of a statement if it was on one side, more of a 'Fuck you.' But it didn't look bad, so I figured we'd just go with it."

While Sheen's new hairstyle was eye-catching, Dennis Haysbert's created an entirely new identity. With his thick black mustache and goatee fully grown in, the time had come for Haysbert to fully immerse himself in his role and completely shave his head. But he wouldn't go through it alone; Sheen, Berenger, Yeager, and Snipes crowded around the chair to watch.

"I knew this was going to be a kick," Haysbert says. "Nobody'd seen my bald head since I was a baby. I had no idea if I was going to have wrinkles on my head or rolls or dents or anything else. So they're all in there holding my hand while I got my locks taken off." Free of rolls, dents, and wrinkles, to his surprise, Haysbert instantly loved the new look. "It was a trip," he says. "And Pedro Cerrano was born."

Corbin Bernsen also desperately needed a trim, but he couldn't get one just yet. Ever since *L.A. Law* finished shooting for the season in the spring, Bernsen had been growing his hair out for his role in *Bert Rigby*. He had just a few days of shooting left on that film when he began work on *Major League*, so he couldn't cut his hair yet. In his initial spring-training shots, Bernsen is wearing a baseball cap, concealing his long locks.

Filming began on Monday, July 18, the start of an ambitious shooting slate consisting of ten six-day weeks at locations stretching from the American southwest to the Great Lakes.

Fittingly, it would start where so many real Cleveland baseball seasons had. And just as so many Indians teams began the bonding process of a long season on arrival in Tucson, the same thing happened almost instantaneously to the cast and crew of *Major League*. "We all hit it off pretty well together," Chelcie Ross says. "It was like going to camp. As soon as we got there, we all became kids again."

For Chris Chesser, it was a special homecoming. After all the movies he'd seen being filmed in Tucson as a kid, now he was part of making one himself. "It was kind of special to me," he says, "being able to bring the guys over to the house I grew up in, which was only a mile away. It all just seemed to fit. But it wasn't like I had the time to really luxuriate in the fact that I was back home."

Ward was much more anxious. "I was feeling the pressure

because if this movie didn't work, my chances of directing again were nil," he says.

As a result, starting in Tucson and carrying through the first few weeks of production, Ward was overly cautious. Although that quality is desirable in most professions, it causes problems on a tightly scheduled film shoot. He shot too many takes, looking for perfection in each one before ultimately realizing there was no such thing. Between that and the crew's not yet having found a rhythm, by the end of the first week, Ward was a day behind schedule, which forecasted being two weeks late by the end of production.

Because they had Charlie Sheen only for five of the 10 weeks of shooting, Ward couldn't afford to fall behind. To save time, they decided to pare a few scenes in the script and shoot the Willie Mays Hayes pajama-running sequence in Milwaukee instead of Tucson, when things would be running a bit smoother.

Although much of the work awaited them in Milwaukee, a quick pace was set in those first few days. Ward's knowledge of baseball helped keep things moving, as did the experience of cinematographer Reynaldo Villalobos, who not only had shot films such as *Urban Cowboy* and *Risky Business*, but had also worked for ABC's *Wide World of Sports*. Villalobos knew how to set up the traditional camera angles that would mirror what viewers were used to seeing when watching a game on television and also captured the action from unusual perspectives to help draw the viewer into the game and the story.

During the Tucson sequences, most of that action was deliberate goof-ups.

Dennis Haysbert had to swing at and miss hittable pitches—but not look like he was deliberately missing them. Sharp-throwing Charlie Sheen had to sail pitches to the backstop and obliterate a metallic replica of a batter. Crisp-fielding Corbin Bernsen had to flub ground ball after ground ball. Baseball novice Wesley Snipes had to figure out not only how to run the bases and slide properly, but then how to slide poorly, so that he came to a stop two feet in front of second base. Yeager had taken him into the outfield the day before to work on his technique, and on his second slide, Snipes got his hand caught in a divot in the grass. He rolled over it, hyperextending ligaments in his left hand. "My hand swelled up like a donut," he says. "And just like at the tryout, I'm thinking, *Well, I enjoyed my flight to Arizona!*"

Even more difficult—especially with a swollen hand—Snipes also had to learn how to hit pop-ups. To emphasize just how hopeless Willie Mays Hayes is at the plate, Ward needed a handful of shots of him popping the baseball harmlessly into the air. Hitting a pop-up on cue is hard enough for an experienced ballplayer, but it's something else again for someone who'd never played the game. "During that two-week mini-camp, Yeager taught him how to hit pop-ups," Ward says. "Here was a guy who never actually swung a bat in competition, and he's hitting pop-ups on demand. And he was good. The first day I thought, *This shot is going to take forever.*" Thanks to Snipes's natural athletic ability, it didn't.

> "WHEN WE GOT TO THE PART OF THE MOVIE WHERE I WAS ACTUALLY SUPPOSED TO HIT THE BALL, THINGS WENT DOWNHILL REAL FAST."

"The old saying about hitting a baseball is that you hit down on the ball," Yeager explains. "This was the opposite. We told Wesley to hit *up* on the ball, to try to hit the bottom side to pop it up. He did a helluva job."

"It's a God-given gift," Snipes chuckles. "There is no acting involved. That was very natural. But when we got to the part of the movie where I was actually supposed to hit the ball, things went downhill real fast."

Another goof-up—this one accidental—slightly altered Ward's script. In Cerrano's first batting scene, after he crushes the first two pitches he sees, Yeager, playing hitting coach Duke Temple, was supposed to shout instructions to the pitcher—Steve Harris, in the script.

After James Gammon wonders aloud why nobody else picked

up Cerrano, Yeager motions to the mound and says, "OK, Eddie. That's enough fastballs. Throw him some breaking balls." It was an innocent mistake—saying "Eddie" instead of "Steve"—but after seeing the scene in dailies, Ward liked that take so much that he changed the character's name so he could use the take (Harris's first name hadn't been spoken in any previously filmed scenes).

With his character renamed, Chelcie Ross was feeling pretty good as the baseball action began in earnest in Tucson. He'd been unable to attend Yeager's mini-camp, so he came into filming a bit rusty. "When I first got to Arizona, I was actually throwing pretty good," he says. "I took it slow and tried to go easy with it, but that didn't last long. I pulled a groin muscle almost right away, so for the entire shoot, I was in a little bit of pain.

"The trainer we had would try to stretch me out, and he'd say, 'God, man, I don't know how you're even walking.' If I hadn't hurt myself, I think I would have looked a lot better in the film. But that's all part of the history of it now."

•   •   •

Just as they would do in Milwaukee the following week, the *Major League* team needed to get extras into Hi Corbett Field to serve as fans while they filmed the spring–training game sequences. Spreading the word through the media, the producers discovered the process was relatively easy for two reasons: The stadium was dramatically smaller than County Stadium, and the residents of Tucson were, if not exactly fans, at least well acquainted with the Cleveland Indians.

Offered little besides prize drawings and free hot dogs—which cost the production roughly $5,400—spectators began arriving at the ballpark around 5 a.m. With 5,000 fans in the stands and 40 ballplayer extras down on the field, all the spring-training game sequences were filmed in one day. And because Hi Corbett was portraying Hi Corbett, the *Major League* crew members didn't have any special set dressing as they would in Milwaukee.

So viewers would know at a glance where the characters were,

Chesser had his brother—a successful landscaper in the Tucson area—bring in and arrange cactuses and other desert plants to the parking lot and around the ballpark. For a longer sequence of Jake Taylor in the Mexican League (which wound up not being used), the production team made the one-hour drive across the border to Nogales to film a couple of scenes inside a rickety ballpark next door to a bullring.

On the drive back to Tucson, Berenger looked over at a car in the next lane and caught a glimpse of the front page of that day's Nogales newspaper. Beneath the bold headline, "Hoy es el Dia" ("Today is the Day"), was a photograph of Berenger with catcher's gear on. Somehow, he—and *Major League*—had become front-page news.

After a week in the desert, where the July daytime temperature regularly hovered near 110 degrees, everyone was glad to get out of the oppressive heat. That Sunday, they packed up and moved on to Milwaukee, where—little did they know—the hottest summer in 75 years awaited them.

EXTRAS . . .

The only scenes taking place in Tucson that were actually shot in Tucson were the parking-lot arrival scene, the baseball sequences inside Hi Corbett Field, and Willie Mays Hayes's dance of jubilation outside the park after making the team. All interior scenes, plus the scene of Hayes running in his pajamas, were shot later in Milwaukee.

•

The only other scene shot in Tucson used in the final film was the quick shot of Jake Taylor getting his phone call from the Indians at a seedy Mexican hotel (La Casa del Campo—translated, "The Field House"). The location used for both the exterior and interior was an actual hotel on Tucson's Miracle Mile (since demolished).

7

Milwaukee's Best

As the laughter echoed through the telephone, Julie Bergman felt her heart sink.

In her first assignment as co-producer on *Major League*, she'd called one of the production assistants from *The Natural* for some tips on how to fill a ballpark with extras for a movie. Bergman and her team would have to do that at County Stadium for the climactic playoff-game sequence. He told her they'd used cardboard cutouts in the stands for long shots in *The Natural*. But when Bergman told him that she didn't have any funds for that, he started laughing and just couldn't stop.

"He laughed at me for like 15 minutes," Bergman says. "He couldn't believe they weren't giving me any money for cutouts. This was before CGI, so there was no computer-generated way to do this. You either shot it real artsy where you never saw the stands, you used cardboard cutouts, or you used real people."

She knew David Ward wasn't going the artsy route, and the cardboard cutouts weren't an option. That left door number three. The 27-year-old Bergman was now faced with a massive challenge on a movie she hadn't expected to work on in the first place. She had come to Mirage from Warner Brothers with Mark Rosenberg and was then dispatched to serve as a co-producer on *Major League*, primarily because Rosenberg wasn't crazy about the idea of spending the entire summer in Milwaukee.

While the cast and crew gathered in Tucson to shoot the spring-training sequence, Bergman and extras coordinator Lisa Beasley headed to Wisconsin to try to figure out how to fill a ballpark with thousands of fans for a movie about a team no one there was interested in.

They faced another pair of roadblocks: They couldn't afford to pay any of the people who showed up, and—even worse in suds-soaked Milwaukee—for insurance reasons, they couldn't serve beer at the ballpark.

THEY COULDN'T AFFORD TO PAY ANY OF THE PEOPLE WHO SHOWED UP, AND—EVEN WORSE— THEY COULDN'T SERVE BEER AT THE BALLPARK.

The one thing they had going for them was the 20-year drought since Milwaukee's last Hollywood experience. "There was no institutional memory of how watching a movie being made is like watching paint dry," Bergman says. "So there was a lot of excitement about this Hollywood movie coming to town."

She quickly devised a radical solution. "I figured out that we were going to have to shoot the entire last sequence of the movie first," Bergman says. "Otherwise the cat would be out of the bag: Everybody would know how boring it actually was to watch a movie being shot, and nobody would come."

Although the cast was able to adapt to shooting the movie out of sequence, the decision held some risks. "It was kind of scary trying to shoot stuff that early," Ward says. "We didn't know if we'd be organized and efficient enough to get everything we needed. And you'd like to give the actors a chance to work into their roles a little bit. We didn't know if the actors really knew their characters well enough yet to react in the same way they'd react when they knew their characters better."

In addition, some of the minor kinks and questions hadn't been completely worked out. For instance, they weren't sure whether the glasses Charlie Sheen would wear in the climactic scene would work visually because they hadn't yet filmed any scenes with them.

Bergman set to work getting the word out, essentially creating a grassroots advertising campaign to entice people to come to County Stadium to not only watch them film, but be part of the movie. The primary target was the first weekend the film crew was in town—Friday, July 29, and Saturday, July 30—when they needed to draw as big a crowd as possible for the wide shots of a full ballpark for the playoff-game sequence.

"I had no experience in doing any of this," Bergman says. "I knew how to develop a script and all that, but I had no idea how to recruit thousands of people to do something. It was like throwing me into the fire."

With assistance from the Milwaukee-based Miller Brewing Company, which proved to be a valuable ally throughout the production, Bergman and Beasley spread the word through radio and newspaper announcements. The production company also offered raffle prizes: televisions, Walkmans, lunch with Charlie Sheen, and a grand prize of a new car awarded on each of the two big nights. "This is your chance to be a part of Milwaukee film-making history," a newspaper ad proclaimed. "Come join in the fun!"

The team also had to figure out how to keep people in the ball-park when they arrived. They hired local bands and comedians from the Second City troupe in Chicago to entertain the crowd during the long stretches between takes and offered a variety of smaller prizes, such as custom-made baseball cards of the actors and signed baseballs, to toss into the stands during shooting. "There would be a show going on around them all the time as they filmed," Bergman says. "It was going to be noisy and horrible, but I told David he was just going to have to get used to it to have that many people."

Even with all of the sideshow activity and entertainment, Ward knew they couldn't afford long delays between shots. "We had to move pretty quickly," he says. "Big crowds won't stay all night, especially if they brought kids with them. You knew that you were only going to have them until about midnight, if you're lucky."

Considering the sun didn't set until around 8 p.m. at that time of year, that would give them, at best, four hours to get a handful of the most important shots of the film.

With the word out and the bells and whistles in place, the cast and crew arrived in Milwaukee, not knowing what to expect. "I felt like I was throwing a party and no one was going to come," Bergman says. "I was terrified that no one was going to show up."

•　　•　　•

For as welcoming and cooperative as Milwaukee had been and would be, it was perhaps the most uninviting summer in the city's history.

Enduring a devastating drought that ravaged much of the U.S., Milwaukee also was plagued by record heat. The temperature would top 90 degrees 36 times between June and August, including six days in which it reached 100, four of them in August when *Major League* was in town.

"Basically it was just as hot as Tucson, and it never stopped," Ward says. "In Tucson, at least you're in the desert and it cools down somewhat at night. We really had to monitor guys to make sure they were drinking water because otherwise they'd cramp up." Adding to the discomfort level, the schedule had switched entirely to night shooting for the next six weeks, requiring a complete reversal of everyone's sleeping patterns.

With the cast and crew slightly dazed and trying to adjust in the oppressive heat, production would begin by portraying October baseball. To do that, they needed a big crowd—twice.

Even with a sound game plan and an effective publicity campaign, Ward and company had no idea how many people would actually show up for the night shoots. They had set 15,000 as the magic number, the minimum needed to get all the shots they wanted. They wound up hitting that number both nights—topping out at 19,000 on Friday—as fans were drawn, according to the *Milwaukee Sentinel*, "by curiosity, the lure of Hollywood, and the possibility of seeing Charlie Sheen."

Bergman's strategy had paid off. "But I don't remember feeling happy about it," she says. "I just remember feeling so relieved that it wasn't a total disaster, and I couldn't really enjoy it."

The crowd was more than they could have hoped for, but the crew still needed to use some sleight of hand to maintain the illusion of a sellout crowd. Fans were massed in strategic areas in the ballpark, depending on the shot, and they were seated in every other row so that when the fans rose to their feet, the empty row behind them wouldn't be seen.

Although the basic plot of the film and the Indians' role in it had been explained, many fans still brought Brewers gear with them to the ballpark. They were quickly stopped at the gate and informed they couldn't bring Milwaukee-themed paraphernalia inside. Later, Indians pennants, hats, and creative signs whipped up by the film's art department were distributed. "As you know," an announcer explained over the public-address system as the crowd settled in, "you're all portraying Indians fans here tonight. Welcome to the world of make-believe."

It was a world the actors embraced immediately. "It was unreal," Corbin Bernsen says. "We had the uniforms, we were under the lights, the field looks beautiful, the lines are there. It was almost like, *Fuck the movie; let's just play baseball!*"

"It was so adrenal," Charlie Sheen says. "It gave me so much more respect for guys who pitch on that level, because suddenly you feel your whole body. If you can talk yourself out of aiming the ball, you can barely throw it. And anything that happens after that is purely adrenaline-driven.

"Somebody said, 'You've been doing this your whole life, just throw a strike.' But I don't remember feeling my shins tingle when I was pitching in high school. It should have been a balk every time because I was never on the rubber—I was five feet above it."

The primary footage shot that first night in front of the massive crowd wasn't baseball action. One of the first setups was the wide shot of the Indians storming out of the dugout and onto the field as the fans rise to their feet and roar behind them. After the crowd was urged to "cheer like there's no tomorrow," the players charged onto the field.

"They were pounding the stadium," Tom Berenger says of the raucous extras. "You could hear their feet pounding. It was exciting. For just a minute there, you had a flash of what it must be like."

As they prepared for the first of many takes and the crowd rehearsed its cheering, Dennis Haysbert was standing beside Steve Yeager on the dugout steps, absorbing the noise and the energy filling the ballpark. Yeager nudged him. "Hey," he said, "look at your arm." Haysbert looked down and saw that it was prickled with goose bumps. Yeager smiled and said, "That's what it's like 162 times a year."

"You just don't understand how big a sound that is until you're down on a baseball field and people are screaming and yelling," Ward says. "It's such a thrill. The actors were just so pumped by it."

"As an actor, you never get that feeling of what it's like to play in a stadium in front of all those people or to be a musician and be playing music in front of thousands of people in an arena," Bernsen says. "You get a little bit of it in theater, but 500 or a thousand people ain't 20,000. It's different. Usually in filming, there are only maybe 20 people around the set."

Haysbert felt the rush much more intensely later when the time came to film Pedro Cerrano circling the bases after his dramatic game-tying home run. Ward, speaking into a microphone linked into the stadium sound system, explained the scenario to the fans, then offered a play-by-play call on an imaginary pitch. At the moment he shouted, "It's gone!" the fans erupted, and Haysbert began rounding the bases, pumping his fist and thrusting his bat at the crowd—which cheered louder each time he did it.

"I didn't have to give him any direction about how jubilant he was or how to play to the crowd or wave the bat or anything," Ward says. "He just did it."

"It's really hard to top running around and hitting all four bags in front of 20,000 people," Haysbert says. "There's nothing quite like that."

In addition to energizing the actors and providing the proper background visuals for the Cerrano homer and the taking-the-field shots, the big crowd also made *Major League*'s signature scene even better than Ward could have possibly imagined.

•   •   •

There wasn't much to it, really. The most memorable sequence of the movie—and the one that would ultimately have the biggest impact on the game of baseball—was essentially nothing more than a guy in a baseball uniform walking 300 feet from the outfield fence to the pitcher's mound. But of course, it was so much more than that.

With the drama of the final game nearing its climax, Lou Brown calls to the bullpen for Rick Vaughn to replace tiring Eddie Harris. The gate in right-center field pops open, and Charlie Sheen emerges, striding intensely to the mound. No dialogue is spoken or needed. Sheen's face carries the cocktail of emotion Vaughn is feeling: confidence, nervousness, and an understanding and appreciation of how far he's come.

But two things set the scene apart: the song that plays in the background, and the fans' reaction to it.

Much like *Major League*, the song that defined its most memorable scene wasn't conceived with any expectation that it would become a cultural icon. Struggling songwriter Chip Taylor was writing primarily country songs when he got a call from the producer of a small band requesting an original tune. The catch was, they needed it the following afternoon. Taylor quickly whipped up a song and improvised some lyrics on the spot, a stream-of-consciousness description of a young woman who had rocked the world of an adoring suitor. The band, fittingly named the Wild Ones, liked the song, but it went nowhere.

The following year, an obscure garage band from England called the Troggs covered the song, originally intending it for the

B-side of a single release. But after recording it in 10 minutes, they liked it so much, they decided to put it on the A-side, and the rest is history.

"Wild Thing" was released in May 1966 and became an instant hit, topping the U.S. charts, and living on through multiple covers nearly as memorable as the original. Jimi Hendrix closed his performance at the Monterey Pop Festival with the song, then set his guitar on fire and smashed it to pieces. In later years, comedian Sam Kinison would record a quasi-parody version, and Animal rocked out the tune on the drums on an episode of *The Muppet Show*.

Another less-publicized adaptation by the punk band X in 1984 had more of a grand sing-along concert feel than previous covers. Exene Cervenka's powerful rendition reversed the original delivery of a guy singing about a girl and opened the song up to a new interpretation, one that fit perfectly with the magical moment in David Ward's baseball fairy tale. "Their version of it was fantastic," Ward says. "It sounded like it was being sung by thousands of people. I thought it was a great fit for the movie."

"I FORGOT IT WAS A MOVIE."

Speaking directly to the fans and providing direction as he would to the actors, Ward gave a quick description of what was about to happen in the movie. The song was blasted over the speakers and the lyrics were put up on the scoreboard so the crowd could sing along. But they were directed to look down at Sheen as he walked to the mound, not up at the scoreboard. Five roaming cameras would wander around the stadium to capture everything. When the bullpen door opened and Sheen emerged, that was their cue. "We just didn't know how they would react," Ward says.

They delivered in spades, providing more than Ward could have hoped for. They sang. They danced. They jumped, cheered, and waved.

"That was just *Wow!*" Snipes says. "I forgot it was a movie."

Ward spotted a group of young women in the front row climb

atop the dugout and begin jumping and dancing, completely unin-structed. He ran over to cinematographer Reynaldo Villalobos. "Do we have a camera on that?" he asked, breathlessly. "If we don't, we should, because this is fantastic!" Villalobos smiled at his amazed director. "We're getting it, we're getting it," he replied.

Sure enough, the roaming cameras captured fans reacting in a myriad of ways, ultimately to be spliced together in a quick, effective montage. "They really felt like they were participating," Ward says, "because they actually were. They were just so caught up in the moment, but they were taking direction and nailing it. It just sort of turned into a party." Like singing karaoke with 19,000 people.

Each night, the party wound down around midnight when the fans began trickling out and heading for home. Ward had gotten the shots he needed, but he also showed a lot of people a fantastic evening.

"I'll never forget that," Ward says. "And I don't think any of the actors will ever forget it."

•   •   •

Although the massive crowds vanished back into the Milwaukee night as quickly as they had appeared, the energy they created persisted as the other pieces of the final-game sequence were put together in the next few weeks.

The most lasting legacy of the big crowd was a core group of fans that remained well after the novelty of the promoted evening faded away. For the 22 days and nights of shooting at County Stadium that followed, Ward never really knew how many people would show up. Some nights had a bigger turnout than others, and the numbers generally tailed off as the shoot continued, as Julie Bergman had predicted, but each time, a small group of roughly 250 fans continually returned to the ballpark.

"They so enjoyed that experience that they wanted to come out and watch every night," Ward says. Their consistency ensured that even if nobody else showed up (and some nights, that was pretty much the case), Ward would be able to get some shots with a smattering of a crowd in the background. Admittedly, it required creativity. The fans were moved to various parts of the ballpark to create the illusion of a jam-packed stadium in every shot.

Although they weren't being paid or plied with freebies, the extras had a blast. They brought food to share and turned each long night of shooting into a backyard barbecue, a feeling strengthened between shots by broadcasts of Brewers' road games and *Late Night With David Letterman* on the scoreboard replay screen. "We moved them around so much," Ward says, "but they were such good sports about it."

"A couple hundred extras over the course of a shoot would have cost a lot of money," he continues. "It saved us a ton. And they got to know the actors. They eventually knew each other by name, and the actors would come over and talk to them between takes. It was great."

Some of the fans later sent Ward photos they'd taken during shooting. Others sent Ward and Chesser Christmas gifts for years afterward.

Toward the end of shooting, one couple told Ward they were trying to decide whether to watch the last two days of shooting or fly to South Korea for the Olympics. "I asked, 'Are you kidding? Go to the Olympics!'" Ward says. "They said, 'But we love it. We don't want to miss the end of it.' They were so into it. You can't buy that."

So although the crowd size might have diminished as the summer wore on and the remaining shots and scenes of the final-game sequence were filmed, the enthusiasm never did. In the final cut of the film, for example, the viewer has no idea that while the shot from behind Charlie Sheen as he walked to the mound was filmed on the night with 19,000 fans, the shot of Vaughn actually emerging from the bullpen was shot about three weeks later, in a very different environment.

"It's about four in the morning and there's nobody there," says Sheen, who was nodding off in the bullpen just before cameras rolled. "You know that exhale I do as I just clear frame? I was so tired it was ridiculous, like I'd just come out of the salt mines. And my arm was hurting so bad. But that exhale was just, *I'm so glad I didn't trip.*

"It's kind of a shame because I own that moment, but when I see it in the movie, I think, *OK, that's three weeks later.* So I can't really get involved. When I saw it opening night, that was the only time I was actually excited by it. Since then, when I see it I feel how I felt then and I know that it was all smoke and mirrors."

Although the march from the bullpen was the most memorable part of the sequence, Sheen loved the moment just before the at-bat when he stood alone on the mound, paying homage to one of the character's templates.

"I completely stole Al Hrabosky's back-of-the-mound thing," he says. "Getting pumped up, slamming the ball into the glove and doing the quick turn. That was total Hrabosky. I'd grown up at Dodger Stadium watching him, and it seemed like the right moment. Then David does that nice little push as I'm coming up on the mound.

"Pretty dramatic shit."

*   *   *

Things were all fun and games for Wesley Snipes when he was just popping the ball up into the air back in Tucson. When it came time for him to deliver an actual hit in the ninth-inning sequence of the playoff game in Milwaukee, things changed quickly.

"The people in the stands didn't know that I didn't know how to play," he says. "They just knew I looked the part. Once I started to hit, I kept swinging and missing. I just couldn't get a good hit for the camera. They started making catcalls and heckling me. It was brutal."

Conversely, when Dennis Haysbert stepped in for the at-bat in which he blasts the game-tying homer, he truly delivered what was needed.

"I told Dennis he had to get one in the air that's from a certain angle and looks like it's hit hard so we can show it going out,"

Ward says. "Well, he got it in the air, all right." On the swing that's ultimately used in the final cut of the movie, Haysbert actually knocked the ball 370 feet, clearing the fence in left-center—the first time in his life he'd hit a baseball over a fence.

"That was electric," Haysbert says. "It was a lot of fun."

However, there were two things that would bother hardcore baseball fans about that scene. First, in the film, Cerrano hits the ball completely out of Cleveland Stadium—over the bleachers and out of the ballpark, which, of course, was impossible unless you were from the planet Krypton. In the 62 years baseball was played at Cleveland Stadium, nobody even hit a ball into the center-field bleachers, let alone over them. To do so would have required a blast traveling well over 600 feet on the fly.

The other issue was Cerrano carrying his beloved bat around the bases after the home run. Most baseball fans cite this as completely implausible; that in reality, Cerrano would have automatically been called out for carrying his bat out of the batter's box. (Long-suffering Cleveland fans can't help but sigh and agree that this is the type of karmic technicality that would have cost the Indians the game.)

But that's actually not true, and has become something of an urban myth. The official rules of Major League Baseball don't state when and where a batter must drop his bat before becoming a runner. In fact, when Babe Ruth was chasing his own home-run record in 1927, he'd take his bat with him around the bases after knocking one out of the park to prevent it from being stolen. So while carrying a bat around the bases defies common sense, by rule, as long as it isn't used to interfere with a defensive player, it's legal. Cerrano's run would have counted, and thus the climax of the film wasn't tainted by baseball geekery.

Just as Haysbert showed off his genuine physical prowess on cue, Wesley Snipes again demonstrated his natural athleticism to make a play that wound up in the movie. His leaping catch over the fence to rob the Yankees of a home run (in reality, a ball thrown by Yeager) was real—again, amazingly impressive for someone who'd just picked up the game that month.

Snipes was more surprised than anyone. "On the take they ended up using in the movie, my reaction was really natural because I didn't know I had actually caught the ball," he says. "I pulled my glove down and looked, and the ball was in it."

Unfortunately, because of the angle of Snipes's glove, you couldn't really see the ball on film. In post-production, technicians went frame-by-frame and "enhanced" the ball before it disappears into the glove.

Later, Snipes wasn't pleased when Ward made him do a few extra takes of his slide into home plate to score the game-winning run, a practice he'd quickly become weary of.

"The hardest thing Wesley had to do was slide," Yeager says. "We must've run that take of him sliding into home plate about four or five times. He had a big strawberry on the side of his hip. Once you slide and you get a strawberry on your side, you don't want to slide there anymore. It just gets bigger and bigger and bigger. He said, 'Yeag, I don't know how many more times I can do this.'"

> **"ONCE YOU SLIDE AND YOU GET A STRAW-BERRY ON YOUR SIDE, YOU DON'T WANT TO SLIDE THERE ANYMORE. IT JUST GETS BIGGER AND BIGGER."**

Snipes thought they'd gotten it on the first take, and with his hip throbbing, he wasn't excited about doing a third and then fourth take. "I think David was getting a kick out of it," he says. "I was hurting so much, part of me wanted to curse this dude out, but it was too early in my career." But Ward knew they still hadn't gotten it and needed another. "He did it," Yeager says of Snipes. "And he didn't complain."

It was worth it because the fourth take was the one used in the film. From that point on, Snipes slid head-first.

.   .   .

For Charlie Sheen, it was like one of those nightmares in which you inexplicably show up at school in your underwear.

During filming he'd developed a bad case of hemorrhoids. He battled through, eventually turning to acupuncture because nothing else was working. The following evening, with a few thousand fans packed into the center-field bleachers behind him, he was on the mound and feeling a little better. His leg kick was a bit higher and he thought the acupuncture had helped alleviate the discomfort.

"Then I felt one of them break," he says. "I called the first assistant director over and said, 'I need to go to the restroom right here, right now.' I had to crab-walk off the field so nobody could see my backside. I got into the clubhouse and looked and there was blood coming through my uniform. I immediately made a diaper out of towels and got a new pair of pants on and went back out there. But I knew it was done, the acupuncture had worked, and I was happy again."

And so, just like George Brett during his much-ballyhooed battle with hemorrhoids in the 1980 World Series, Wild Thing returned to the field to help his team achieve October glory.

*   *   *

The celebration scene at the conclusion of the movie would require a cast of thousands, with extras storming out of the stands to surround and celebrate with the primary actors. Although staging the celebration might seem simple, it required thought and logistics to coordinate several hundred people swarming and jumping around the actors with the cameras rolling.

Amid the chaos, Corbin Bernsen notes, David Ward's direction led to a subtle conclusion to Roger Dorn's character arc. "If you look, I'm kind of wading through the crowd on my own when I spot Charlie," he says. "Then he punches Charlie and hugs him and now he's part of the whole thing. He looks a little lost in the celebration, and then he punches Charlie and you feel he's a part of it. That's probably the first enlightened moment of his life. In the script, it's a wonderful example of David Ward really understanding the character beyond comedy. It's a great moment for Roger Dorn, where he becomes human. And that's what the story is. He's part of the team; he's not an outsider."

Making the moment even more memorable was Bernsen accidentally connecting when he threw what was supposed to be a fake punch at Sheen. "I got caught a little bit, like one knuckle, just at the very bottom of my chin," Sheen says. "And it rang my bell just enough that my reaction on film is not fake; it's me trying to get my bearings." In fact, Bernsen's punch caught just enough to leave a small red mark on Sheen's face, and Ward remembers that they had to pay attention to the camera angles they used when shooting Sheen over the next few days to prevent his souvenir from showing up on film.

Bernsen experienced another odd moment when filming the scene just after the Wild Thing montage, when Dorn confronts Vaughn on the mound, better known as the "strike this mother-fucker out" scene. Ward kept having Bernsen repeat the line with different inflections and verbal emphasis.

"That was the freakiest moment of the whole movie," Bernsen says. "I felt I wasn't getting it right. David would say, 'Try it this way, try it harder.' And I'd think, *Shit, am I not getting it?* It's a huge beat. It was one of those moments as an actor where you think, *What do I do?* You could just tell that line was going to be a moment."

After Ward had nearly a dozen different takes on film, he struggled with which one to pick. And it seemed each person he asked had a different opinion. The one he finally chose undoubtedly worked, as Bernsen would discover in the years to come.

"When I sign autographs, everybody wants me to sign 'Strike this motherfucker out,'" he laughs. "Which is about the longest, hardest thing to write when you're at a signing. It takes long enough to sign my name and 'Dorn #24.' And some of them actually want the beginning of the line, 'I've only got one thing to say to you' on there, too."

•   •   •

Fittingly, through all its perils and pitfalls, the filming of the play-off-game sequence contained its own subtle epilogue.

Just hours after David Ward oversaw the filming of thousands of faux fans rocking at a Tribe playoff game, back in Cleveland, the real Indians of 1988 dropped below the .500 mark—for good, it would turn out, essentially ending the outside possibility of inter-ference from reality. Although Tribe fans rolled their eyes at yet another letdown, Ward breathed a sigh of relief.

Cinderella was still waiting for her fairy godmother.

EXTRAS . . .

Whenever County Stadium's huge scoreboard clock appeared in a shot, its time had to be adjusted. Still, a couple of continuity lapses occurred. During the playoff game, the clock is visible several times as Eddie Harris is removed, Rick Vaughn comes in, and Jake Taylor knocks in the winning run. In real time, that would have taken about a half-hour, but each time we see the clock it reads 10:20. Also, in the opening-day afternoon game, just after Vaughn gives up the grand slam to Clu Haywood, the clock seen behind Charlie Sheen as he picks up the rosin bag reads 10:40—betraying the time in the morning when the scene was shot.

•

All the scoreboard animations—for example, Chief Wahoo sending smoke signals or riding a rocket emitting smoke that spells out "Away We Go"—were actual animations used by the Indians on the Cleveland Stadium scoreboard in the 1980s.

•

Another scoreboard feature did tip the film's hand (at least to Mil-waukeeans and Clevelanders): A banner across the top advertised WTMJ Channel 4—Milwaukee's NBC affiliate.

•

During filming in Milwaukee, one of the regular hangouts for the cast and crew in their off hours was Stormin' & Vuke's, a bar on Milwaukee's south side owned by Pete Vuckovich.

•

Vuckovich, a former pitcher, hits two home runs in the movie as the villainous Yankee first baseman. But he hit no homers in his own major-league career.

MAJOR LEAGUE

Original Screenplay

by

David S. Ward

REVISED
~~First~~ Draft ~~(2)~~
~~March 1, 1985~~ November 13, 1987
Producer: Chris Chesser

1. Title page for the revised first draft of *Major League*. *(Morgan Creek Productions)*

2. A young David Ward outside his home in Cleveland Heights, Ohio. It was here that he would watch his beloved Indians get swept in the 1954 World Series and begin their epic downfall . . . which ultimately led to the inspiration for *Major League*. *(David S. Ward)*

3. Producer Chris Chesser *(left)* and writer/director David Ward get a bird's eye view of filming at Milwaukee's County Stadium. *(Chris Chesser)*

4. Juggling its schedule between Milwaukee Brewers games, the *Major League* crew would take over County Stadium whenever possible, often shooting all night long. *(Milwaukee Journal Sentinel, Michael Sears, © 2015 Journal Sentinel Inc.)*

5. David Ward directs the crowd at County Stadium. *(David S. Ward)*

6. Nearly 20,000 fans showed up at County Stadium on each of two back-to-back nights, enabling the crew to get the crowd footage needed for the film's playoff-game sequence. *(Julia Miller)*

7. Cleveland Municipal Stadium, 1993. The Indians' home ballpark couldn't be used for filming *Major League*. Milwaukee's County Stadium was selected as a stand-in because of its similar appearance. *(Wasted Time R, Wikimedia Commons)*

8. The primary template for the Wild Thing character was bespectacled Ryne Duren, who'd been a successful relief pitcher in the 1950s before off-field issues derailed his career. *(National Baseball Hall of Fame Library, Cooperstown, New York)*

9. Charlie Sheen, as Rick "Wild Thing" Vaughn, goofs around on the mound between shots at County Stadium. *(Milwaukee Journal Sentinel, Michael Sears, © 2015 Journal Sentinel Inc.)*

10. Production designer Jeffrey Howard inside the cockpit of the "Indian Express" DC-3. *(Bill Rea)*

11. Corbin Bernsen, as Tribe third baseman Roger Dorn, with Julia Miller, David Ward's assistant—who would have a memorable cameo in the film. *(Julia Miller)*

12. David Ward and Tom Berenger, who played Indians catcher Jake Taylor, in the press box during a break in filming. *(David S. Ward)*

CHARLIE SHEEN
"RICK VAUGHN"

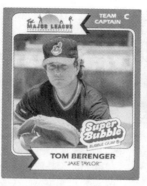

TOM BERENGER
"JAKE TAYLOR"

CORBIN BERNSEN
"ROGER DORN"

WESLEY SNIPES
"WILLIE MAYS HAYES"

DENNIS HAYSBERT
"PEDRO CERRANO"

CHELCIE ROSS
"STEVE HARRIS"

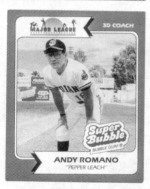

ANDY ROMANO
"PEPPER LEACH"

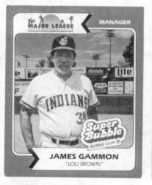

JAMES GAMMON
"LOU BROWN"

STEVE YEAGER
"DUKE TEMPLE"

ANDY ROMANO
JAMES GAMMON
STEVE YEAGER

CHARLIE SHEEN
DENNIS HAYSBERT
TOM BERENGER
WESLEY SNIPES

13. A set of trading cards created as a prize give-away for extras during filming. (Chelcie Ross's character is still "Steve" on his card; he became "Eddie" on the set by accident.) *(Morgan Creek/ Super Bubble is a registered trademark of Ferrara Candy Company, Oakbrook Terrace, IL 60181)*

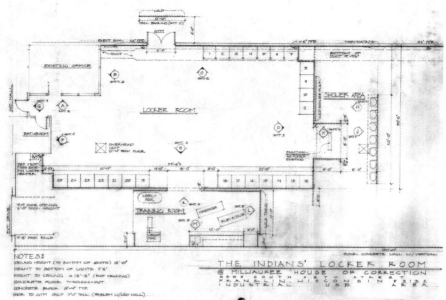

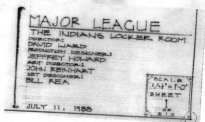

14. Blueprint of the design for the Indians locker room. *(Bill Rea)*

15. The final result (built in the recreation room of a Milwaukee-area prison). *(Bill Rea)*

16. One of the most iconic "characters" of the film, Jobu today lives comfortably in retirement, still with his cigar and rum nearby. (*Brian Robinson*)

17. The crew films a scene in which Tribe catcher Jake Taylor and his teammates meet Lynn (played by Rene Russo) at the church on her wedding day. The scene, scripted to appear just before the Indians' playoff game, was eventually cut—one of several changes made to the end of the film just before its release. *(Milwaukee Journal Sentinel, Ernie Mastroianni, © 2015 Journal Sentinel Inc.)*

18. One of the Indians' most recognizable fans, Sister Mary Assumpta made two brief appearances in *Major League* that launched her into celebrity status. Here she smiles with real Tribe outfielder Mel Hall. *(Maryhelen Zabas)*

19. *Top:* Corbin Bernsen and Wesley Snipes are the center of attention at the world premiere of *Major League* at the Ohio Theater in downtown Cleveland on April 4, 1989. *(Cleveland International Film Festival)*

20. *Bottom:* A ticket to the Milwaukee premiere of the film on April 5, 1989. *(Julia Miller)*

'Major' Big Hit In First Inning

By LAWRENCE COHN

NEW YORK — Rash of new product yielded few winners, with "Major League," "Cyborg," "The ~~Dream Team~~" and "Dead Calm" dominating boxoffice here this frame. Spate of horror pix flopped

NEW YORK

mightily while many holdovers shape up as fast folds.

Par's **"Major League"** opened well across the board with $146,-000 due at Astor Plaza, N.Y. Twin, Orpheum, 34th St. Showplace and 84th St. Sixplex.

Cannon's **"Cyborg"** dominated action trade with muscular $103,-500 debut at Criterion 2, Manhattan and Orpheum.

Universal's **"The Dream Team"** opens fair with $101,500 at Nation-

Cinema 2, Gramercy, G St. and 84th St. Sixplex.

"Heathers" hot with sighted in second week Twin, 34th St. Showp 84th St. Sixplex.

"Rain Man" hefty w in 17th frame at 34th St. and Paramount, as wel moveover week at Tow

"Dangerous Liais cooking with $58,388 68th St. Playhouse, Festival, 84th St. Sixp ieland 8th St.

"The Adventure Munchausen" doi $48,000 in fifth we combined with debu wich.

"Working Girl" $45,000 in 16th la 15th at 34th St. East

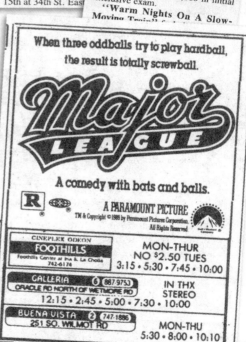

'Major League' Hits B.O. Homer

SAN FRANCISCO — "Major League" slammed a homer with $50,500 in season opener in three parks, as a lot of new films arrived to generally good results, though overall b.o. is soft.

"Dead Calm" is breezy $31,000 in three boats in first sail.

"The Dream Team" wakes

SAN FRANCISCO

alertly with $23,500 in three beds the first time.

"Cyborg" crushes bold $18,000 in two-house debut.

"Murmur Of The Heart" reissue beats healthy $11,000 in initial exclusive exam.

"Warm Nights On A Slow-Moving Train"

21. *Top, bottom:* Box office reports from *Variety*, April 12, 1989.

22. *Center:* A newspaper advertisement following *Major League*'s release in April 1989.

'Major League' Wins Pennant With Warm 61G

By JIM HARWOOD

SAN JOSE — First hot spell plus Spring fever dried up boxoffice, bu "Major League" still hit mighty $61,000 in first time at two bases.

"The Dream Team" also play tough $42,000 in initial outing four.

"Rain Man" boasts bu

SAN JOSE

$33,000 in 17th lap on two field (last week, $46,230).

"Cyborg" fearless $26,000 six assaults for openers.

"Fletch Lives" finds happ $17,000 in three rackets in four ($32,940).

"Bill & Ted's Excellent Adve ture" remains tender $15,500 seven touches in eighth co ($19,051 in six).

"Dead Calm" still $15,00

'Major' Bows To Big-League 26

By HILARY HUNT

CHICAGO — Big week for openers this round as **"Major League"** tops the roster with major $266,000 in first inning at 18.

"The Dream Team" next at bat with rosy $125,000 in bow at 18.

"Dead Calm" shows with okay

fourth lap at 15 after $78,00 week at 18.

"Leviathan" bleak $30,0 fourth scare at 10 after $67,3 time at 17.

"Lawrence Of Arabia"

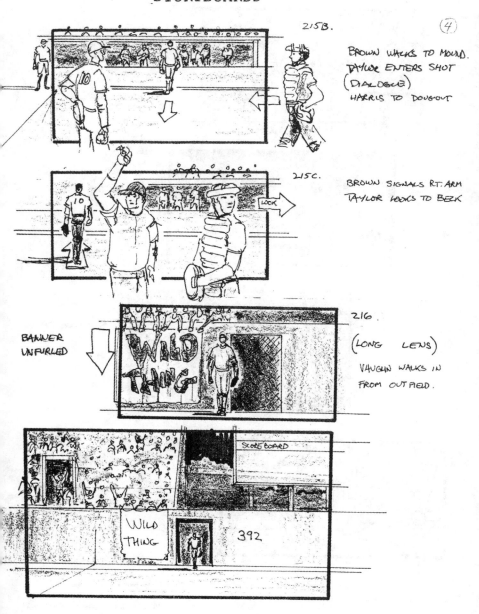

215B.
④

BROWN WALKS TO MOUND.
TAYLOR ENTERS SHOT
(DIALOGUE)
HARRIS TO DUGOUT

215C.

LOOK

BROWN SIGNALS RT. ARM
TAYLOR LOOKS TO BEZK

BANNER
UNFURLED

216.

(LONG LENS)

VAUGHN WALKS IN
FROM OUTFIELD.

WILD
THING

SCOREBOARD

WILD
THING

392

23. Most of the on-field action in *Major League* was storyboarded before filming, including the most memorable scene of the movie: Rick Vaughn walking out to the mound and striking out Yankees slugger Clu Haywood. *(Morgan Creek Productions)*

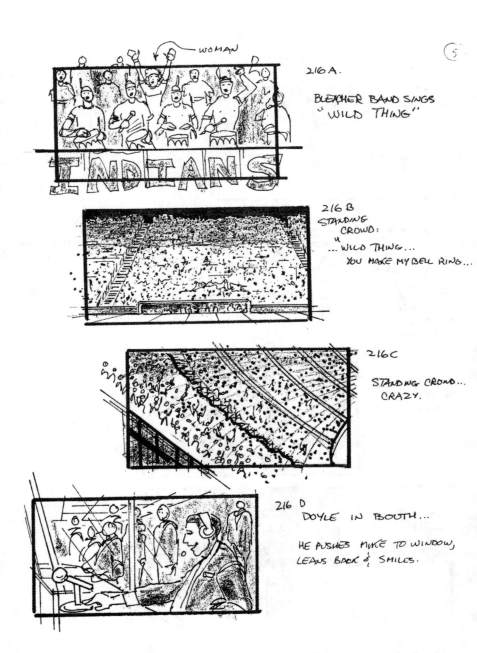

WOMAN

(5)

216 A.

BLEACHER BAND SINGS
"WILD THING"

216 B
STANDING
    CROWD:
"...WILD THING...
    YOU MAKE MY BELL RING...

216 C

STANDING CROWD...
CRAZY.

216 D
DOYLE IN BOOTH...

HE PUSHES MIKE TO WINDOW,
LEANS BACK & SMILES.

INDIANS

24. *(Morgan Creek Productions)*

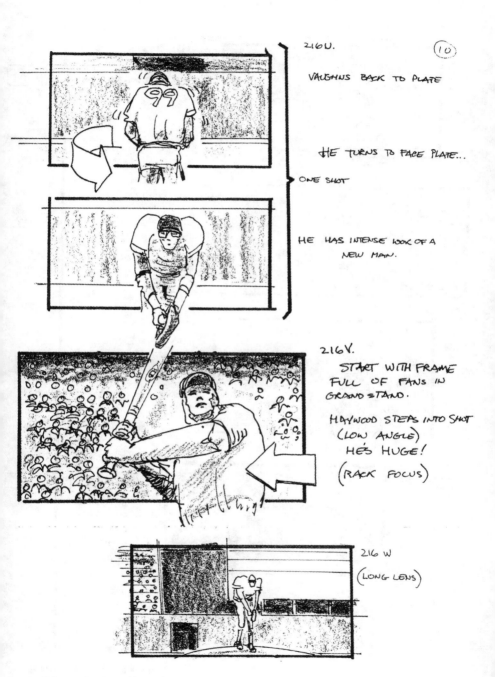

216U.

VAUGHNS BACK TO PLATE

HE TURNS TO FACE PLATE...

ONE SHOT

HE HAS INTENSE LOOK OF A
NEW MAN.

216V.
START WITH FRAME
FULL OF FANS IN
GRAND STAND.

HAYWOOD STEPS INTO SHOT
(LOW ANGLE)
HE'S HUGE!
(RACK FOCUS)

216 W
(LONG LENS)

25. *(Morgan Creek Productions)*

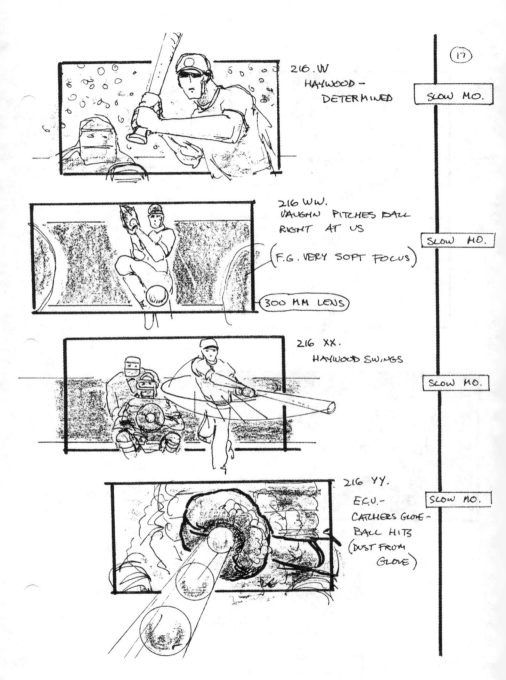

216.W
HAYWOOD —
DETERMINED

SLOW MO.

(17)

216 WW.
VAUGHN PITCHES BALL
RIGHT AT US
(F.G. VERY SOFT FOCUS)
(300 MM LENS)

SLOW MO.

216 XX.
HAYWOOD SWINGS

SLOW MO.

216 YY.
E.C.U. —
CATCHERS GLOVE —
BALL HITS
(DUST FROM
GLOVE)

SLOW MO.

26. *(Morgan Creek Productions)*

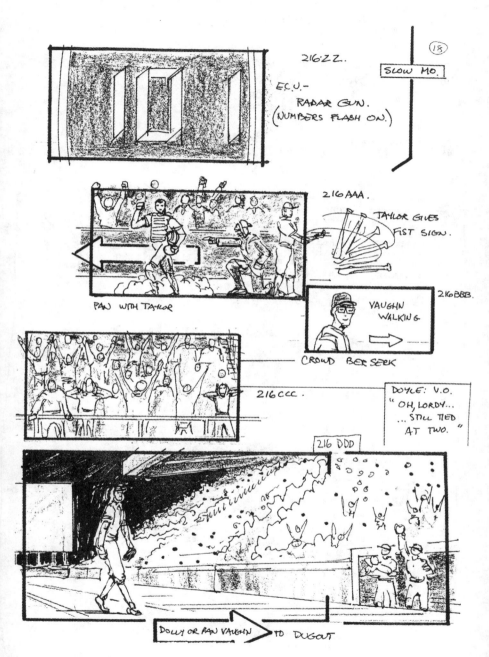

216.ZZ.

E.C.U. -
RADAR GUN.
(NUMBERS FLASH ON.)

(18)

SLOW MO.

216 AAA.

TAYLOR GIVES
FIST SIGN.

PAN WITH TAYLOR

216 BBB.

VAUGHN
WALKING

CROWD BER SERK

216 CCC.

DOYLE: V.O.
" OH, LORDY...
... STILL TIED
AT TWO. "

216 DDD

DOLLY OR PAN VAUGHN TO DUGOUT

27. (Morgan Creek Productions)

                    TAYLOR (Cont'd)
          Forget the other stuff. It coulda
          happened to anybody. Besides, Haywood
          didn't hit it that good. That ball
          wouldn't have been out of a lotta
          parks.

                    VAUGHN
          Oh yeh, name one.

                    TAYLOR
                  (after a pause)
             Yellowstone.

Vaughn just looks at Taylor a second and then smiles in spite of
himself.

                    VAUGHN
             Shit...

43   INT. CLEVELAND SUBURBAN MALL - AFTERNOON   43

Hayes and Vaughn sit at a table outside a sporting goods store in
the mall. Above them hangs a banner which says, "Meet Your
Indians" and below that "Future Stars Willie Hayes and Ricky
Vaughn." On the table are several baseballs, waiting to be
autographed. So far they're moving like radioactive toe jam.

                    HAYES
          How long we been here?

                    VAUGHN
                  (checking his watch)
          Couple hours.

                    HAYES
          How many we given away so far?

Vaughn counts up the balls.

                    VAUGHN
             None.

                    HAYES
          Shit, we gotta get aggressive here.
          We're supposed to be promoting the
          club.

A 14 year-old BOY wanders by, a record album under his arm.

                    HAYES
          Hey kid, how'd you like an autographed
          baseball? Impress your friends at
          school.

The kid thinks it over a second.

                    KID
             Yeh, O.K.

                    HAYES
          Great. How would you like me to
          sign that?

                         KID
                 To Brian, a great guy...

Hayes starts writing.

                         KID (Cont'd)
                 Your friend...Reggie Jackson.

Hayes stops writing.

                         HAYES
                      (pissed)
                 I can't sign that. It's gotta be
                 my name.
                      (softening)
                 I'll tell ya what. You take one
                 of these balls,
                      (whispering)
                 I'll give you two bucks.

                         KID
                 O.K. Can I have one without an
                 autograph? .

Hayes stands up and grabs the kid by the lapels.

                         HAYES
                 Look you little creep, I saw you
                 lift that album from the record store
                 down there when the manager wasn't
                 lookin'. You take one of these balls
                 with my god-damn autograph on it,
                 or I'll see to it that you get the
                 chair. You understand me?

The kid nods in terror. Hayes lets him down and presses two
baseballs into his hands, and for good measure, two more under his
arms. The kid hurries off, leaving his record behind.

                         HAYES
                 Now we're cookin'

28–30. Script pages containing the "Yellowstone" joke that was included in the trailer but ultimately cut from the final version. Many fans believe it was in the film. It's followed by a scene, never filmed, of Rick Vaughn and Willie Mays Hayes at a disastrous autograph signing—one of several scripted comical moments that didn't make it into the movie. (*Morgan Creek Productions*)

① BALL HIT
② BECK ENTERS
③ PICKS UP BALL—THROWS
④ PAN/ZOOM TO 1ST
   HES OUT.

PAN & ZOOM

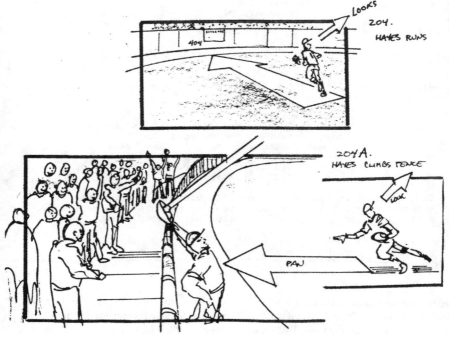

LOOKS
204.
HAYES RUNS

404

204 A.
HAYES CLIMBS FENCE

LOOK

PAN

31, 32. Storyboarding the often-complicated baseball action helped speed up the process of setting up multiple camera angles during a hectic day of shooting. The above panels from the playoff game show third baseman Roger Dorn (labeled by the character's original name of "Beck" in the notes) and Willie Mays Hayes making sterling defensive plays. *(Morgan Creek Productions)*

216 EEE

(BROADCAST BOOTH)

DOYLE:
"CAN YOU BELIEVE
THIS, MONTY?"

MONTY TAKES SWIG.

INT. MUNICIPAL STADIUM PRESSBOX - NIGHT   41

We get our first glimpse of HARRY DOYLE, the Indians' 55 year-old
radio announcer. Harry's never walked past a bar in anger.
He's been with the Indians through thin and thinner.

> DOYLE
> (on the air)
> Hello, everybody, Harry Doyle here,
> welcoming all you Friends of the
> Feather to another season of Indians
> baseball.
> (pouring some Jack Daniels
> in his Coke)
> ...he tribe this

> DOYLE
> So, the Sons of Geronimo, still
> suffering a bit from propellor lag,
> are nipped by the Tigers tonight,
> 11 to 0. The only excitement for
> the tribe provided by Rick Vaughn
> who set an American League record
> by throwing 4 wild pitches in one
> inning. For the Tigers, 11 runs,
> 18 hits, and no errors. For the
> Indians, no runs, and, let's see, one
> hit.
> (to his stat man)
> Is that all we got, one fucking
> hit?

> STAT MAN
> (whispering)
> You can't say "fuckin'" on the air.

> DOYLE
> Don't worry about it. Nobody's
> listening anyway.

33-36. The Harry Doyle character
was changed during shoot-
ing, with his on-air drinking
toned down considerably. *Top:*
Storyboard shows color man
Monty taking a swig of Doyle's
ever-present bottle of Jack Daniels.
(Morgan Creek Productions) Middle: First description of Doyle in the script. *(Morgan Creek Productions) Bottom right:* One of Doyle's original scripted lines that Bob Uecker modified to eliminate the "f-bomb." *(Morgan Creek Productions) Bottom left:* The crew filming Uecker inside the broadcast booth at County Stadium. *(David S. Ward)*

MARANO

(1) PAINTS FACE, ALWAYS DOES VOODOO IN HIS
                                        JOCK.

(2) OFFERS GIN TO GODS

(3) SPREADS RAW EGGS ON ALTAR

(4) CHANTS WITH SNAKE AROUND NECK
(5) DRIPS BLOOD OF A RAT
(6) DRIPS BLOOD OF CHICKEN ON ALTAR
(6) DANCE AROUND PUDDLES OF BURNING GIN
(7) BURN GUN POWDER ON ALTAR

9   INT. CHARLIE DONOVAN'S OFFICE - DAY

Donovan's on the phone to another player.

                    DONOVAN
          Rick, we heard about your pitching
          out at Portland last year...

RICKY VAUGHN

Good looking, muscular, 19 year-old. Sleeveless black T-shirt.
Talking on a wall phone in a non-descript room.

                    RICK VAUGHN
          I'm, ah, not with them anymore...

Vaughn has been working, sweating slightly. He takes off his cap
to mop his brow - revealing a MOHAWK HAIRCUT. He sports a ring
in his left ear.

                    DONOVAN
          We'd still like to take a look at
          ya at our spring camp in Arizona,
          March 1st.

LONGSHOT OF VAUGHN

In the background, Vaughn is on the phone. In the foreground, we
see SECURITY BARS. Vaughn's in a Youth Authority prison.

                    VAUGHN
          Yeh, well, I'm not sure I can make
          it by then.

                    DONOVAN
          Don't worry, we're gettin' you out
          on a sort of work furlough deal.
          Any questions?

                    VAUGHN
          Yeh. Where's Cleveland?

37, 38. *Top:* David Ward's original character notes for Pedro Cerrano, who was originally
named "Marano." *(Morgan Creek Productions) Bottom:* Rick Vaughn's scripted debut in the
film. *(Morgan Creek Productions)*

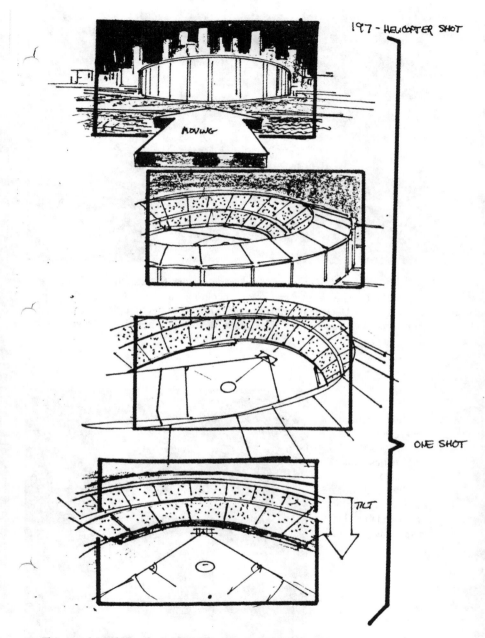

197 - HELICOPTER SHOT

MOVING

ONE SHOT

TILT

39. The storyboards for the long helicopter shot over a packed Cleveland Stadium prior to the film's climactic playoff game. While the actual filming of the shot (the first of the production) was relatively simple, arranging it proved to be much more complicated. *(Morgan Creek Productions)*

40, 41. After the real-life Indians' 1990s renaissance followed the release of the film, *Major League* became even more recognized and celebrated by the franchise. *Left:* Bob Uecker, aka Harry Doyle, throws out the first pitch at an Indians game. *(Cleveland Indians) Right:* A popular Rick Vaughn bobblehead given away to fans at Progressive Field in 2009. *(Cleveland Indians)*

42. The cap Charlie Sheen wore in his role as Rick Vaughn and the baseball he used during the final strikeout scene are carefully preserved in a glass case in his home. *(Jeff Ballard)*

8

Vampire Baseball

Like an enthusiastic young fan staying up way past his bedtime to watch his favorite team play a game on the west coast, filming of *Major League* toiled endlessly into the steamy Milwaukee nights, with each day's work often wrapping up just before sunrise.

Not surprisingly, working from 3 p.m. to 6 a.m. for six straight weeks quickly took its toll on the cast and crew.

"Your body clock had to adjust," Ward says. "You never really get used to sleeping in the daytime. You just don't sleep as well. Your body keeps thinking, *This is all wrong.* After a while, everybody got grumpy."

Even when the Brewers were in town and production bounced around Milwaukee for other location shoots, the cast and crew maintained their nocturnal schedules. Because so much of the shooting was set at night for the baseball scenes, most of the rest of the movie—even scenes taking place during the day—was also shot at night to maintain the same schedule.

Although fatigue set in, a big-picture attitude persevered. "We were getting paid to play baseball, so that wasn't a problem at all," Dennis Haysbert says. "That's why they have blackout curtains."

For James Gammon, it felt more like a family vacation than work. His wife Nancy was from Milwaukee, so she and their two daughters joined him and spent the summer visiting relatives and bringing them to the set to watch Gammon work. Adding to the vacation feel, the Gammons, like many members of the cast and crew, rented an apartment in Juneau Village Towers, just downstairs from where Haysbert and Wesley Snipes were staying, and they'd often spend off-hours together. The young Gammon girls latched onto the massive Haysbert in particular, jumping onto him as he'd lift the giggling kids into the air.

In that spirit, for as long as the days were, there were still moments of childlike joy. Each afternoon the cast and crew would wake up and head down to the ballpark, where they would take infield and batting practice as if they were actual ballplayers.

"We were all like kids in a candy store," Corbin Bernsen says. "We'd even play during lunch. It'd be two in the morning and after we'd get a bite to eat, we'd come back into the stadium and start throwing balls around, or Yeager would hit us balls."

Even Margaret Whitton got into it, playing pepper in high heels with Yeager between takes and learning how to throw a curveball. Throughout filming, Ward and Chesser kept their gloves nearby and would slip away for a game of catch, just to take the edge off.

With Yeager honing the actors' skills, the baseball action at County Stadium ticked along like clockwork. So did life around the ballpark.

"There was this tannery that fired up every day and made the air all around smell horrible," Charlie Sheen says. "We called it the 'anus factory.' It was like a shit cloud every day at four o'clock." Indeed, between the various factories and numerous breweries around town, members of the production crew soon began calling Milwaukee "the city of a thousand smells."

While there was much emphasis on the on-field action, Ward and company spent just as much time and effort preparing the off-field scenes, starting with scouting and preparing locations and building a handful of small sets in a former trolley factory (then being used for school-bus storage) offered for use by the city of Milwaukee.

The largest and most important of the few sets that were built was the Indians' clubhouse, constructed to mirror the dimensions and layout of a typical big-league locker room in the 1980s (which, of course, meant it was dramatically better than the actual Indians' clubhouse back at decaying Cleveland Stadium). The clubhouse set was actually a common room at the Milwaukee County House of Correction, spruced up by set designers and carpenters. Another part of the facility was used for the players' spring-training barracks.

County Stadium was a bit of an upgrade from the Indians' real home park, especially once the *Major League* crew got to work. Prior to each round of shooting, the Brewers' green outfield-fence padding was replaced with blue padding to match Cleveland's, and a large teepee was erected in the left-field bleachers as the symbolic home of the quartet of die-hard Tribe fans who serve as the film's Greek chorus. Similarly, Rachel Phelps's patio-like perch for watching the games was simply a private box spruced up and decorated to provide a bit more panache (prop details that would prove to be important later). County Stadium was also occasionally modified to resemble other ballparks for shots of the Indians' road games.

Of course, each time the actual Brewers returned to town, the fence padding was swapped out, the makeshift teepee was taken down, Rachel Phelps's box was de-blinged, and all evidence that a movie was continually being filmed at County Stadium vanished in the summer breeze.

•　　　•　　　•

One of the most important moments of filming came not on a night when the crew was shooting baseball, but during Rene Russo's first day of work, for the scene that also marked her character's debut in the film.

The reunion of Jake Taylor and Lynn Westland was filmed at a posh Milwaukee restaurant called Gritz'z Pizazz, closed for the evening and filled with extras and equipment. Russo, embarking upon a new and very different chapter in her career, was visibly nervous. As they went through the first few takes, she continually moved her hands around in random fidgets and motions, accompanying every line with a gesture.

After pointing it out to her and seeing little change, Ward eventually decided to rehearse the scene while holding Russo's hands to her sides. It worked. Although residual hand motions appear in the final version of the film, Russo had managed to control her nervousness and delivered the performance needed for the scene. Ward sighed with relief, assured that his female romantic lead was going to work out.

"It was really intimidating working with all these big actors," Russo says. "But David kind of pulled me through that. I think he had more confidence in me than I did. I don't think I would have been able to get through it with some of the directors I've worked with since."

"IT WAS REALLY INTIMIDATING WORKING WITH ALL THESE BIG ACTORS."

The other female lead also faced a challenge on her first day on the set. Margaret Whitton's initial scene was Rachel Phelps's confrontation with Lou Brown in the Tribe clubhouse—filled with half- and fully naked men. "I came in and just thought, *I have to take this room*," Whitton says. Wearing a two-toned wig that reflected Phelps's Palm Beach–socialite aspirations, Whitton then took control of a complicated scene that required her to hit several specific marks and recite her lines while strutting through the clubhouse.

Although it was her first day, she improvised several additions that spiced up scenes. In one case, as she dismissively responds to Brown's complaints, she prods her players as if they were her boy toys, casually poking the top of Willie Mays Hayes's head with her finger, then causing Jake Taylor to spill hot coffee on his bare leg.

Whitton also came up with the idea of knocking on Rick Vaughn's protective cup and adding the line: "Oooh—cups still work, though." Ward wasn't so sure it was a good idea, fearing that the audience might not get the joke. Whitton remembers: "David was a little nervous about it, and Charlie said, 'Leave her alone. It's funny.' So Charlie helped me get a little room to run."

Similarly, as she strolled past the massive Pedro Cerrano, standing like a statue with arms crossed and wearing only a jock-strap, she gave him a light slap on the derriere. "It was kind of like Mount Everest," she says. "It was there."

After knocking on Charlie Sheen's junk and smacking Dennis Haysbert's caboose during her first few minutes on the set, Whitton had announced loud and clear that Rachel Phelps had arrived.

.   .   .

Like Rene Russo, Haysbert was also affected by nerves as he shot his first big scene. The passionate prayer in front of Cerrano's locker at the end of the first day of spring training took 25 takes. To make matters worse, Haysbert had the added pressure of speaking an unfamiliar language with a made-up accent while sporting a bald head for the first time.

He also had to share his debut moment with Jobu, who was making his own cinematic debut. Described in the script only as a "primitive fetish doll with a cigar in its mouth," the figure was sculpted from clay over a wire frame by the film's art department and embellished with a beaded necklace, red sash belt, and jagged straw hair. Although fragile, the final product was good enough to steal every scene it was in.

Then, on top of everything else, Haysbert very quickly had to overcome his fear of snakes.

During his first evening's shoot, he had to handle a large python that Cerrano uses in two shots to ward off the red tag placed in players' lockers in spring training to indicate they'd been cut from the team. Haysbert was terrified of the snake and hated the idea of wrapping it around his arm and even kissing it at one point.

Eventually, he overcame his fear. "I learned a lot about snakes and what the system of control was for them," he says. "You just had to keep them cold to make them as dormant as possible. Then you can do just about anything with a snake. They basically had them on ice, and they didn't move around much." Haysbert eventually became friends with Cerrano's slithery companion, and no sign of trepidation appears in either scene.

Then there was the heat. In a summer of uncomfortably hot days, the one on which Haysbert made his debut (and made friends with a python) was undoubtedly the worst.

All of the scenes in the Indians' spring-training clubhouse were shot on the night of August 9 in the basement locker room of Nicolet High School in suburban Glendale. Although the visual contrast between this site and the "Cleveland Stadium" clubhouse set worked, the sweatbox conditions made work difficult. Even in the dead of night, the temperature in the locker room topped 90 degrees.

It was so hot during filming of the scene in which Jake Taylor discovers he's made the team, that over the course of the take Tom Berenger continually sweated through his Indians t-shirt. Only one other shirt was available, so between takes, Berenger took off the shirt and a production assistant dried it with a hair dryer for the next take. Of course, the shirt would be dry, but also now hot, causing him to sweat even more.

Ironically, the scene that followed shortly after—the only non-baseball "action" scene of the film—resulted in injury.

After mistakenly confronting Lou Brown about the red tag Roger Dorn had placed in his locker, Vaughn storms back into the clubhouse and throws himself at Dorn. Stuntmen were used for the initial shot of the two characters toppling over a table, but both Sheen and Bernsen were used for the next shot, which turned out to be more realistic than intended. They tackle each other again and go flailing over a bench and onto the floor. During the fall over the bench, both Sheen and Bernsen got a bit battered.

"I'm on top of him," Sheen says, "and we're whispering to each other: 'You OK?' 'Yeah. You OK?' 'Yeah. Good, keep going.' It was enough to feel it the next day and compare bruises."

"We felt pretty beat up," Bernsen says. "We did that on our own and paid the price for it."

• • •

Fear of injury slowed down the shooting for another scene.

After Eddie Harris tempts fate by drinking Jobu's rum, he comes out to the playing field and gets cold-cocked by a wayward bat. For the take, Steve Yeager climbed a stepladder with a rubber bat that had a steel rod down the center of it to give the illusion of firmness. He was to double-hand twirl the bat across the field to hit Chelcie Ross in the back of the head.

"He was scared to death to do that," Ross says. "He was so afraid he was going to hurt me. We did it a couple of times, and he hit me down on the shoulders. I had to convince him that it really wasn't hurting. Then he finally got one right and it was fine. He'd just seen enough guys get hit with bats that he was a little bit scared of it."

The physical gag of getting hit by the bat was overshadowed by the two lines Ross spoke just before—both of which have been repeated *ad nauseam* ever since: "Up your butt, Jobu," and "Hey, bartender! Jobu needs a refill!"

"NOT A WEEK GOES BY THAT SOMEBODY DOESN'T ASK ME TO EITHER WRITE OR SAY ONE OF THOSE THREE LINES FOR THEM."

"The 'Up your butt' line is just funny," Ross says. "There was no problem making it funny. It was just good writing. 'Jobu needs a refill' was actually an ad-lib."

Combine those two lines with his earlier chestnut—"You tryin' to say Jesus Christ can't hit a curveball?"—and Chelcie Ross joins Bob Uecker as the most-repeated actor in an often-repeated film. "Not a week goes by," Ross says, "that somebody doesn't ask me to either write or say one of those three lines for them."

Perhaps it was only fitting that one of Ross's most memorable moments of filming came when he found himself standing in line to eat with Uecker. "We didn't have any scenes together," Ross says, "but one night at about three in the morning, they told us to go to lunch and stuck me in line right behind Bob Uecker. I had not met the man yet. He turned around and introduced himself, as if I didn't know who he was. He said, 'Was that you hurling down there?' And I said, 'Yeah, I'm afraid so.' He said, 'Oh no, no, man. It was inspirational.' I asked, 'It was?' He said, 'Yeah, I'm not kidding. Made *me* want to hurl.'"

Bob Uecker, ladies and gentlemen.

* * *

Although he would become one of the most iconic, most influential participants in *Major League*, Mr. Baseball was on the set for a grand total of two days. But in those two days, Bob Uecker made movie magic.

Because the film was being shot in the middle of the baseball season, Uecker's schedule was already full, broadcasting actual games almost every day and criss-crossing the country with the Brewers. However, as a result of a quirk in the team's schedule, Milwaukee was off on both Tuesday, September 6, and Thursday, September 8, enabling Uecker to cram all of the Harry Doyle scenes and voiceovers into two long sessions.

Making it a bit easier was that these scenes were shot inside Uecker's normal work space, the Brewers broadcast booth, requiring only wardrobe changes, a handful of extras to fill out the press box, and the occasional set decoration tweaks to make it look like a different ballpark.

Uecker was actually given very little script and very little direction. "Basically, David told me to be Harry Doyle," he says. "Do whatever; just be this guy. Having a baseball background and being a broadcaster, that was easy for me."

Keeping the script on the floor by his feet, Uecker would review it before each scene to get a sense of what it was about, then toss it back down on the floor and go to work—although not necessarily by delivering the lines as Ward had crafted them. "David gave me the freedom to do these other lines that weren't written," Uecker says. "There was a lot of stuff that I thought, *This is not what I would say. This is what I would say. This is Harry Doyle to me.*"

The result was a handful of lines not in the script that wound up in the final movie, such as:

"We don't know where Hayes played last year, but I'm sure he did a helluva job."

"When this guy sneezes, he looks like a party favor."

"This guy threw at his own kid in a father-son game."

Doyle: "Haywood's a convicted felon, isn't he, Monty?" Monty: "Doesn't really say it here." Doyle: "Well, he should be."

"I don't think I did anything that I don't do on a regular broadcast," Uecker says. "When you're not winning, you have to do something to keep people listening. So if I have to do comedy, then I do it. I think people come to expect it. Nothing making fun of players—I don't do that on the air because I know how hard it is to play the game. But most of it was stuff I'd do to keep people listening when you're not playing very good. It was easy for me to do."

On the contrary, he knew when to play it straight when doing actual broadcasts, and could deliver lines to match the dramatic climax of the film's playoff game. "I can be serious when I have to be serious," he says. "I don't screw around when we have a good game going."

But for most of his work on *Major League*, he was there for laughs, and laughs he delivered. He'd cook up new lines on the spot, do several takes, then scoop the script up off the floor and read over the next scene. But it took time—much longer than if Uecker had simply delivered the lines as written.

"If you're doing the script straight, you can go through it a helluva lot faster," he says. "When you're ad-libbing, you do one, and David says, 'Do more like that.' Then you've got to sit for a minute and think of something weird again. But when you've done play-by-play when your team is not having a good season, those weird things come to your mind rather easily. Then David picks the ones he wants."

Perhaps Uecker's best—and most repeated—line wasn't in the script, either.

When Rick Vaughn makes his big-league debut in the Indians' first regular-season game against the Yankees, his first pitch is supposed to be high, prompting Jake Taylor to leap up to catch it.

Harry Doyle's subsequent scripted line was humorous, but subtle: "First pitch is a little high . . ."

The day of filming, Ward and Uecker cooked up a better idea. Based on a previous shot of a Vaughn pitch sailing so far off the plate that even a diving Taylor couldn't reach it before it pounded into the backstop, they improvised a gem which, with Uecker's perfect delivery, became an instant classic:

"*Juuuust* a bit outside—tried the corner and missed."

It was certainly a funnier moment than the one intended, but neither Uecker nor Ward had any idea how much impact that line would have.

Part of what made the line funny was the unabashed sarcasm in Uecker's delivery, uncommon in the generally dry, just-the-facts-ma'am sportscasting of that era. Still, there was a kernel of truth in the hometown announcer trying to make his ballclub seem less ridiculous than it actually was without visual evidence betraying him.

"I did that all the time anyway," Uecker confesses. "If I'm on the radio, nobody can see what I'm describing. If we had a pitcher out there who was wilder than hell, I'd do that on purpose.

"People who bring radios to the games think, *What the hell is Uecker watching?* That's what makes the radio part of it so much fun."

Over the course of those two days, Ward got reels of hilarious Harry Doyle lines he simply couldn't use, either because there wasn't room for them or because they were a bit too saucy. "He'd say some stuff every once in a while that even for Harry Doyle was a little out of bounds," Ward says. But they were still funny, such as casually calling an incoming pitcher a "pervert by trade" or capping the call of an opponent's home run with: "Let's hope we still have diplomatic relations with the country that baby lands in."

Another gem preceded Rick Vaughn's professional debut: "Rick Vaughn, a short-tall right-hander who was treated by the trainer today for a boil on his ass, is now working for the Indians."

When Yankees' bullish reliever Duke Simpson enters the playoff game, Uecker turns to his partner and asks, "What about his drug rehab program this summer, Monty?" The dumbfounded colorman glances at his notes and shrugs his shoulders, to which Uecker replies, "He graduated? All right!"

But perhaps his best unused improv, cooked up after Roger Dorn lets a potential game-ending grounder roll past him, caused the set to break up in laughter and Ward to cut the take: "Boy, I wanna tell ya," Harry Doyle sighs, "Rachel Phelps's dog is gonna take a whipping tonight."

Harry Doyle didn't really seem to care what he said. After he's scolded by Monty for swearing on the air, Doyle pivots directly to, "Let's take a break here for identification—that'll stop the shit. Ten seconds on the Indians radio network."

Even in the brief time it took to shoot Uecker's scenes, Ward had to alter the character a bit. From his introduction in the script, it's clear that the Indians' long-suffering announcer liked to imbibe during the games primarily as a method of survival, a trait embellished during filming by Uecker's comical reactions whenever he'd take a swig. But in the final version of the movie, his reactions were cut, and after he pours a cup full of Jack Daniels in his first scene (and slips a few droplets behind his ear in a casually natural motion demonstrating his love for the whiskey—also ad-libbed by Uecker), there's less emphasis on Harry Doyle's alcohol consumption, to the point that you never get the sense it's affecting his broadcasting.

"You can't make the guy an alcoholic on the air," Uecker says. "There's no way a guy could operate like that and keep a job. Taking a hit every once in awhile is OK, but they were right in deciding to cut it back."

Uecker also put another limit on the character. "One of the first things I told David when we talked about it was that I wouldn't use any f-bombs," he says. "I've never used that word because I think I can be funny without it." So in the scene in which Harry Doyle is wrapping up another embarrassing Indians defeat, the original line "That's all we got—one fucking hit?" was changed to "one Goddamn hit."

In his whirlwind two-day experience, Uecker *became* Harry Doyle, turning him into the kind of entertaining, devil-may-care announcer who could call it however he saw it, figuring that, as Doyle says: "Nobody's listening anyway."

In reality, Uecker's lines would not only be heard, but remembered and repeated for decades to come.

•　•　•

Just as Uecker added real-life flavor, actual Indians history was incorporated into the small army of extras who had been cast. Ken Keltner, a Milwaukee native and Indians star of the 1940s, was a regular at County Stadium and often came down to watch the filming and mingle with the cast and crew. His grandson Paul became part of the movie when he was cast as a batboy.

By and large, casting and then maintaining the extras was an ongoing challenge. "One of the problems we had was that being ballplayers, not being actors, they didn't understand that you needed to show up every day for continuity," Ward says. "A guy wouldn't show up one day, and we didn't have the same shortstop or left fielder or something from an earlier shot in the same sequence. So we had to make sure we didn't shoot that way."

In one case, a no-show allowed Chris Chesser to live out a childhood dream. When the extra slated to be the Yankees' pitcher during the opening-day sequence failed to show up, Ward needed a lefty to fill in. Like Lou Brown, he motioned to Chesser and intoned, "Go put on a uniform." Thus, on the day before his 40th birthday, Chesser got to be the New York Yankees' ace pitcher. Although he had no lines, he got to strike out Pedro Cerrano and pick off Willie Mays Hayes from first base with a throw to Cy Young Award–winner Pete Vuckovich. Later, Vuckovich signed the baseball to Chesser as a souvenir: "To Chris—for the best pickoff move ever."

•　•　•

Some cheating was necessary to augment the velocity of Rick Vaughn's fastball. Whenever Ward set up a scene of Vaughn pitching from behind home plate, the camera was placed about 10 feet in front of the plate. At that distance, Sheen's pitches—which from a distance of 60 feet, six inches crossed the plate around 84 miles per hour—appeared to be coming in somewhere in the mid-90s.

Similarly, for the scene in which Vaughn strikes out Clu Haywood, the catcher's glove used in the close-up was coated with dirt. So when the ball hits the mitt, a cloud of dust floats up, illustrating the violent impact and, by extension, epic speed. Another shortcut was taken when Sheen's arm began to tire over the course of principal photography by using a lighter, soft-stitch baseball.

And of course, in what would become a sensational revelation, Sheen admitted enhancing his abilities and physical appearance by taking steroids prior to and during filming. "It was a two-part combo, not like one of these crazy cocktails," he says. "Three days a week oral Anavar and every fifth day I shot a Winstrol, which is what they give to fucking horses."

Sheen's steroid use was unknown until he revealed it years later. "I had no idea," Ward says. "At the time, I'm not even sure I knew what steroids were. Had he told me he was taking steroids, I would have thought it was for a rash or something."

> **"AT THE TIME, I'M NOT EVEN SURE I KNEW WHAT STEROIDS WERE. HAD HE TOLD ME HE WAS TAKING STEROIDS, I WOULD HAVE THOUGHT IT WAS FOR A RASH OR SOMETHING."**

Ward wasn't alone. Most of America wasn't introduced to the topic until September 1988, when Canadian sprinter Ben Johnson was stripped of his gold medal in the Seoul Olympics after steroids were detected in his system through a drug test. Of course, in that more innocent time, performance-enhancing supplements were casually passed around major-league clubhouses without fear of repercussions.

"I don't talk about it in any type of judgmental way or try to shy from it, but I used them for the movie," Sheen says. "That's why I'm a little bloated, but also why my fastball went to 84 [mph]. A 160-pound guy from Malibu should not be throwing 84. I wanted to deliver something better for a snapshot in time. It was a sacrifice I made to make the film better. But I didn't continue with them and didn't need to rely on them. In fact, I got in shape for *Hot Shots 2* with just diet and exercise."

Not surprisingly, there were side effects, primarily in his overall mood. "Oh my gosh, it changes everything," Sheen says. "Somebody would say, 'Can you pass the salt?' And I'd say, 'Fuck you!' You are on edge. It's crazytown.

"The big problem was the haircut. I'd be out in bars and people would be making fun of my haircut. I'm not a fighter; I'm a lover, but I'd be on the verge of fistfights with people because they're making fun of my hair. And I'm thinking, *OK, this is not me. This is the additive.*"

Still, Sheen was enjoyable to be around.

"Charlie was Charlie," Bernsen says. "He's always been a magnet for fun. We'd follow him around. He was definitely the leader of the pack."

Well, Sheen was fun to be around as long as you didn't comment on his haircut or confuse him with his dad. "I remember he would get so mad that people would call him 'Martin,'" Wesley Snipes says. "People would come over to him and say, 'Oh, Martin, I loved you in that movie.' And he'd say, 'I'm not my fucking father!'"

"We were always a little worried about Charlie, let's face it," Julie Bergman says. "There were girls visiting him from various cities around the world. But ballplayers do that shit, too. So I guess he was just staying in character off screen." Sheen actually had an assistant with him on the set whose sole job it was to coordinate the visiting girls' flights to ensure that the one who was flying out didn't see the one who was flying in.

The magnetic Sheen had one weakness. One day, after spotting a cute extra he wanted to meet, he asked Ward if he could find out her name for him. Knowing Sheen's impressive on-base percentage with the ladies, the surprised director asked why he didn't just ask her himself. It turned out Sheen had a very slight verbal tick—there were certain groups of consonants that, when combined, made Sheen stutter and stumble over the word. So he'd always check out a girl's name before approaching her to make sure he could pronounce it without stuttering. If he couldn't, he wouldn't approach her.

This one's name passed the test. "So he gave it a shot," Ward says. "And I have no doubt that he succeeded."

·   ·   ·

While the cast members had to adjust their body rhythms to the night shooting and were often exhausted by the time each day of filming was over, whenever they had a night off—and with Sheen leading the way—they made the most of it.

"We had carte blanche to wherever we wanted to go," Sheen says. "Somebody always had an emergency jersey in their trunk, so if we couldn't get in somewhere, we'd just throw that shit out there and then it was, 'Hey, guys, c'mon in!'"

"We'd go out at night and we were rock stars," Bernsen says. "It was a bit mixed for me. This was everything I ever wanted: I'm in a big movie, and I've got everything going, and the potential was all around. But I'd just gotten married and my wife was pregnant with our first son. So to put it in baseball terms, I couldn't follow through. My swing stopped a little short."

"Corbin was the only one we never had to worry about," Bergman says. "The others gave us schpilkas from time to time."

It was a full-blown circus with a handful of ringleaders. "You'll always have guys who have got to stir it up and got to get some-thing going," Chelcie Ross says. "Yeager was a master of that. He lived for it. He'd been playing professional baseball for 19 years and was still a kid. And good old Jimmy Gammon—he was a char-acter, too. He always had the card game going, just like Dennis Hopper on the set of *Hoosiers*."

"It was a blast," Haysbert says. "People were just wondering,

What are you guys doing here? We basically hung out with ourselves and had a great time. As corny as it may sound, we were a team, and we acted like it. Not too many people messed with us, I'll tell you that."

*   *   *

While many members of the cast and crew had fun when off the clock, David Ward was focused merely on survival. "I didn't go out and socialize with the actors or hang out," he says. "I was so tired, I just went home and went to bed.

"If I wasn't shooting, I was home looking at my storyboards and my shot list, making sure I could make the day. And cutting stuff out if I thought I wasn't going to be able to make it. And then just trying to get some sleep so I could keep going. There was nothing else in my world for those 10 weeks."

The strain took its toll. Midway through the shoot, Ward was taken to the hospital, where he was diagnosed with exhaustion and dehydration. He remained there overnight but was back on the set the following day. There simply was no time for him to recuperate.

"It was a killer, and it particularly killed David," Chesser says. "His big concern was just getting through some of those days."

Especially toward the end. "I got to the point where a scene would end," Ward says, "and I'd be asking, 'Did he say the lines? Were those the lines I wrote?' I couldn't quite tell. You get a little loopy after awhile. You had to fight to maintain your focus and make sure you're not letting things slip just because you're tired."

*   *   *

Tired or not, even the little things often became challenges.

One example was the smallest, hairiest member of the cast. The small brown Pekinese playing Rachel Phelps's beloved Cha-Cha appeared briefly in only three scenes but caused problems in each one, moving around and ruining multiple takes.

Margaret Whitton had trouble in the opening scene of the

movie, when she strolls into the conference room with the dog straddling her arm. It kept squirming, and she struggled to hold it still until the owner offered a tip: Place the dog's testicles between its leg and her arm, and if it started to squirm, apply quick, sharp pressure. Whitton, an animal lover, was hesitant but soon realized she had no choice. It worked like a charm—although it's worth noting in the scene how quickly she hands the dog off.

> **"WHITTON, AN ANIMAL LOVER, WAS HESITANT BUT SOON REALIZED SHE HAD NO CHOICE."**

There are no reports of this method being used on any other cast members.

·   ·   ·

In late August, Charlie Sheen was robbed.

While Sheen was filming one afternoon, someone used a passkey to enter his room at the Marc Plaza Hotel and make off with about $1,500 worth of items. It wouldn't have been a big deal had it just been his CD player, two Walkmans, and AC-DC, U2, and Whitesnake tapes. But Sheen hadn't locked the room's safe, and the loaded .357 Magnum he carried with him when he traveled also was taken. Although Sheen hadn't violated any state laws or city ordinances, the incident was splashed all over the local news.

"A few years later, I got a call saying the weapon had been retrieved, not used in a crime or anything," Sheen said. "The guy saw the movie and felt so bad that he either turned himself in or dropped it off anonymously. Rather than flying all the way back to Milwaukee, I donated it to the police.

"It was just one of those odd things that happen while you're at work—your gun gets stolen."

·   ·   ·

Other "little" problems emerged while working with the largest prop in the movie. The introduction of the rickety "Indian Express" airplane required some unexpected maneuvering and negotiation. At the Milwaukee airport, the prop department found an old DC-3, well past flying condition, and had it painted and wheeled into place so it could be slowly taxied into the frame as a comic reveal to the disbelieving ballplayers about to embark on a road trip. The interior of the DC-3 was also used for the in-flight scenes.

To add the necessary beat to the joke of the plane's reveal, Ward wanted a regular, state-of-the-art jetliner as the decoy the players initially think is their plane. They struck a product-placement deal with Northwest Airlines to use one of its planes with the caveat that it be on the screen alone for a minimum of three seconds before the Indian Express came limping into frame. In return, Northwest provided vouchers for flights that enabled the cast and crew to travel to and from Milwaukee during filming.

There was more airport drama when a Federal Aviation Administration official noticed the shot of an airline mechanic duct-taping one of the propellers on the DC-3. He quickly informed Ward that no airport would let a plane take off with duct tape on a propeller. Ward replied that they knew that, but explained that they were shooting a comedy and it was just a joke. The official persisted, insisting that it would never happen. Ward shrugged and shot it anyway.

For a movie depicting the Indians as champions, a duct-taped airplane propeller was hardly unrealistic.

•　　•　　•

Just as Jake Taylor was the leader of the fictional team, Berenger became the leader of the cast.

"The actors had a couple disagreements, and when we did, Tom was like the Sarge," Chelcie Ross says. "He'd say, 'C'mon guys, my trailer.' And we'd sit down and talk about whatever it was. Sergeant Tom would sort things out, and we'd go back to work. I think that's just part of who he is. He's one of those people that guys naturally look up to and listen to."

Still, Charlie Sheen couldn't help but seize an opportunity to take some good-natured payback.

"There was a day when I was really struggling, and he kept throwing back to my left and my right and my feet," Sheen says. "I was exhausted and it was like 100 degrees, and he finally threw one so far over my head, I didn't even jump. I just stared at him. It was my way of saying, 'C'mon, bro. I'm out here working hard enough, y'know?'

"It was also payback for a finger poke he gave me in the middle of a scene that wound up in *Platoon* that he hadn't done in rehearsal. He poked me in the chest so hard I think he bruised my heart, literally and emotionally. So that was my payback to him."

.　　.　　.

For all the glory and childlike enthusiasm in pretending to be ball-players, there was a downside. By August, pain—in a variety of packages—had begun to set in.

"I looked like a Devil Dog," Snipes says. "There were parts of my legs that were black, and there were other parts that were white. I rubbed off the skin on my ass and my side. And I had pads on. I even put another pair of pads on and *that* didn't work. I still have the base-sliding burns on my butt. It's like having the memories of a beautiful tattoo on my ass."

For others, the discomfort was less visible: primarily sore shoulders, knees, and elbows, further inflamed by the herky-jerky schedule.

"You'd be ready to go, then you'd sit there for a while, then you'd go out and get loose again," Yeager explains. "The baseball stuff was so quick and so easy that we'd only do one or two takes and then move on to the next one. So they'd sit around a lot. They had to turn it on and turn it off when they needed to. It was a long shoot, no doubt about that. It was like a long season."

Especially for Charlie Sheen, who would would sometimes throw more pitches in a week than an actual big-league pitcher.

"You want to talk about shoulder pain?" he asks. "God, the amount of pain on each pitch. My elbow was from another galaxy." To help him get through, Sheen would regularly stop off on the way to the set for a cortisone shot in addition to his steroid regimen. "How I remembered a single line of dialogue is beyond me."

"The actors had to be treated like athletes," Julie Bergman points out. "That was hard for them because a lot of them were young and they wanted to party, but they couldn't because they had to wake up the next day and play."

Indeed, at one point Tom Berenger, peppered with bruises and blisters, staggered over to Yeager and, almost in disbelief, asked, "You guys really do this?"

Yeager smiled. "Every day, pal."

•   •   •

And every day, through the heat, the logistical nonsense, the cranky arms and shoulders, there was Yeager. "If there was baseball going on," Yeager says, "I was out there making sure it was going on correctly."

"You'd see a character at the plate swinging at what looked like a tremendous home run," Chelcie Ross explains, "and Steve and his trusty fungo bat would actually hit it out. He could do that. He was a master of the trade. He coached everybody; he was just right there all the time."

Charlie Sheen, for one, noticed a difference whenever Yeager filled in. "There's an old adage: Never make the pitcher work harder than he has to," Sheen says. "For most of Tom's throws to me on the mound, I was on the verge of dislocating rib cartilage trying to catch what was coming back. Then Yeager jumps in and everything back at me was just dead center, and I thought, *Oh, that's how these guys play.* I was so excited to pitch to Yeager that I threw harder and I threw more accurately. I didn't want to let him down."

Only once did Bernsen not take Yeager's advice.

"In those days, they were very tight-fitting uniforms," Bernsen explains. "You wouldn't see it on the field, but I always felt like the cup stuck out in this weird way on camera. So I said, 'I'm not wearing a cup. It might work for baseball, but not for this.' Yeager said, 'I'm going to be hitting you some zingers down there. You better wear a cup.' I said, 'I'm not going to do it. It'll look stupid.' So I beat him on that one, and I never got hit in the balls."

Helping Bernsen's cause, for the shot in the pennant-fever montage when he gets bombarded with grounders that bounce all over his body, Yeager was hitting rubber baseballs.

•   •   •

But Yeager wasn't the only one adding realism to the proceedings.

Not only did he deliver visually as Clu Haywood, Pete Vuckovich also added a bit to the script, improvising several lines with actual digs from his playing days. For instance, he introduced the derogatory nickname "Meat" used among actual ballplayers.

But his most memorable contribution was his greeting to Jake Taylor when Clu Haywood strolls to the plate in the first game: "How's your wife and my kids?"

"I'd asked him what he would say to a guy to really mess with him," Ward explains. "Ballplayers would say that kind of stuff to each other in jest. But I'd never heard it before, so I felt it was something he'd say just to be an asshole."

"That was Vukey," says Uecker, who'd known him when Vuckovich played in Milwaukee. "That's the stuff he did with the Brewers. It was like a bunch of players standing around shooting the shit with each other. That's how they talk."

"HE LOOKS LIKE SOME KIND OF MONGOL BARBARIAN INVADING THE ROMAN EMPIRE, BUT HE'S REALLY A SWEET, NICE GUY."

Although Vuckovich might have looked the part of the villain, in reality he was anything but. "He's a lot of fun and a lot nicer than he looks," Berenger says. "He looks like some kind of Mongol barbarian invading the Roman Empire, but he's really a sweet, nice guy."

And still true to his roots as a ballplayer.

Vuckovich always kept a case of beer on ice in the trunk of his

Mercedes, and after a long night of shooting, he and members of the cast and crew would sit on the bumpers of cars in the parking lot of County Stadium, drinking beer and watching the sun rise.

•   •   •

It wasn't until the last minute that Ward and company knew whether they'd be allowed to use one of the most memorable bits of the film. During the pennant-fever sequence, Ward scripted an American Express commercial to mirror one of the most iconic ad campaigns of the 1980s. For weeks, Chesser negotiated to get permission to shoot it.

"We kept putting it off because we didn't know if we'd be allowed to use it," Ward says. "They kept going back and forth about whether or not it was a good thing for them."

Just in case, Ward adapted a backup version, using essentially the same dialogue for the fictional "Red, White, and Blue Card."

Ultimately, the hang-up wasn't the actual use of the card or its logo, but the adaptation of the tagline. So they shot two versions, one with Wesley Snipes saying the scripted, "Don't *steal* home without it," and the standard, "Don't *leave* home without it." Even after it was filmed, Chesser spent months trying to get an official sign-off from American Express. Finally, with the movie in editing and the release date creeping closer, American Express agreed to both the sequence and the modified tagline.

•   •   •

Even with barely contained chaos swirling around him, Ward managed to maintain his sense of humor and keep the tone light.

On an off-day in late August, Berenger arranged a private screening for the cast and crew of his just-released film *Betrayed*, in which he plays the leader of a white supremacist order. "This film is so fucking intense," Sheen says. "Tom is so good and the film is so brutal, it's hard to watch. At the very end of it, we're all sitting there in stunned silence. David Ward stands up, claps his hands, and goes, 'All right, let's go make some more comedy.'

"It just showed his ability to keep everybody smiling and happy and focused. It was pretty cool."

•　　•　　•

The most difficult day of shooting occurred on the final weekend. On Saturday, September 24, production moved from Milwaukee to just outside Chicago, where they would film the walk-and-talk dialogue scene between Jake and Lynn at the Northwestern University library.

Taking a nonunion production into Teamster-strong Chicago presented a potentially prickly situation. Chris Chesser assumed he'd headed any problems off at the pass by calling the local Teamster contact he'd worked with on a previous film of his that had shot in Chicago. Would it cause any problems or provoke retaliation if the production was in and out of town in just one day? His contact implied that everything would be fine, but that he couldn't officially know about it.

And technically, everything did go fine. A parked car suspiciously caught fire with a crew member in it catching a nap in the wee hours of the morning before shooting began, but he got out unharmed, and the rest of the day transpired without further incident.

With the library packed full of extras, Ward had to quickly decide how to construct and choreograph the scene. There was a lot of work to do and only one day in which to do it. "We were trying to keep the actors from feeling like we were getting frantic," Ward says. "We *were* frantic, but no matter how frantic you are, you don't want the actors to feel it. You don't want to put that pressure on actors."

Between takes, Berenger alternated between lying flat on the large wooden study tables and pushing the crew to keep moving so they could get the day over with. "They just let me because they were so tired, too," he says. "But it kept me going."

"That was probably one of the hardest scenes I've ever done," Russo says. "It went on for quite a few pages, and in that time I had to stop, pick up books, turn around, talk, hit marks. It was like rubbing your stomach and patting your head at the same time."

It was a long day that took a lot out of everyone involved, particularly Russo, who hadn't yet developed the necessary stamina. By the time they reached the final setup, where Lynn brushes Jake off and walks into her office, Russo was utterly exhausted. After the last take, as the office door closes behind her, she broke into tears.

"She was just done," Ward says. "We had gone through so much."

Finally, after a couple of make-up days the following week, principal photography wrapped—fittingly, at the same time the Major League Baseball season came to an end.

EXTRAS . . .

Other than the two daytime ballgame sequences—opening day and Vaughn's debut with glasses—the small handful of daytime scenes were shot mostly toward the end of principal photography.

•

When searching for back issues of the comic books that Jake Taylor uses to catch up on his literature, production assistants had a difficult time finding the *Classic Comics* version of *Moby-Dick* that was the centerpiece of the joke. That was an original copy of issue no. 5, published in September 1942, which today sells upward of $200. The other issues that are literally tossed around in the movie (*Song of Hiawatha*, *The Deerslayer*, and *Crime and Punishment*) were later editions and easier to find. (Careful viewers will note they were from the later reincarnation of *Classics Illustrated*, not the original *Classic Comics*.)

•

Cut from David Ward's first draft: When Willie Mays Hayes spots Jake Taylor reading *Classic Comics*, Hayes asks, "*Moby-Dick*? What is that, porno?"

9

Cut the Windup

The week after principal photography wrapped in Milwaukee, David Ward, Chris Chesser, Irby Smith, and Julie Bergman traveled to Cleveland to oversee second-unit photography in the downtown area and at the stadium, which would add ambiance and flavor to the movie.

Standing in the parking lot outside Cleveland Stadium, they spotted one of the most charming things any of them had ever seen. As they gathered footage that sunny October afternoon, they spotted a nun in a black habit and a Cleveland Indians Starter jacket walking out of the ballpark.

Ward was instantly intrigued. *Here's something I couldn't make up*, he thought. It was simply too priceless not to capture on film. He sent an assistant over to her.

"Are you an Indians fan?" the assistant asked the nun, motioning to her jacket.

"No," she replied wryly. "The pope makes us wear these for penance."

He smiled and explained what they were up to, asking whether she had an hour to spare. And in that hour, Sister Mary Assumpta would transform from a mildly recognizable face at the ballpark into something of a legend.

After moving to Cleveland from Chicago and becoming a nun

in 1963 at the tender age of 17, Sister Mary Assumpta quickly became a huge Indians fan. She was a fixture at Tribe games in the 1970s and 1980s, standing out in the minuscule crowds in her habit and large glasses. During a particularly grim era in team history, her presence at the ballpark was both inspiring and comforting to long-suffering fellow Indians fans: If she had faith, they should, too.

As a thank-you for some of the players who'd been gracious enough to meet with nursing-home residents whom she and her fellow sisters had brought to the game, she baked cookies for them. It soon became a tradition, with her bringing cookies for the players at the start and finish of the season, then at the beginning of every home stand.

"They were in such bad shape at the time," she says of those Tribe teams. "We did that just to show them that somebody cared." She says she baked hits and strikeouts into them for hitters and pitchers, respectively, although she admitted sometimes the guys ate the wrong cookies.

The cookies earned a special distinction in the Tribe clubhouse and were not just enjoyed, but almost revered. A few years later, the Indians' ill-tempered slugger Albert Belle, frustrated by a lousy batting practice, swiped his bat across the team's buffet table, knocking everything on it—including Sister Mary's cookies—to the floor. Teammate Omar Vizquel, who like the rest of his teammates was used to seeing such outbursts from Belle, couldn't believe it.

"Oh, man," Vizquel said. "You can't do that."

"Why not?" Belle snarled.

"The cookies were on the table," Vizquel replied.

"So?"

"You know who baked the cookies?"

"Yeah," Belle huffed.

Vizquel paused, still not sure Belle really understood.

"You know who she works for?"

On the afternoon that Ward spotted her in the Cleveland Stadium parking lot, she was, in a way, on an errand for God. For a fundraiser for the Jennings Center for Older Adults in Garfield Heights, which was supported by her religious order, the Sisters of the Holy Spirit, the Indians had donated a load of leftover promotional giveaway items—which, in this era, were often plentiful. "The first 10,000 fans would get a thermal mug," she says, "and there weren't 10,000 fans."

This particular trip to the ballpark wound up being a bit more memorable. In the next hour, she and several other extras were filmed walking through a stadium turnstile for a shot that would be inserted just before the climactic playoff game. It was fun, but that, she thought, was that.

One day later, she got a call from another production assistant inviting her to join the film crew for lunch downtown, where they asked if they could film her for another scene. "Doing what?" she asked. "Well," the assistant replied, "what would you do if you came down early to a game?" She thought about it for a moment and said she'd probably stop to feed the birds in Public Square. "OK, we'd like to film you doing that." This all seemed quite strange, but Sister Mary's schedule was open, so she agreed.

At lunch that day she met Chesser and Ward, who gave her the lowdown on the film—which, of course, she'd heard about the previous summer. Once again, she agreed to be filmed, and for the rest of that gray autumn afternoon, she stood in front of the Old Stone Church in Public Square in her Indians jacket, which she'd received that summer as a present on the 25th anniversary of joining the order, tossing chunks of bread at pigeons and freezing her habit off.

"It was about 45 degrees, and then there was the wind chill off the lake," she says. "They had to keep powdering my nose because it was so red." But it was worth it. She was promised the standard extra fee, $25, but Morgan Creek wound up making a $2,000 donation to a new building fund for the Jennings Center.

Months later, Sister Mary got a call from Chesser, with whom she'd formed a strong friendship, telling her that both of her scenes made the final cut of the movie, with the bird-feeding shot in the opening-credit sequence. Even if you didn't know who she was or what she represented, it's a nice, almost Norman Rockwell-esque piece of photography.

Her other cameo, smiling with pride as she walks through the turnstile for the climactic playoff game, was a nice bookend, showing how the faith of these long-suffering fans had finally been rewarded. But for Clevelanders, it wasn't a gimmick. It was a tribute to one of the most beloved Tribe fans of all time. And, in the years to come, it would launch her into an entirely new world.

In addition to snagging Sister Mary Assumpta, over the course of those two days in Cleveland, the second unit collected a variety of shots, primarily for the opening montage.

Generally they were simple, such as exterior shots of the stadium and the city skyline (particularly the Terminal Tower, which photobombs almost every shot), but also the more esoteric visuals: the freighters along the Cuyahoga River, the statue of Moses Cleaveland in Public Square, kids playing baseball on a brick-covered hill just outside downtown, and the too-good-to-be-true baseball diamond nestled between smokestacks that was used for the title-card shot.

Although the majority of the movie had already been filmed in Milwaukee, this footage—and Sister Mary Assumpta—ensured it would contain an unmistakable Cleveland flavor.

.   .   .

Once the second unit returned from Cleveland, shooting was complete and the un-sexy, primarily technical process of post-production began.

The largest undertaking was assembling the musical soundtrack. Fittingly, just as the *Major League* cast was sprinkled with talented actors just about to hit it big, David Ward found another talented artist on the brink of his breakthrough to compose the score.

James Newton Howard was a relative newcomer to the business, but Ward had heard his stuff and saw the potential there.

Because Howard was still a few years away from becoming one of the biggest names in the business, *Major League* could afford him.

Ward didn't want a big orchestral score, but a smaller one with more texture. Visiting Howard at his home studio, Ward listened and provided feedback as Howard played sections of his score on a synthesizer. Although the score isn't a huge element in comedies such as *Major League*, it was a quietly important piece of the puzzle. Howard created a subtle, well-balanced score that juggled the physical comedy, the upbeat montages, and the final-game intensity.

He also expanded the romantic theme into a melody that was developed into the accompanying "Most Of All You," a sentimental song of reflection for the Jake/Lynn relationship. The lyrics were written by the Academy Award–winning duo of Alan and Marilyn Bergman—co-producer Julie Bergman's parents.

She floated the possibility of having them pen the lyrics, and Ward thought it was a good idea, particularly when former Righteous Brother Bill Medley, a longtime friend of the Bergmans, was brought in to sing it. The song was played briefly during the movie and then in its entirety during the end credits, and the melody weaves through Howard's score.

Although "Most Of All You" might have been the heart of the soundtrack, two other songs proved far more important. The first was X's cover of "Wild Thing," which proved relatively easy to acquire the rights to with the band broken up (they later reunited).

Even before production had begun, Ward had known that Randy Newman's tongue-in-cheek ballad "Burn On" was going to open the movie and play over a montage of images of Cleveland and the Indians' troubling history. He wanted it not only because it perfectly fit the tone of the film, but also because it was the only song Ward had ever found about Cleveland. It was so perfect, in fact, that for years afterward, people assumed Newman had written the song specifically for the movie.

Released on his "Sail Away" album in 1972, "Burn On" is a musical depiction of Cleveland's Cuyahoga River catching fire three years earlier. The story made the national news and further dinged Cleveland's reputation.

Appreciating the song's endearing wit and charm, Ward simply had to have it for the opening credits. The problem was, Newman *knew* he had to have it and put a steep price tag on the rights. "He knew he had us over a barrel," Ward remembers. "No matter how much we tried to pretend we could take it or leave it, he knew better, and he held out for the highest possible price. And we had to pay it. I remember having a meeting with Joe Roth and Joe saying, 'God, isn't there another song that's cheaper?' And I said, 'Joe, believe me, there is no other song. Even if there were, it couldn't possibly be better than this. It sounds as if it was written for the movie.'"

Consequently, Morgan Creek wound up paying nearly $90,000 to use "Burn On"—more than it had paid for the rest of the music on the soundtrack combined. In addition to the nice check, just the misconception of the song's origin helped propel Newman's career as a film composer. After writing the scores for four movies prior to *Major League*, including *The Natural*, he'd write nearly 20 more over the next two decades, finding his niche in a handful of acclaimed Pixar films and winning a pair of Oscars.

It was just another example of what would become a recurring trend over the coming years: an undoubtedly talented but relatively unknown artist using *Major League* as a springboard to bigger and better things.

•   •   •

David Ward had known that the script was strong and the performances he'd filmed were terrific. Yet when he watched the first cut of the movie, he quickly came to a startling conclusion.

It wasn't funny.

It looked right, and the performances and deliveries were fine, but the movie just didn't seem to have any energy. Once again turning to the seasoned filmmaker who'd become *Major League*'s proverbial godfather, Ward showed the cut to Sydney Pollack. And Pollack immediately identified the problem.

"David," he explained, "the stuff is all there. The thing is, you're getting into the scenes too early. Each of your scenes has a beginning, a middle, and an end. So you're stopping and starting every time, and it feels like a bunch of little stories connected together. You have to keep the audience falling forward, keep them chasing the movie."

To do that, especially in a comedy, Pollack told Ward he had to jettison the setup and get into the scenes later and pull out earlier. The humor was there all along; there was just too much sandwiching it.

WHEN HE WATCHED THE FIRST CUT OF THE MOVIE, HE CAME TO A STARTLING CONCLUSION: IT WASN'T FUNNY.

"That other stuff might be funny," Ward says, "but when you have too much, it slows the movie down."

Pollack, who'd never been to a baseball game, nevertheless put it in perfect hardball terminology. "You're building every scene with the windup, then the pitch, then the ball being thrown back to the pitcher," he told Ward. "Cut the windup and getting the ball thrown back and just get to the pitch."

Once Ward began cutting the windups, the film began to come together like soft butter, finding both its energy and its comedy.

"It started out being hard to cut things," Ward says, "but once I adopted that attitude, I was ruthless. They had to stop me after awhile. I was a locomotive."

Along the way, a handful of lines, scenes, and even entire characters were left on the cutting-room floor. Although the tight editing is one of the primary reasons *Major League* draws viewers in and keeps them in, some of what was lost for the overall good of the film was intended to explain or justify details in the story.

For instance, Lou Brown's initial hesitation to take the job as Indians manager—"Let me think it over, will ya, Charlie? I got a guy on the other line about some whitewalls"—was to be played out further during a subsequent phone negotiation scene with Charlie Donovan. It wasn't that Brown thought the Indians were such a joke that he didn't want the job (which is how it plays in the final version), but rather that he didn't want to be part of a big organization where baseball was a business and not a game, and the players are millionaires who think they know everything.

"Look, Lou, you been in baseball 30 years," Donovan says. "Don't you wanna advance some?"

"I used to coach the unwed mothers' softball team," Brown replies. "I have advanced some."

Donovan tries to explain that Brown certainly won't have to worry about dealing with any high-priced prima donnas.

"Don't you have any proven major-league talent?" Brown asks in disbelief.

"Not that I know of," Donovan sighs.

"Well then," Brown replies, "I'll be up in a couple days."

The script also called for more focus on Jake Taylor in Mexico. Following the prank phone call bit in the seedy hotel, Taylor was to get another call from Donovan in the ballpark's bathroom that served as the clubhouse and agree to come to the Indians' camp. He tells his manager he's heading back to the States, and he's required to leave his uniform,which is all he has to wear. Wearing only his boxer shorts, he boards a bus loaded with Mexican immigrants and chickens bound for the U.S.

Although the sequence in the initial rough cut was funny, Ward decided it had to go, as did a similar unfilmed sequence introducing Willie Mays Hayes working at a burger joint.

"It was slowing everything down," he said. "We didn't need all this backstory. We get it pretty quickly when we see them all showing up at Hi Corbett." Thus, the production's entire day trip to Nogales wound up on the cutting-room floor.

Such was the case for the work of an actor who later won three Emmys. Then-unknown actor Jeremy Piven, who went on to have a nice film career and carve a niche on the television series *Entourage*, had been cast as an antagonizing bench jockey who never saw the field, but would comically ridicule opponents from the Indians dugout. Again, Ward thought Piven's stuff was funny, but when it was blended into the film, it felt out of place, as if they'd continually cut away from a game sequence to somebody doing a stand-up routine in the dugout. So all of Piven's scenes were cut and no trace of him remains in the film.

Another minor character was axed in the middle of the movie. The quick "jukebox" scene in which an attractive young lady approaches Rick Vaughn in a bar and seductively recites a line from the "Wild Thing" song was all that remained of a much-longer scene intended to fuel the fire between Vaughn and Roger Dorn.

The team is in Milwaukee, and the players are hanging out in a bar. Dorn is awaiting the arrival of Arlene, his Milwaukee girl, played by Ward's assistant, Julia Miller, in a last-minute casting decision. When she arrives, she's more interested in Vaughn's potential upside as a ballplayer and blows off Dorn, citing his age and poor batting average. Ward decided the scene was too long, but kept the last snippet of Arlene approaching Vaughn at the jukebox and reciting the opening line of the "Wild Thing" song.

Similarly, the Jake-and-Lynn hookup scene was trimmed down when production fell behind schedule early on. In the script, Jake spots Lynn in the middle of a game and conspires with the umpire to get himself thrown out so he can follow her. Borrowing the Indians' bullpen car, he then trails her to the Cleveland Athletic Club, where she jumps in the pool and begins to swim the individual medley, her former speciality. Jake hops in and races her, loses, and they begin the conversation seen in the final version. Halfway through, she climbs out of the pool and heads back to her car, where she tries to lose Jake—still in the bullpen car—in the streets of Cleveland. She arrives at her apartment thinking she's lost him, but he pulls up moments later, and the scene finishes the same as in the final version. After Ward tightened the sequence, Jake spots her after the game is over, and their entire conversation takes place in Lynn's apartment.

Before the swimming scene was cut, Charlie Sheen took the initiative to find a body double for Russo's swimming sequences by scouting out the local strip clubs. "I was supposed to OK the body double," Russo says. "He'd bring back these big-breasted girls and I'd say, 'Um, that doesn't really look like me.' It was classic Charlie."

The pennant-fever montage also included a few other moments. There's a newscast segment of Indians fans burning doormats, reminiscent of feminists' bra-burning in the 1970s, as their way of telling the rest of baseball that the surging Tribe won't be stepped on anymore. (In the first draft of the script, fans show up on opening day wearing doormats around their necks.)

There were also supposed to be quick scenes showing the impact the Indians were having on their hometown: a shot of a crowd at a strip joint enjoying the show while wearing radio earphones to follow the Tribe and another of opera attendees secretly listening to the playoff game and then stomping their feet along with the ballpark crowd. Both were cut from the script when the price to shoot in the selected locations proved too high.

Two longer scenes designed to complete the romantic story arc were eventually cut. Instead of Chicago, the Indians' final game of the regular season was originally scripted to take place in Detroit. After the victory, Jake is informed that an old flame is waiting to see him—a blonde named Darla (the "Miss Fuel Injection" Lynn refers to in their discussion in the library). He unenthusiastically goes with her.

The scene of him finding Lynn's apartment empty, and the realization that she'd moved in with her fiancé, were slated to run at an earlier point than in the final version, just after their one-night stand. Jake calls it off before he and Darla can hop into bed, telling her he just can't do this anymore. Darla is understanding, knowing it means Jake has grown up and has found a keeper.

Just as Jake and Darla leave the hotel room, they encounter Lynn in the hallway, who tells him she was in town for a conference but stopped by the hotel to congratulate him. Making the obvious assumption, she quickly leaves. The following afternoon, Jake meets Lynn at the church, he in full Indians uniform, she in her wedding gown. His teammates line the sidewalk to the church, holding bats up to form an arch for her to walk through. Jake tells her nothing happened the night before in Detroit, and unlike all the other times, Lynn believes him. They wish each other good luck and Jake and his teammates leave for the ballpark.

These deletions joined a handful of other details or quick scenes that were cut from the script and never filmed or changed significantly:

- When Jake first spots Lynn at the restaurant, he follows her into the bathroom and their conversation takes place with her sitting on the toilet. Consequently, Jake is arrested and uses his one phone call to try to get in touch with Lynn—then he finds out she gave him a fake number.

- After seeing that Hayes has cut up his hands sliding, Jake suggests he wear gloves on the base paths. There was a scene of Hayes buying 100 pairs of black calfskin gloves at Saks Fifth Avenue for $110 apiece.

- Another scene followed of Hayes negotiating his contract with Rachel Phelps. He starts by comparing himself to Rickey Henderson and asking for a million dollars. He winds up at $32,500—barely enough to cover the cost of his gloves.

- Harry Doyle originally had a tape recorder with cassettes of crowds cheering that he would play into the microphone during games. When it breaks, he begins making the cheering sound effects himself.

- The quartet of bleacher fans whipped up a fight song to the tune of the "In the Land of Sky Blue Waters" Hamm's beer jingle, changing the lyrics to "In the Land of Burning Waters."

- Before the Indians' turnaround, there's a scene of Hayes and Vaughn at an autograph signing at a sporting goods store. After two hours and no requests, Hayes offers to pay a kid—then threatens him—to get him to take a few signed baseballs.

- In a precursor to his request for a live chicken, Cerrano proclaims he'll be sacrificing unborn children to appease Jobu. This draws the ire of Harris until he sees Cerrano is referring to a raw egg he cuts with his knife.

- Harris originally drank Jobu's gin (later rum) in front of the entire team. "You gonna try and stop me?" he asks Cerrano, who replies, "It is your problem, not mine." Later, Harris shuts his locker door too hard, which causes a rusty overhead pipe to fall and land on his head, knocking him unconscious.

• The scene in which the "Indian Express" bus is introduced was more elaborate, centered around an immigrant bus driver named Philbey who's racing to get the team to New York in time for the game. The bus blows a tire, which the players help change, and then does a 360-degree skid (toppling on its side in one draft) when Philbey slams on the brakes after nearly falling asleep at the wheel. Lou Brown eventually winds up driving the bus.

• After Vaughn is lit up by Haywood a second time in New York, Harris enters the game and is instructed by Lou Brown to hit the next batter with a pitch to wake up the Indians. He does, and a comical bench-clearing brawl ensues.

• Once Taylor finds out what Rachel Phelps is up to, he storms into her office and threatens to tell the press. She coldly notes that because of the Indians' history, no one will believe him. Even if they did, she's covered her tracks: The books will show that everything she's done was because of revenue problems. All he'd do by talking to the press is irritate her, she says, for which she'd send him to the minors.

Interestingly, a handful of the cut scenes and additional dialogue that were filmed wound up in trailers for the film, which were put together as the final film was being cut.

The most notable of these instances was a line delivered by Taylor when he tells Vaughn that the first homer he gave up to Clu Haywood wouldn't have been out of most parks. "Name one," Vaughn demands. "Yellowstone," Taylor replies dryly. And the line—or lack thereof—became something of a controversy for years to come. "People swear it was in the movie," Ward says. "I've had arguments with people."

Funny as it may have been, the Yellowstone line, like several others, had to go for the overall good of the movie. "If comedies get slow, they lose their edge," Ward explains. "You gotta get in and get out. Hit 'em with it and move on."

Finally, after weeks of Ward working feverishly with editor Dennis Hill—and even bringing in a second editor to work exclusively on the playoff game, then bouncing between editing suites—*Major League* was ready for an audience.

All of it, that is, except the ending.

.   .   .

Want to know the worst-kept secret in Hollywood?

Directors hate previews. And, to some extent, preview audiences.

"You do all of this work," Ward says, "and then all of a sudden the opinions of a bunch of off-the-street knuckleheads are going to determine how the movie is cut, and maybe even how it's released."

Paramount passed out flyers at malls and shopping centers around Los Angeles inviting people to attend a free screening of the film. On a Tuesday evening in January, 230 volunteers showed up at a theater on the Paramount lot to preview *Major League*.

Ward sat nervously in the crowd, eager to see how it would play. In fact, he was so eager—and so nervous—he twitched whenever people got up from their seats for popcorn or a trip to the restroom just before key moments in the movie.

At one point, Ward actually grabbed a guy headed for the lobby and told him to stay—there was a good part coming up. "That's how paranoid I was," Ward says. "I'm thinking, *He's going to go out and miss the best scene, and he's going to come back and think this movie doesn't make any sense.*"

Even with the occasional drifter, the movie played well. People laughed at the right moments and seemed to be enjoying the film. But as the movie approached its climax, Ward could tell something was wrong. He just couldn't quite put his finger on exactly what.

Things started to get weird when the big twist of the story was revealed. Just before the playoff game, Lou Brown storms into Rachel Phelps's office and announces he'll resign in protest after what she's put him and the players through over the course of the season. But Phelps, now behaving in a completely different, more sincere manner, comes clean. There never had been an offer from Miami, and she never intended to move the team. The truth was that the franchise was broke. Phelps told him she knew when she took control that if the team endured another miserable season, she would be forced to sell it, likely to someone who would indeed move it elsewhere.

It turns out Rachel Phelps isn't just a two-bit Vegas showgirl looking for a quick buck. She knows baseball, is committed to the franchise, and personally scouted every player the team invited to camp.

"They all had flaws that concealed their real talents or I wouldn't have been able to afford them," she says, adding that she knew that Brown—whom she'd also scouted—would be able to straighten them out and turn them into a good team. She'd deliberately taken on the veil of the cruel owner to give the players the motivation they'd need, contingent on her prediction that Charlie Donovan would eventually clue Brown into what was really going on with the Miami deal and the attendance ploy.

"You tryin' to make me believe you wanted us to win all along?" Brown asks, and Phelps nods in reply. "Bullshit," he snaps. "What about the plane, the bus, the bad hotels . . ."

"We were broke," she explains. "We couldn't afford anything better. Donald left the team nearly bankrupt. If we'd had another losing season, I would have had to sell the team. I knew we couldn't win with the players we had, so I decided to bring in new players and see how they'd do with the proper motivation."

She even points out that had she truly wanted them to lose, once some of the younger players began to improve, she could have just ordered that they be sent down to the minors. But she didn't. And now she warns him that if Brown tells anyone the truth, she will indeed fire him. With a newfound respect for his would-be nemesis, Brown leaves the office, as Phelps—nearly in tears—looks up to the sky and says, "OK, Donnie . . . here we go."

As the scene flickered across the screen, Ward could feel the air going out of the balloon. There was no laughter, no gasps of astonishment, no palpable sense of shock. Just nothing. Ward tried to figure it out. Were they silent because they were surprised by it? Moved by it? Not exactly. "They were being quiet there," he says, "because they're going, 'What the *fuck*?'"

But at the time, he didn't know that. And, for that night at least, he didn't want to know. Typically, at a preview screening, directors, producers, and studio executives all stay after the film is over to hear any comments from the audience and get a quick read of their comment cards and focus-group feedback. That night, as the credits rolled, so did David Ward.

"Like before they could string him up," Morgan Creek president Jim Robinson says. "It was with that sense of urgency."

It wasn't that Ward didn't want to hear the feedback. He knew something was wrong and that the ending hadn't played the way he'd wanted. But in his pressurized, highly sensitive state of mind, with his directorial career hanging in the balance, he just couldn't deal with it at that moment. In addition, regardless of the preview scores, Ward remembered all too well how things had turned out on *Cannery Row*.

"I'd been through a preview where I got great scores and the movie went down the toilet," he recalls. "I didn't even want to know. I didn't want to sit around and go through a big postmortem. So I just left."

He knew some changes had to be made, particularly with the twist ending. He thought he'd just constructed the reveal scene wrong, that maybe if he recut it or delivered the twist differently, it might play better.

The next day, Ward got his answer.

Major League had scored 74 on a 100-point scale—slightly above average, but certainly not great (*Cannery Row*'s had been 93). It was the kind of score that prompts notable revisions before release. And in most cases, even that doesn't do much good. Generally, if an audience doesn't like a movie, it's because whatever they don't like is already baked in. You can't just fix it by adding something or taking something out. But looking at the comments, the solution presented itself, loud and clear.

They didn't like the twist ending. Check that—they *hated* the twist ending. And the response was overwhelming. In a process that usually results in wildly differing opinions and suggestions, almost every comment card noted the same problem. They loved the characters, they loved the romance, they loved the comedy. They just despised the clever twist, partially because it seemed unrealistic, but mostly because they loved hating Rachel Phelps and didn't like missing out on seeing her agony of defeat.

When they saw the cards, Ward, Chesser, and everyone else involved with the making of the movie slapped their proverbial palms against their skulls. In the time it had taken to cook up the concept, write the script, shop the script, and produce the movie, it had never dawned on anyone that the surprise ending might be a huge mistake.

"It was so ubiquitous that I almost felt like a fool for not realizing that would happen," Ward says. "I thought I was being clever. But they didn't want clever, dammit; they wanted to see her go down."

"I don't think any of us were surprised," Julie Bergman says. "We were sort of relieved because we knew there were things that weren't working, and we weren't sure exactly what the answer to that was going to be."

The good news was that everybody agreed with what had to be done and that it was a relatively easy fix. But they had to move quickly.

•   •   •

Margaret Whitton, meanwhile, was baffled.

She put down the phone and tried to comprehend what she'd just been told, that not only was she going to have to do a quick reshoot for *Major League*, but that her favorite scene in the movie was being shit-canned.

She'd loved the twist ending and felt it made both Rachel Phelps and the entire movie something special. "I thought it saved it from being another 'they-win-the-big-game' film," she says. "I think David was trying to make a sports movie that was a little less predictable."

The reveal scene in which Whitton felt she and James Gammon had "caught fire" would have to be deleted, along with the collage of shots of Rachel Phelps cheering wildly in her private box during the playoff game, even dancing along to "Wild Thing" when Rick Vaughn came in from the bullpen. To replace them, Ward would have to hop the pond to London, where Whitton was temporarily stationed as she traveled around Europe shooting the television series *A Fine Romance* for ABC. Her Rachel Phelps wig was shipped over from the States, and she reluctantly prepared to reprise the role.

For one day's work, the owner's private box was reconstructed in the corner of a soundstage at Pinewood Studios, where Morgan Creek was filming the ill-fated horror movie *Nightbreed*. To save money, Ward had the *Nightbreed* crew build the set and film the additional shots, coordinating across the ocean how the box should be built.

"It was just really weird," Julie Bergman says. "David and I were communicating with that production designer and his crew. The fact that it actually looked like what we thought it needed to look like was a small miracle."

Another trick was making sure the lighting matched the exterior lights of County Stadium as much as possible, then equalizing the sound. Once everything was worked out, Whitton—pulled in on her day off—sat beside Charles Cyphers to redo the scenes of them cheering that had been filmed six months earlier, this time with Whitton moping through the final game. That wasn't difficult, Whitton explained, not only because she didn't agree with the new take on the character, but because she was so tired from shooting *A Fine Romance*.

"It was so bizarre going back and doing that," she says, "and really kind of depressing because I had so carefully calibrated how she was plotting all of this."

Ward returned to America with the new ending, cut it into the movie, and *Major League* was ready to take another swing. At a second preview just over a month before the release, the difference was unmistakable. The average score jumped up to an 88, and both Ward and Morgan Creek knew they had dodged a bullet and now had a potential hit on their hands.

•   •   •

Although the new ending rescued the movie by giving the audience what it wanted, it also changed the basic premise of the plot. Whether it was better or not depends on who you ask.

"There are rules in storytelling, and if you break them, the audience is going to feel cheated," Corbin Bernsen says. "One of those rules is that you can't suddenly have the antagonist be faking it. In really good storytelling, you can switch who's good and who's bad, but you can't have them faking it."

Whitton thought part of the reason the test audience—particularly the men—didn't like the ending was that they weren't comfortable with the aesthetic of the gender role portrayed in the original ending. "Very often it makes men nervous when women know too much about sports," she says. "That's their all-male club, and a smart woman coming in who knows a lot about it rocks their little world. In their unconscious minds, they didn't want the woman to be the hero."

"I STILL PREFER THE ORIGINAL ENDING. I WISH IT HAD WORKED A LITTLE BETTER."

Coincidentally or not, within the original preview audience, the movie scored higher with women than men.

"I still prefer the original ending," Chesser admits. "That's one of the things that helped us to get Embassy to develop it to begin with. That twist was so clever—that she knew what she was doing."

Although Phelps suddenly becoming a good guy was somewhat unsatisfying and perhaps implausible, it added a level of verisimilitude to the rest of the film and helped fill some of the logic gaps. Most notably, it addressed the question of why motivation alone was the only thing that instantly turned the Indians into a contender. In the original script, it wasn't—the resurgence was all part of a master, if far-fetched, plan.

"She was left with a bankrupt team," Whitton says. "What was she going to do? It didn't make sense that she was going to move it to Miami. She walks in and says, 'Here's a list of people we're going to invite to spring training.' Nobody's that lucky. If it were that easy, everybody could do it. So she made herself the target, which I thought was quite brilliant. Without that, I don't think the movie really adds up."

The twist also inadvertently forecasted a new baseball philosophy that would eventually take the game by storm. To today's baseball fans, Phelps's cunning personnel strategy no doubt sounds familiar: The owner brings in players other teams thought were only marginal and tries to get the most out of them primarily because he can't afford to do otherwise.

More than a decade before Oakland Athletics general manager Billy Beane decided to blow up the modern front-office baseball mentality, and 22 years before Brad Pitt depicted Beane on film, Rachel Phelps was—in the original version, at least—playing Moneyball. Just as for Beane and the Athletics, it worked. And when it did, Ward couldn't help but think of Rachel Phelps.

"I came up with it as a comic conceit, not because I thought it was a real model for Major League Baseball teams to use," he says. "I can't say I was a savant about playing Moneyball. But I thought it was funny that it did turn out to be a philosophical approach to building a team. Who would have thunk it? Rachel Phelps was a pioneer." But because she was also such a delicious villain, nobody would ever know it.

With the windup cut, the story tightened, the right music inserted, and the ending fixed, the time had come for *Major League* to face the world.

EXTRAS . . .

Wesley Snipes, unlike Willie Mays Hayes, wasn't a fast runner. So the spring-training scene in which Hayes sprints in his pajamas required creativity. Filming it in slow motion helped. That allowed Snipes to run at full speed while his opponents ran more slowly. Still, the scene needed some choreography: the two players Mayes runs past squint their eyes, grit their teeth, and puff out their cheeks while maintaining the motion of a full stride without actually running hard.

•

One of the most important sound effects of the film was created for Rick Vaughn's three-pitch strikeout of Clu Haywood. David Ward asked his sound technicians for something unique, something that suggested that the baseball might actually be breaking the sound barrier on its way to home plate. The effect they created sounded like a combination of a jet engine and a tidal wave. The second he heard it, Ward knew that was the one to use.

•

After filming, when there was no time to get Pete Vuckovich to loop a new line of dialogue in his first scene, David Ward simply did it himself. He carefully watched a few clips of Vuckovich and had himself recorded imitating Vuckovich's voice. The sound engineer then tweaked the line a bit so it had the right pitch, and Ward placed it in the film. When a smiling Hayes dusts off his new shoes at first base and Haywood grunts, "Really knocked the crap outta that one," it's actually the voice of David Ward.

•

It seems Hollywood can't make a baseball movie without including a newspaper-headline montage. *Major League* had two. For both, permission was granted by *The Plain Dealer* for use of its masthead and layout template. Fake headlines were created and spliced into the pennant-fever montage, and broader headlines encompassing the Indians' gradual demise ("Indians Hit Skids, Finish 6th") were grafted onto actual *PD* sports pages from the past for the newspaper sequence during the film's opening credits.

10

"Like Watching a Home Movie"

It was a boyhood dream come true. Clad in an Indians cap and jersey, David Ward stood just off the baseline at Cleveland Stadium, exchanging warm-up tosses with Chris Chesser in preparation for throwing out the ceremonial first pitch of the Tribe's 1989 season.

More than 40,000 fans were packed into the colossal ballpark for the home opener on an overcast, chilly Monday afternoon, and Ward was beginning to think about each of those pairs of eyes settling on him. Not wanting to humiliate himself or jinx the Indians' season (which they generally liked to take care of themselves), Ward was both nervous and intense, focusing solely on the quality of his throws. So focused, in fact, that he didn't notice when the 40,000 fans silently rose to their feet, nor when the familiar music began playing a moment later. He just continued to throw, thinking about the magnitude of where he was and what he was doing. He'd be throwing from the same mound on which the heroes of his childhood had once stood: Bob Lemon, Early Wynn, Herb Score, heck—Bob Feller, for goodness' sake. Here in this mammoth, sacred ballpark that he had once seen as the playground of the gods and had revered for as long as he could remember, Ward would etch his own place in its storied history.

His nostalgic and grandiose thoughts were interrupted by a brash, irritated voice from the crowd:

"Take off your hat, you asshole!"

It was then that Ward realized the national anthem had begun to play and he was still playing catch. He quickly removed his Tribe cap, placed it over his heart, and faced the flag, now thinking about what a surprise it was going to be for the fans when the asshole who hadn't taken his hat off was introduced as their guest of honor.

Moments later, he stood atop the mound, and before it could really sink in how different it was to throw from up there, he fired a pitch to home plate. To his enormous relief, it didn't sail to the backstop, nor did it bounce to the catcher. Perhaps appropriately, not unlike Rick Vaughn, Ward's pitch was high and inside. He received a nice ovation, and the Indians took the field in what would be an impressive victory over—coincidentally—the Milwaukee Brewers.

Aside from his whirlwind stop for second-unit photography six months earlier, Ward hadn't been back to his home town in nearly 15 years. Now, he was a celebrity. Because of him, for that week, at least, and for the first time in nearly three decades, the Cleveland Indians were genuinely cool.

With *Major League* set to open nationwide that Friday, and the opening day of the baseball season marking the symbolic end to another brutal Cleveland winter, that first week of April became a sort of mardi gras in northeast Ohio. Mayor George Voinovich declared it "*Major League* Week," and fittingly, the film would have its world premiere right down the street from the ballpark.

Ward and his colleagues were on hand at the Ohio Theater in Playhouse Square the following evening, April 4, when *Major League*'s premiere kicked off the annual Cleveland International Film Festival before a crowd of more than one thousand. Corbin Bernsen, Wesley Snipes, and Bob Uecker were there, as was an entourage from the Indians' front office and nine actual Indians players.

Perhaps more than any member of the Indians' contingent,

Bob DiBiasio was interested in seeing how the final product would look. Since that winter day in his office more than a year ago, he'd known what the basic elements of the story would be, so he was able to absorb the film a bit more and appreciate how the written words on the page had been translated to a visual medium. "From start to finish, I was watching it a bit more critically," he says. "I just sat there and kept thinking, *This is fun*." He wasn't the only one.

Before the film began, Ward addressed the crowd and assured the players none of the characters were based on them. "If you find any similarities," he told them, "you should seek professional help."

He went on to thank the many people who'd helped him bring his baseball fantasy to life, not realizing until after he'd left the stage that he'd forgotten someone absolutely essential to the project. He quickly rushed back on stage to offer a quick, breathless tribute to his dad for instilling his love of the game and the Indians.

Then celebrated local singer Rocco Scotti belted out the national anthem, and the movie flickered up onto the screen.

From the opening notes of "Burn On" and the montage of downtown Cleveland through the next 106 minutes, the crowd clearly liked what it saw. When credits rolled and the lights came up, the audience rose and offered a rousing ovation. To be sure, they were inclined to like the film anyway, but it was clear that any fears they had had of being mocked had faded away. This was, among other things, a film for Cleveland by a Clevelander.

Even the players, able to see it with more objectivity, loved the film. Pitchers Tom Candiotti and Doug Jones both said they thought *Major League* was better than the previous summer's *Bull Durham*. Catcher Joel Skinner—who would one day manage the Indians—was impressed with the actors' honed baseball form. Pitcher Bud Black, also destined to become a big-league skipper, was particularly impressed with Charlie Sheen's pitching mechanics, so much so that Black wryly confessed, "I'm going out tomorrow to get a pair of glasses and get my hair cut just like him."

Dick Jacobs, who had purchased the team with his brother

three years earlier and would soon engineer the creation of a new ballpark that would be named for him, also was on hand, and complimented Ward for a job well done.

Sister Mary Assumpta was unable to attend the premiere to celebrate her film debut but told reporters by phone that she was praying for the success of the film. "May it also be a portent of good things to come for the Indians," she wrote in a letter to Chesser prior to the release.

Over the course of that celebratory evening, there was only one mild criticism.

As the ovation rolled through the theater at the film's conclusion, Bob DiBiasio stood up to applaud along with the rest of the front-office contingent sitting in front of him, including team president Hank Peters and his wife Dottie. Smiling, she turned to face DiBiasio.

"Hank told me that you had script approval," she said.

"Yes, I did," DiBiasio said.

"My goodness," she replied, still smiling. "Do you kiss your mother with that mouth?"

DiBiasio could only chuckle.

At the after-party at Cafe Sausalito in the Galleria, a tall, silver-haired gentleman stepped up to Ward and introduced himself. Before Ward could digest that he was talking to Hall of Fame pitcher Bob Feller, the legend he'd watched as a child, Rapid Robert complimented him on a job well done.

"I think it's a funny movie," he said. "I just think there's too much swearing. We don't swear like that."

Ward could understand Feller's view. He'd played in a different era and had always been a forthright, religious person. He had no doubt Feller hadn't sworn as much as any of the characters in the movie, but still . . .

"I think what he probably meant was that he hated to see the image propagated that the guys swear a lot," Ward says. "But they do." Indeed, if you aren't prepared for it, the spicy language within *Major League* could sour your overall impression of the movie.

If you're keeping score at home, there are 99 verbal obscenities in the movie, an average of roughly one per minute (and a tally that could be interpreted as a deeply encrypted homage to Wild Thing). Although there are long stretches, particularly toward the end, without any foul language, there are others downright saturated with swearing. Most notably, during the sequence in which Rick Vaughn attacks Roger Dorn after the red-tag prank, there's a machine-gun spray of seven profanities in 17 seconds.

> "I WAS SHOCKED AT ALL THE SWEARING THAT WAS IN [THE MOVIE] BECAUSE I NEVER SAW IT IN MY SCENES."

There's a wide selection of expletives to choose from throughout the movie, but the clear champions are "shit" (including derivatives "shitty," "bull-shit," "horseshit," and the instant classic, "shitburger") with 37 uses, and "fuck" (including "fucking," "motherfucker," and new-comer "fuckwad") with 23, including one in Spanish. Neil Flynn kicks off the festivities with the construction worker's "Who are these fuckin' guys?" at the five-minute mark, and the Yankees' third baseman rounds it out with a slow-motion "Shit!" upon seeing Jake Taylor's surprise bunt in the final moments.

"Honestly, I was shocked at all the swearing that was in it because I never saw it in my scenes," Bob Uecker says. "I think it was a shock to a lot of people, and some didn't particularly go for it. But it wasn't like *The Babe Ruth Story* or *Pride of the Yankees,* where there's no cursing and everybody's going to church. It's not like that in reality."

The issue also came up during the two preview showings. Older attendees noted the movie had too much profanity, which was reflected in the scores and kept the movie from reaching the low 90s. But neither Ward nor the producers had any intention of trimming the language. "We felt like for that core audience of young men, that made the film feel real to them," Ward says.

Even Sister Mary Assumpta agreed.

"Knowing baseball players and guys, it was natural," she says. "I just regretted that a lot of the little kids I knew couldn't watch it."

Although there were a few moments when Ward concedes they might have gone a bit too far (such as Rick Vaughn inviting the umpire to blow him after he's ejected from the game), Ward still thinks the language adds more than it takes away.

"I've had some fathers come up to me and say they wanted to take their 10-year-old sons, but there was just too much swearing," he says. "The feeling was, we might have lost some business there, but I think it's a trade-off. We might have lost some other business by not doing it. It's a hard thing to quantify."

• • •

On Wednesday, the *Major League* train returned to Milwaukee for another premiere, which was preceded by a black-tie reception sponsored, not surprisingly, by the Miller Brewing Company at the Marc Plaza Hotel (the site of Charlie Sheen's break-in seven months earlier).

With tickets priced at $100 apiece and the proceeds going to charity, more than 800 people attended the gala, transported by limousine and tour bus two blocks to the Grand Cinemas theater for Milwaukee's Hollywood moment. But it was a much more substantial, intimate experience for many in the crowd. "Like watching a home movie," as one attendee described the experience.

In Los Angeles or New York, it might have seemed silly, but in Milwaukee, as in Cleveland, it was a big deal. "There are a lot of people who said we shouldn't be so excited about this movie; that it shows we're unsophisticated in Milwaukee," one Milwaukee County executive said. "If that's the case, I vote for being unsophisticated."

If not more sophisticated, certainly a less invested audience awaited the premiere in Los Angeles on Friday night, where Ward and his comrades would watch the film for the first time with a neutral audience at the Bruin Theater in Westwood.

Recalling the painful memory of *Cannery Row*'s premiere seven years before, Ward didn't plan to attend. He knew the movie was good and that, so far, people had liked it, but he just couldn't imagine going through another disappointment like that. Throughout the day on Friday, he kept getting phone calls from Joe

Roth and others telling him he simply had to attend; that there was nothing to worry about.

Finally he relented, but to his horror, when he arrived, the theater was once again nearly empty. As the lights dimmed and the coming attractions lit up the screen, Ward was ready to bolt, sensing another disaster. "Joe basically had to tackle me to keep me there," he says. Roth and others tried to remind him that this was just how it worked with late-arriving L.A. crowds.

Sure enough, by the time the title of the movie flashed onto the screen, the theater was full. And as they watched the movie, members of the crowd repeatedly laughed and appeared to enjoy themselves. When the end credits rolled, the audience applauded, and Ward breathed a sigh of relief. It was not *Cannery Row* revisited.

"This is why I got into this business," he says. "A totally different experience."

As it turned out, it was a totally different experience at the box office as well.

•   •   •

Even without word of mouth, it was difficult not to know *Major League* was coming. In addition to the two-and-a-half minute theatrical trailer and a variety of TV spots, in conjunction with Miller Lite, signs and placards promoting the film were displayed in supermarkets, convenience stores, and bars across the country. Clips were shown on the scoreboards of big-league ballparks as the new season began, and free passes to the movie were distributed through radio shows, events, and contests across the country. A San Diego nightclub even hosted a "Wild Thing" dance contest as a tie-in to the movie.

Further announcing the film's arrival was its distinctive logo, cooked up by the Paramount marketing department: a baseball adorned with reflective sunglasses, a red Mohawk, a large gold hoop earring, and feathers. Although there was really no connection between elements of the logo and anything in the movie, the graphic delivered a clear message: This movie was going to be fun and a little bit badass. Its impact was spoiled somewhat by the eye-rolling tagline—"When these oddballs try to play hardball, the result is totally screwball"—but redeemed by its clever subtitle: "A comedy with bats and balls."

Overall, Paramount had done its job, carpet-bombing the proper demographics and making the eventual arrival of *Major League* an event from coast to coast.

Even as Ward was sweating out the size of the crowd at the Bruin on opening night, the coffers were filling up. On Friday alone, *Major League* cashed in more than $2.7 million, followed by an even better showing on Saturday. By the end of the weekend, the film had tallied $8.8 million in an era when a massive blockbuster would generally rake in around $20 million in its opening weekend, and earned an average of $5,734 per screen.

THE LOGO DELIVERED A CLEAR MESSAGE: THIS MOVIE WAS GOING TO BE FUN AND A LITTLE BIT BADASS.

It was the highest-grossing film of the weekend, capturing the No. 1 spot over the Michael Keaton comedy *The Dream Team* and the suspense thriller *Dead Calm*, both released the same day. Playing at more than 1,500 theaters nationwide—better than *The Natural*, *Bull Durham*, or *Field of Dreams* in their opening weekends— *Major League* remained No. 1 through the following weekend, topping newcomer *Say Anything* before being knocked from the top spot by the film adaptation of Stephen King's *Pet Sematary*.

By the time *Major League* dropped out of first-run theater circulation in mid-June, it had collected $46 million domestically. After its late-summer turn in the second-run theaters, *Major League* had raked in a grand total of $49.8 million, making it at the time the third-highest-grossing baseball film ever and 26th among all films released in 1989.

With a budget of $11 million, it had proven an unequivocal profit-maker.

Major League also did big business overseas, particularly in South Korea, Mexico, and baseball-mad Japan, where Rick

Vaughn's Wild Thing character became almost a cult figure and led to a handful of profitable endorsement contracts for Charlie Sheen.

On the whole, not too bad for a concept that had been laughed out of almost every office in Hollywood.

*　　*　　*

Sister Mary Assumpta had never laughed so hard in her life.

Unable to attend the Cleveland premiere because of a previously scheduled religious retreat, she was visiting cousins in Santa Fe on vacation, when they surprised her by taking her to the local theater so she could see the movie that she'd become part of by chance.

From her debut in the opening moments to the image of her beloved Indians being crowned in the final shot, she loved every second. And as she came out of the theater wearing her Indians jacket, the other filmgoers' eyes widened with the realization that they'd just seen her in the movie. They flocked to her like moths to a flame, asking whether she was really a nun or a Hollywood actress.

And, of course, requesting her autograph.

*　　*　　*

Despite its financial success and warm audience reception, as with many films that ultimately develop a long-term cult following, *Major League*'s initial reviews were not especially good.

Sports Illustrated labeled it "Too Bush for the Bigs," comparing it to a triple-A-level product.

"The worst part of watching *Major League* is knowing that there is a higher intelligence out there somewhere," it said, adding that the accomplished David Ward "does a little too much slumming." Although conceding the movie redeemed itself at the end, *SI* wondered how the fictional Indians would have done in the American League Championship Series.

"You might also leave wondering what the movie had been

like had it not been quite so silly," the review continued. "If their long-suffering fans are going to be teased by *Major League*'s creators into thinking they have a chance to win the American League East, they deserve a little better. So do the rest of us."

SI did find qualities to praise, citing Charlie Sheen as "entirely believable as Wild Thing" and declaring James Gammon so convincing as skipper Lou Brown that he could probably land a real-life managing job. Of course, there was a big thumbs-up for Harry Doyle "doing an impersonation of Bob Uecker."

Time was more forgiving, admitting the film "doesn't try too hard or aim too high, but it is pretty funny" and its climax "is as predictably uplifting as *Rocky*'s and as surefire effective as *Damn Yankees*." Interestingly, *Time* crammed its reviews of both *Major League* and *Field of Dreams*—released two weeks later—into the same quarter-page article and stated its preference for *Major League*.

In that spirit, the *Los Angeles Times* grudgingly admitted that the film "had its own ingratiating charm."

Surprisingly, the *New York Times* endorsed it, though in its usual vaguely condescending manner. Ultimately calling it "wonderfully unpretentious, uningratiating, and uninspiring," the review applauded the actors' performances as "quirky and lively" while noting that *Major League* "trots out the standard formula, but has the wit to make fun of it now and then."

A common theme in nearly every review was a comparison to the previous summer's hit baseball movie, which also contained a storyline about a downtrodden veteran catcher trying to nurture a young, inexperienced, hard-throwing youngster. Because *Bull Durham* had hit theaters almost exactly a month before principal photography began on *Major League*, the comparisons were to be expected.

Naturally, Ward had seen *Bull Durham* right away. Although he couldn't help but notice subtle similarities between the two principal characters, he wasn't concerned because they were marginal and, with his $11 million production three weeks away from kickoff, there wasn't much he could do about it.

The one detail in *Bull Durham* that did concern him was minute but enough to prompt action. Early in the film, there's a quick voodoo joke in which a Puerto Rican player rubs his bat with a chicken-bone cross to snap out of a slump.

Ward called *Bull Durham* writer/director Ron Shelton, first to tell him how much he liked the movie, then to let him know he was about to roll cameras on a baseball movie that included a character who believed in and practiced voodoo.

"I just didn't want him to think I had watched his movie and thought, *Voodoo! That's a great idea!*" Ward says. "The other similarities I just chalked up to the fact that most baseball movies have a romance, and there's also usually a relationship between the pitcher and the catcher."

Another similarity had ultimately taken care of itself.

The defining characteristic of one of *Bull Durham*'s ballplayers was his devout Christianity and persistence in bringing his teammates into the light. Likewise, in early drafts of the *Major League* script, Eddie Harris's religious leanings were a prominent part of his character. However, the fervor was sanded off somewhat as the writing progressed because Ward saw that the more religious he got, the less funny the character became. Thus, in the film, Harris's religiosity is contained to the ill-fated clubhouse prayer before the Indians' first game and the "Jesus Christ can't hit a curveball" tête-à-tête with Cerrano.

Regardless, critics latched onto the similarities between the two films—and the proximity of their releases—to compare and contrast them. And because *Bull Durham* had been a hit the year before, *Major League* generally lost this cinematic interpretation of the Pepsi Challenge.

"No one, not even baseball fans, should go to *Major League* hoping for *Bull Durham*'s sex, raunch, and sophistication," the *Los Angeles Times* reported, repeating a popular sentiment.

Most reviewers seemed convinced that *Major League* was trying to ride the coat tails of *Bull Durham*'s success—most of them unaware that not only was *Major League* written five years earlier, but that many of the elements celebrated in *Bull Durham*'s release had been repeatedly rejected by studios when *Major League* made the rounds.

"It was just a great irony," Chesser notes, "that it was developed so much later but came out first."

•   •   •

Although it received lukewarm critical praise nationally, *Major League* was embraced in the two places it hit home.

The *Milwaukee Sentinel* gave it a glowing review, noting: "David Ward has composed an affectionate paean to baseball and in doing so, has organized a likable group of misfits to act out his vision of a winning season for the, in real life, beleaguered Cleveland Indians."

The only thing that might disappoint local viewers, the *Sentinel* concluded, was the difficulty in picking out recognizable Milwaukee landmarks, which the paper attributed to Ward's efforts to create the illusion that the movie had been filmed in Cleveland.

The Plain Dealer review also was adoring, likening the film to a "perfect day at the ballpark" and comparing its virtues with those of *The Sting*.

It appreciated Ward's "affectionate, spoofing, and slightly nostalgic" tone and predicted that "this comedy of haplessness is so sweet and unassuming that . . . even non-fans will be won over."

Special praise also was given to Sheen in his first truly comedic role. What made Rick Vaughn so interesting, the *PD* explained, is that "Sheen plays him tight and inhibited, a guy who dies with every mistake, and wants most of all to be completely in control."

On the day the film was released, the hard-barked *Plain Dealer* editorial staff published a column about *Major League* and the impact it was expected to have on the city and the Indians.

Sandwiched between a piece warning about the fragility of Namibia's newfound independence and another about Poland's battle against communism, the editorial praised the film for topping out with the Indians winning the divisional title, rather than showing them advancing in the playoffs and/or World Series.

Had *Major League* portrayed such fantasies with the same effective strokes with which it captured the division title, the essay stated, "such triumphs, should they arrive in real life, would be anti-climactic."

The editorial asserted that the movie had indeed helped to fill the three-decade chasm the franchise had created, combining "Hollywood's brand of fantasy with one Tribe followers have entertained year after dismal year."

Noting Cleveland "photographs well and exudes vitality," it predicted the film would also do well outside of northeast Ohio, even if Cleveland became an unwitting accomplice in another joke at its expense.

Still, the editorial concluded, it was worth it. "To trade fantasy for mere wishful thinking," it said, "the closing minutes might just give America a preview of the long-awaited baseball revival."

Incredibly, it did.

EXTRAS . . .

On the weekend that *Major League* opened, the real Indians swept the real Yankees in a three-game series in New York—the Tribe's first sweep at Yankee Stadium in 23 years.

•

The 92-70 record posted by the fictional Indians in *Major League* would have been the franchise's best mark since going 88-66 in 1956.

•

Until it was mentioned in the plot of *Major League II*, many fans wondered how the Indians of *Major League* would have fared in the playoffs after vanquishing the Yankees to win the division title. But David Ward had never even considered it. "I always intended it to just end with them winning the division," he says. "Anything else would have seemed like an anticlimax."

11

Major League Strikes Back

Major League turned out to be a lot like Watergate.

Any time there's any whiff of a political brouhaha, reporters reflexively tack on a "-gate" suffix and, if it goes on long enough, they dutifully point out similarities with the two-year carnival run by the Nixon White House in the early 1970s. Likewise, at the dawn of the 1990s, whenever the Indians did anything of note, local and national reporters couldn't resist drawing parallels with *Major League.*

It started from inside the walls. In 1990, to promote the first full Indians season since the release of the film, the team introduced a new marketing slogan, which would be printed on pocket schedules and incorporated into a radio jingle: "A Major League Good Time." The word choice was subtle, but not coincidental.

"We were having fun with it," Bob DiBiasio says with a smile.

There was more allegorical fun that summer. A comically optimistic prediction for Indians success in 1990 by columnist Mike Downey in *The Sporting News* provided 90 reasons why the Tribe would make the playoffs. Number 11 was: "Cleveland's pennant success already has been recorded for posterity on film, which saves the club a lot of time and money. Trust me, by the year 1991, they'll be listing the movie *Major League* as a documentary."

That sentiment was reflected in mid-June when the Milwau-kee Brewers came to town. Before the opening game of the series, Bob Uecker walked up to the cage to watch batting practice, and Indians rookie catcher Sandy Alomar spotted him.

"Hey," Alomar said, pointing at Uecker, "Harry Doyle."

A month later, few, if any, Indians fans noticed when the team traded for an obscure minor-league outfielder named Alex Cole, and his major-league debut drew little attention two weeks after that. But when he stole five bases in his eighth big-league game and led the Tribe to a victory over Kansas City, the rail-thin, goggles-wearing Cole became the talk of Cleveland, not only for tying a team record that had stood for 59 years, but for becoming the real-life personification of one of their fictional heroes, right down to the out-of-nowhere, "we-don't-know-where-he-played-last-year" detail.

When Cole returned to his locker after the game, he saw that his teammates had taped "Willie Mays Hayes" across his nameplate and attached five sliding gloves beside it, just as Hayes had done with his own gloves after each successful stolen base.

"Yeah, I saw the movie," Cole replied when reporters asked the obvious question. "I can identify with him."

Although Cole turned out to be a solid player in his seven-year career in the majors, his sudden, explosive debut—and perhaps his conspicuous connection to the movie that had cemented so many fans' allegiance to the team—did more harm than good.

After Cole batted .300 and stole 40 bases in 63 games to round out the 1990 season, the Indians' front office decided to build the team philosophy around Cole's speed. They moved the Cleve-land Stadium outfield fences back for 1991 and vowed to win with pitching and speed, rather than power (not that they had all that much of any of the three).

The plan backfired. Despite playing in nearly twice as many games as in his debut season, Cole managed only 27 steals, and the Indians hit a mere 22 home runs at home in a franchise-worst 105-loss season.

It was a great example of why David Ward becomes a bit

nervous whenever parallels are drawn between his team and his movie. "It's a double-edged sword," he says. "It's fun, but if it goes south, does it give people a negative association with the movie? Sometimes you want the movie to stay in the movie realm and the baseball to stay in the baseball realm."

But the year of the disastrous Alex Cole experiment also marked the arrival of the primary core of players who would lead the long-awaited resurgence.

Up-and-coming sluggers Carlos Baerga and Albert Belle became full-time starters. Scrawny third baseman Jim Thome made his big-league debut. Charles Nagy evolved from a minor-league prospect to the most promising young pitcher on the staff. In June, the team used its first-round draft pick to select promising slugger Manny Ramirez, and in the next few months, the Indians would trade for athletic center fielder Kenny Lofton and pitcher Jose Mesa, soon to become the most dominating closer in franchise history.

With a new ballpark on the horizon, the team had the financial security to lock down all of these players to long-term contracts, and the Indians showed flashes of promise over the next two seasons. The team was poised to take off in 1994.

Coincidentally, that's precisely when *Major League* re-entered, stage left.

·   ·   ·

The motivation for doing a sequel didn't originate with a grand, inspired idea or story concept, but with a junior-high mentality: Everybody else is doing it, so we might as well do it, too.

Morgan Creek saw other studios cranking out sequels to successful comedies and figured it could work for *Major League*.

"There was always talk about a sequel because the first one did pretty well and made money," Corbin Bernsen says. "Then you get into, *What are they going to do in this one?* It's tough because we've done the underdog story, so the best you can do is have them all become Roger Dorn and fall prey to their success, then have to start all over again."

The problem was that, partly because of a dispute between Morgan Creek and Paramount over the VHS release of *Major League*, nearly four years had passed before the ball started rolling for a sequel. And by the time it did, it was too late.

FOUR YEARS HAD PASSED BEFORE THE BALL STARTED ROLLING FOR A SEQUEL. AND BY THE TIME IT DID, IT WAS TOO LATE.

"You either do it right away or you do it way later," Ward says. "You don't do it in that five-to-ten-year period after. That's not the right sequel window."

With Ward stacked up and unable to tackle the responsibility of writing a script for the sequel, Morgan Creek threaded a few ideas together and commissioned a script. Ward wasn't happy with it, and Chris Chesser referred him to R.J. Stewart, an old friend and established screenwriter who was about to make his mark on television by developing the cultish *Xena: Warrior Princess* series.

Stewart jettisoned essentially everything from the original script and developed the idea of the players coming back the season after the events of *Major League* and struggling with their sudden success.

Ward and Stewart presented the basic story, subplots, and new characters to Morgan Creek in early 1993, and the wheels began turning. Ward had never planned to direct the sequel, but a little more than a month before filming began, he changed his mind.

"The more I thought about it," he says, "the more I felt like I couldn't let somebody else go off and make a movie with my characters."

Already worn out from wrapping up writing and directing *The Program*, a drama about big-time college football, Ward rushed into pre-production on *Major League II*.

"It was a very hectic, intense pre-production," he says. "It helped that I had already made a *Major League* movie, but it was just tough trying to get everything done. We were behind the eight ball from the beginning and were always playing catch-up."

In addition, it was a completely different production with a completely different team. Chesser had never had sequel rights built into his contract for the first *Major League*, and he was busy working on a movie in Canada, with another on deck. After producing the hit comedy *City Slickers* and then *Rookie of the Year* and *Angels in the Outfield*, Irby Smith had retired from full-time production work. Joe Roth had become the chairman of 20th Century Fox and was about to take the same role at Walt Disney Studios.

This time there was no Mirage development, so no Sydney Pollack, and Mark Rosenberg had died of a sudden heart attack the previous year. But the new team had aligned the stars, signing most of the primary actors from the original, albeit with subdued enthusiasm.

"On the first one, I read the script and thought it was gold," Bernsen says. "On this one, it was, 'OK, we're making another *Major League*,' rather than that we were working with a great script."

More problems emerged just before shooting began when Stewart was laid up with a kidney stone, forcing Ward to step in to do some last-minute script work when he was already tied up with a harried pre-production. There just wasn't time to get everything right, and even with Stewart on the set between hospital visits, they wound up rewriting portions of the script on the fly—not the ideal way to make a movie.

Naturally, the first priority of the script was to capture the spirit of what everyone had liked about the original.

Fresh from their triumph, the Indians find themselves ill-prepared to pick up where they left off as the predictable factors of arrogance, injury, age, and lack of hunger set in. Jake Taylor calls it quits as a player and becomes a coach. Roger Dorn, who has bought the team from Rachel Phelps, also has retired. Willie Mays Hayes is more focused on nurturing a movie career and hitting home runs than stealing bases. Pedro Cerrano has given up Jobu for Buddha, but his pacifism adversely affects his game. Most notably, Rick Vaughn reinvents himself. Trading the thick glasses for contacts and his crazy haircut for a neat coif, Vaughn dumps his "Wild Thing" image and blazing fastball for a more mature, career-oriented persona and a series of more esoteric, less-effective pitches.

There are also new players with new problems. Rube Baker is a backup catcher who can't throw the ball back to the pitcher without reciting model profiles from an issue of *Playboy*. Overly intense Japanese outfielder Isuro Tanaka—a last-minute addition to the script—provides spark but has a propensity for knocking himself unconscious running into the outfield wall. Finally, the new nemesis comes from within the ranks: superstar catcher Jack Parkman, whom the Indians sign as a free agent. But after antagonizing everyone in the Cleveland clubhouse, Parkman is traded to the rival White Sox because of the team's poor financial state.

Things unfold predictably, with the Indians slogging through the first half of the season, led by Vaughn, who lands in the bullpen after several shellackings. Reconnecting with an old flame from his carefree days (a subplot intended to stand in for the Jake/Lynn storyline of the first film), he begins to find himself and turn the corner, but can never quite get there.

After infighting and strife, things turn around for the Indians at the film's midpoint. Dorn is forced to sell the team back to Phelps, whose sole mission now is revenge, her plot for moving the team apparently abandoned. Affected by all the stress, Lou Brown suffers a heart attack that knocks him out of action, and he asks Taylor to take over managing duties. Finally, the Indians find the magic of the previous season and put it all together. They charge to another division title and reach the postseason, where they face Parkman and the White Sox.

The Tribe charges to a commanding three-game lead in the American League Championship Series and is one win away from the World Series when—prompted by Phelps's psychological tinkering—they fall apart.

Chicago wins the next three to set up a decisive Game Seven in Cleveland. Just as in the playoff with the Yankees in the original movie, each character steps up to contribute in the climactic game, with Cerrano again hitting a dramatic go-ahead homer in the eighth. Vaughn is then called upon to close it out in the ninth.

He emerges from the bullpen to his "Wild Thing" anthem with his hair chopped and wearing the thick black glasses and leather vest from the first movie, having finally found himself. He promptly strikes out Parkman on three pitches (faster than the three he threw in the climax of the original), and the Indians are headed to the Fall Classic as credits roll.

While a bit predictable, the sequel didn't have many other story avenues to choose from. "It would have been hard to do the underdog thing again," Ward says. "In retrospect, we might have been able to do it more because of how long we'd waited, but we couldn't do the whole Rachel Phelps thing again in the same way. It sort of took the same direction as the third *Rocky*, after he won."

Another mistake, in retrospect, was roping Wild Thing into a romantic subplot. "We couldn't quite get that to work," Ward admits. "In a way, it felt like something from another movie. I think people didn't really want him in a significant relationship. That's not really Wild Thing."

While tactically they were on shaky ground from the get-go, the actual process of making the film was as enjoyable as the first. The band was back together, and everybody was having a good time.

"It was actually more fun making the sequel than the first one," Bernsen says. "The first one was seriously down to business. By the time we got to the second one, it was, *All right, we're rock-and-roll stars—let's take the stage.*"

But there was also less enthusiasm.

"I wasn't as excited about it because David didn't write it," Sheen says. "You could feel it. I wasn't in shape, and midway through the movie I was out smoking cigarettes."

With lessons learned from the first movie, shooting the baseball action went a little quicker the second time, and production was relatively smooth. Ward even dropped in a ghost from the first movie by adding the "Yellowstone" joke that had been cut from the original into a scene between Vaughn and his would-be girlfriend in the only sequence of the movie shot in Cleveland. "So many people thought they'd seen it that I decided I'd better actually use it," he laughs.

Evidenced by its PG rating, *Major League II* was far more tame in its language, with barely a third as many profanities. Even before Stewart began writing the script, he was instructed to include less swearing to allow the movie to stay within PG boundaries.

"Jim [Robinson] kept talking about all the fathers who couldn't take their sons to the first movie because of the R rating," Ward says. "They wanted a PG rating, so there was an effort to tone down the profanity. I think that took away some of the edge of it. It just wasn't quite as in-your-face as the first one."

With the toned-down profanity came far more subdued humor, and some felt the two elements went together.

"The vital mistake was they made it PG," Corbin Bernsen says. "It took out some of the reality. The first one just felt real. You take that stuff out of the second one, and it adds to the lack of success. I agree with it conceptually, but in that movie it needs to be there, and when you take it out, it doesn't feel real. Quite frankly, I think you lost more audience because it's not there."

Bob Uecker's Harry Doyle contributions, so vital to the first film, weren't quite as sharp, and the addition of Randy Quaid (best known as Clark Griswold's buffoonish cousin Eddie in the *National Lampoon's Vacation* films) as a bellicose heckler did little more than overshadow the whip-smart contributions of the established bleacher Greek chorus.

In the end, *Major League II* felt very different from its predecessor—a bad sign for a film that essentially set out to match the original. Although it brought back most of the recognizable faces, a notable absence was Wesley Snipes, who didn't reprise the role of Willie Mays Hayes.

Right after he'd heard the sequel was ready to go, Bernsen was on the 20th Century Fox lot where he shot *L.A. Law* and spotted Wesley Snipes. Bernsen ran up to him to say hello.

"Hey, man, we're doing *Major League II*!" he said. "Isn't this great?"

Snipes, who had just starred in consecutive hits *New Jack City*, *White Men Can't Jump*, and *Passenger 57*, looked at him coldly and asked, "You're going to do that shit, man?"

Bernsen's eyebrows rose slightly. "C'mon, man," he said. "It's gonna be fun."

"Nah, man," Snipes replied. "Not me."

Bernsen was both surprised and disappointed. *How quickly we forget*, he thought. *He must be a star now.*

"My recollection of that period is that I was busy," Snipes says. "I think it came around at a time when I had a chance to do another project and the other project was better for me. I could play a lead role versus a co-starring role. So I gotta go with the lead role."

To this day, Snipes has never seen *Major League II*.

Up-and-coming Omar Epps, who had worked with Ward in *The Program*, was cast in his place, and, like Snipes, used the role as a springboard to a successful career.

A less noticeable recasting was done for the city of Milwaukee, which had played an effective Cleveland in the original movie. The sequel was filmed primarily in Baltimore, with gorgeous new Camden Yards standing in as Cleveland Stadium in what might have been the funniest joke in the movie.

Although news of the sequel prompted excitement (in Cleveland, if nowhere else), expectations were understandably subdued. The rule of thumb with sequels—particularly comedies—is that they're rarely as well done as the originals.

"The loosey-goosey energy and joy wasn't really there," says Margaret Whitton, who admitted she wasn't excited to reprise the role of Rachel Phelps.

Sheen agrees: "Not to disrespect anybody who was involved, because there were a lot of good performances and a lot of hard work, but there's only one *Major League*. Period, the end."

Naturally, *Major League II* didn't receive much critical praise. *The Plain Dealer*, which glowed about the original when many other reviews were lukewarm, noted that the second film "wears sequel fever like a rash," and called it "a full-length comedy that offers sitcom-sized jokes."

Roger Ebert was less diplomatic: "The humor is so predictable, forced, and awkward that the actors sometimes seem like helpless bystanders." And the *New York Times* brought down the hammer: "There has rarely been such a steep and strange decline between a movie and its sequel as the one between the fast, silly original and the dismal, boring *Major League II*."

"Some of the criticism I accept," Stewart says, "but some of it pissed me off. A lot of the reviews said, 'Isn't this just like the first *Major League*? Aren't they just going for the pennant again?' Well, what are they supposed to do? Take out the guns of Navarone or something? It's a movie about a baseball team."

Major League II struggled at the box office. It beat the competition when it opened that Easter weekend, drawing slightly more than $7 million, but pulled down a modest total of $30.6 million for its entire domestic run. Despite playing on more than 500 additional screens and earning more per ticket, *Major League II* made $19 million less than *Major League*. It still was profitable after collecting nearly $10 million in Japan, where Sheen was still a big draw, and Takaaki Ishibashi, who played Tanaka, was one of the country's biggest television stars.

"The movie was more jokes and less heart," Ward says. "I think that's why it wasn't as good a movie and why it didn't do as well. People just didn't hook into it emotionally the same way as they did the first one."

The reviews and initial impressions certainly played major roles in *Major League II*'s struggles, but, in Cleveland at least, another factor likely dampened enthusiasm for the sequel right off the bat.

Just over 48 hours after *Major League II* had its premiere at the Palace Theater in Cleveland's Playhouse Square, Jacobs Field opened its gates for the first time for a Saturday-afternoon exhibition between the Indians and Pittsburgh Pirates.

Essentially all of the buzz around Cleveland that early spring was about the new ballpark and the bold new era the Indians franchise was about to embark on. With a core of young players on the verge of developing into stars and the celebrated signings of free-agent pitcher Dennis Martinez and slugger Eddie Murray, the

Indians were instant contenders. And with the much-ballyhooed "wild-card" playoff format that allowed twice as many teams to reach the postseason, it appeared the Indians' ship had finally come in.

They had a new home, new uniforms, and a new outlook. Their fans didn't need *Major League* in quite the same way anymore. Like teenagers opting to go to a party with friends instead of staying home for a movie night with mom and dad, they no longer leaned on the fictional vision of the Indians as a contender. Thanks to the new ballpark and the new landscape of Major League Baseball, they'd finally become one.

"The reality of the Indians had changed quite a bit," Ward says. "They weren't seen as the same sort of underdog team. I think that had something to do with it."

In retrospect, the original film was Cleveland's Mary Poppins: It served its purpose, got long-suffering fans through a troubled time, and now that all was well, it was ready to be whisked away by the west wind.

In other words, it wasn't the right time to trot out a sequel. Had *Major League II* been released a year or two earlier, when the Indians' bright new future was still on the distant horizon and the window of successful "sequel-ability" was still open, it likely would have done better, or at least been welcomed with more enthusiasm than it was on the doorstep of the Jacobs Field era. As it is, it still holds a special place on the DVD shelves of many fans of the original, like a photo of a relative who's not exactly the family's favorite.

And for Tribe fans, there was little time to dwell on a disappointing sequel because, before their eyes, the pennant-fever montages of both films had suddenly become real.

•   •   •

After a slow start, the '94 Indians caught fire in May and surged into first place with a 10-game winning streak in mid-June. They won a franchise-record 18 straight in their new home, which was now rocking with 40,000-plus in the stands for every game. The lonely nights at Cleveland Stadium were quickly becoming a distant memory. The Tribe was neck-and-neck in a tight division race with the White Sox as a new rivalry emerged, giving *Major League II* credit for a prescient glimpse into the future.

Then the players went on strike in mid-August, wiping out the remainder of the season. It was heartbreaking and difficult to get over. But 1995 made up for it.

The Indians picked up where they had left off, then found another gear, cruising to a 100-44 record and their first postseason appearance in 41 years. No longer were the Indians the plucky overachievers comparable to their *Major League* counterparts. They were a behemoth out to avenge four decades of abuse.

"It was nice to see the Indians get good and to feel that, in a way, we were a good-luck charm for them," Ward says.

The weekend after they clinched the division title, Chris Chesser came to Cleveland to visit Sister Mary Assumpta. As they strolled around town, Chesser was amazed by how many people were proudly wearing Indians gear.

"I can't believe it," he said, astonished. "It's just like the movie."

Sister Mary smiled. "No, Chris," she replied, "the movie was so popular because people knew that this is what it would be like if we ever got there."

Still, the allusions were impossible to miss. Once the playoffs began, Tribe fans couldn't help but smile when switching on the NBC television broadcasts of the games to see Harry Doyle himself calling the action. Technically, it was Bob Uecker serving as the color commentator alongside play-by-play man Bob Costas, but Uecker's presence only helped to fuel the imagination and fantastical landscape of this golden turn of events.

"Every time there was a pitch that was way outside," Uecker says, "Bob would say, 'Uke?' And I'd say, 'Juuuust a bit outside.' It went on through the whole series."

Even on the field, there were similarities. In the first game of the Division Series with Boston, the Indians were on the brink of defeat in the 11th inning before Albert Belle smashed a Pedro Cerrano-esque tying homer. Citing Belle's suspension for using a corked bat the year before, the Red Sox asked that the umpires examine Belle's bat, and it was eventually sawed in half by baseball commissioner Bud Selig and found to be cork-free. In the heat of the moment during the game, the irascible (and, this time at least, justified) Belle responded by glaring into the Boston dugout while flexing his right biceps and pointing to it—all of it feeling like a deleted scene from *Major League*.

After sweeping the Red Sox, the Indians stumbled to a two-games-to-one deficit to upstart Seattle in the ALCS, and Belle was out of the lineup with an ankle injury. With the dream season on the verge of collapse, the nervous crowd—wondering whether the '95 Indians were following the same course as their 1954 predecessors—began to perk up when scenes from *Major League* were flashed on Jacobs Field's giant scoreboard prior to Game Four. Then, moments before the first pitch, the Indians' bullpen door popped open and, as X's "Wild Thing" exploded over the speakers, Rick Vaughn came marching out, wearing a vintage 1989 Indians jersey with his name on the back and a fresh chopper haircut.

The remaining tension in the ballpark vanished in a heartbeat as the sellout crowd roared to life in a realistic depiction of the ending of *Major League*. Although technically it was neither Rick Vaughn nor Charlie Sheen—rather, a Sheen impersonator from Dallas—it was exactly what was needed. Tipping his hat and acknowledging the adoring audience as red and blue streamers were blasted into the air, "Vaughn" took the mound and fired a hard ceremonial first pitch that again sent the fans into a state of delirium. Nobody was going to beat the Indians in this kind of an atmosphere. The signature scene Bob DiBiasio had read on that memorable winter day almost eight years earlier had been brought to life.

"It was just awesome," DiBiasio says. "I never would have thought we'd be recreating this someday before a playoff game with 43,000 people."

With Jacobs Field electrified, the Indians crushed the Mariners 7-0 that night.

Ironically, Sheen himself made an unscheduled appearance

at the Jake the following evening when he adapted his trip to see his beloved Cincinnati Reds after they were swept in the National League Championship Series. "The amount of love and Wild Thing shouts and all the stuff on the scoreboard," he recalls. "I just couldn't believe it." With the real Rick Vaughn on hand, the Tribe won Game Five to take a three-games-to-two lead back to Seattle.

Facing intimidating pitcher Randy Johnson in Game Six, the Indians took a wafer-thin 1-0 lead into the seventh, then clinched the game and the pennant on one of the most memorable plays in franchise history. With runners on second and third, a wild pitch by Johnson allowed a run to score, but to the surprise of everyone in the ballpark, speedy Kenny Lofton motored home from second, sliding just beneath the tag of Johnson to make it 3-0 and put the Indians in the clear. In that moment, and in all the replays that followed in the years to come, some would equate Lofton's daring baserunning and evasive slide with Willie Mays Hayes's streak across the plate in *Major League*'s climax.

Although the Indians lost the subsequent World Series to the Atlanta Braves, the most memorable period in team history had begun. Throughout it all, *Major League* hovered in the background like a friendly specter, coming to the forefront again when the Indians and Yankees met in the postseason for the first time two years later.

New York, the defending world champions, took a two-games-to-one lead in the best-of-five Division Series and was four outs away from eliminating the Indians and advancing to the ALCS. This time it was Sandy Alomar who took on the robes of Pedro Cerrano, belting a dramatic game-tying homer, and—just as in the movie—the Indians won in the ninth when an infield hit scored their center fielder from second base. For good measure, the final score was 3-2, the same as in the final game of *Major League*. En masse, the similarities were notably conspicuous.

"There were times I thought this was crazy," Ward says. "I couldn't believe this was happening."

The Tribe closed out the Yankees with a spirited triumph the following evening, then stunned heavily favored Baltimore in six games to advance to their second Fall Classic in three years. That autumn evening of their Game Six triumph, in the champagne-soaked clubhouse at Camden Yards (which had served as the Indians' home park in *Major League II*), Cleveland general manager John Hart stepped up onto a makeshift stage to accept the American League championship trophy, then was pulled aside for a live interview with FOX broadcaster Chip Caray. It had been an exciting series with a myriad of storylines woven throughout, yet Caray's first question for Hart was perhaps more appropriate: "We've seen *Major League I*, we've seen *Major League II*—is this kind of finish *Major League III*?"

Little did anyone watching know that *Major League III* was already on its way.

*   *   *

The following April, four years after the first sequel was released, *Major League: Back to the Minors* premiered. And virtually nobody was excited about it.

Ward heard about it in an afterthought phone call from Morgan Creek.

"They said, 'You're probably not going to want to do this but we just want to make sure,'" he says. "And I said, 'You're right—I'm not going to want to do this. Why are *you* doing this?'"

They were making another *Major League* movie without Charlie Sheen, without Tom Berenger, and without the Indians. From Ward's—and basically planet Earth's—point of view, it made little sense.

"How is this *Major League*?" Ward wonders. "I thought this was just idiocy. It was an ill-conceived notion from the beginning."

From its oxymoronic title to its B-list cast, *Back to the Minors* unapologetically had no connection to either of the first two movies other than to unnecessarily shoehorn in a handful of the franchise's characters and actors. It focused on a minor-league team called the Buzz, an affiliate of the Minnesota Twins, which are now owned by Roger Dorn (who'd apparently whipped up enough capital to purchase another big-league team after owning the Indians for a disastrous 44 minutes in *Major League II*).

An aging pitcher (played by Scott Bakula as a poor man's Tom Berenger) decides to hang it up as a player and is brought in to manage the club, which is peppered with the same kind of quirky misfits introduced in the original films. Pedro Cerrano and Rube Baker, apparently at the tail end of their once-promising careers, are somehow on the team, and midway through the movie, Isuro Tanaka, the Japanese sensation from *Major League II*, joins the Buzz when the team bus stops by a miniature golf course (in a plot hole as ridiculous as it sounds).

Worst of all, Harry Doyle inexplicably winds up as the radio announcer for the Buzz, with Bob Uecker taking on the role for a third time. But evidently Doyle left all his wit and humor in Cleveland, and his scenes—arguably the best parts of the first two movies—were painfully unfunny and made *Back to the Minors* worse than it already was.

What little story there is, crammed between the threadbare baseball gags, centers on the Buzz challenging the parent-club Twins to a game and ultimately beating them in a meaningless exhibition that brings no resolution to any of the cardboard characters or hackneyed subplots.

"The joke . . . that the long-hapless Cleveland Indians actually become contenders has been decisively outdated," the *Los Angeles Times* review noted. "Now, in its third installment, the *Major League* series itself is the joke."

By any standard, it was a complete dumpster fire: an obviously desperate attempt to squeeze another payday out of the franchise. It didn't fool anybody. As it turned out, the only notoriety *Back to the Minors* earned was for posting one of the worst opening weekends in the history of cinema. Playing on more screens than either of the first two *Major League* films, *Back to the Minors* tallied just over $2 million in its first three days, ranking as the fourth-worst opening ever for an American film playing on more than

2,000 screens. It went on to total an embarrassing $3.5 million in its short-lived run. Although the original two installments hadn't been box-office sensations, *Back to the Minors* managed to bring in just 11 percent of *Major League II*'s total and only 6 percent of that of the original.

"It was an experiment," Jim Robinson says, "and it wasn't worth our while."

Bob Uecker was a bit more succinct. "*Major League III* sucked," he says. "I guess you can use it for skeet shooting."

Ward couldn't bring himself to see it in the theater but finally gave in several months later and watched it on an airplane ("That thing was on airplanes the day we finished it," Uecker quips).

"I just sat there with my mouth open the whole time," Ward says. "I was flabbergasted. Not even from judging the quality of the movie as much as how they could call this *Major League*. This has nothing to do with *Major League*. This team that looks like bumble bees? What the hell *is* this?"

"I think it was a way of saying *Major League* is not about the Indians," Bernsen says. "That *Major League* was about underdogs. You could put it in Little League, you could put it anywhere you wanted."

But for many, even those who weren't Tribe fans, *Major League* *was* about the Indians. To try to turn it into an assembly-line franchise was a colossal mistake. More harmful than its financial infamy was how the sequel sullied *Major League*'s good name.

"I wasn't a big fan of *II* or *III*," Bob DiBiasio says, speaking for the vast majority of fans of the original. "Actually, I almost got a little angry about them, as if it tainted a little bit of what we thought was something really special and fun."

At the same time, the reality of *Back to the Minors* was akin to being a celebrity who's mocked on *Saturday Night Live*—it's the moment you know you've made it. "This little sports movie wound up having two sequels," DiBiasio adds. "That alone speaks to how it grabs people."

●　　　●　　　●

Glowing in this new era where the longtime doormat had become a perennial contender, the Indians went on to four more playoff appearances in the next 10 years, finishing among the top three in home attendance in the American League for seven straight seasons. "When I arrived, the Indians were best known nationally as the inspiration for the movie *Major League*," the Tribe's star shortstop Omar Vizquel wrote in his 2002 autobiography. "When I first headed to Cleveland, the movie didn't seem all that fictional. Now we can look at it and laugh."

As *Major League* approached its 20th anniversary, the Indians' title run tapered off, and they quickly fell back into the familiar role of a franchise in perpetual rebuilding mode. Consequently, this rediscovered sense of frustration and isolation created a new appreciation for the film in Cleveland, and a powerful nostalgia factor began to kick in.

Soon the Indians began to shift from subtle acknowledgment of *Major League* to official partnership. And the movie that no one wanted to make about a team no one wanted to watch began to establish an unexpected but enduring legacy.

EXTRAS . . .

How the three *Major League* movies fared at the box office . . .

	Release Date	Open Wknd	Dom. Total	Screens	Rank/ Year
Major League	4/7/89	$8.8 mil	$49.8 mil	1,615	26th
Major League II	4/1/94	$7 mil	$30.6 mil	2,167	45th
Major League: Back to the Minors	4/17/98	$2.1 mil	$3.6 mil	2,322	165th

12

Making Hearts Sing

When Rick Vaughn marched to the mound from the bullpen with X's cover of "Wild Thing" blaring over the speakers as the crowd went bananas, *Major League* officially entered into the lifeblood of pop culture.

Not only was it the most famous scene of the movie, it was one of the most recognizable sequences of any sports film ever made. Macho, witty, suspenseful, and a bit inspiring all at once, Vaughn's walk ensured that—for better or worse—everybody who saw the film would remember it. Even the original song, which had stood tall on its own for more than 20 years, now has a new meaning. "I think when most people hear that song," Chelcie Ross says, "they immediately associate it with Charlie coming out of the bullpen."

While the staging and magnitude were original, like most other aspects of the story, the seeds were based in reality. Theme songs for relief pitchers in their home ballparks can be traced back to the dawn of relief pitchers themselves. After relievers slowly became an accepted part of the game in the 1950s, by the early 1960s, ballpark organists began to note the arrival of a familiar face from the bullpen by playing recognizable tunes. But even then it was more about being cute than any attempt to fire up the pitcher or intimidate the opposing batters.

It's believed that the first time it happened was in Minnesota in 1963, when Twins reliever (and, coincidentally, former Indian) Bill Dailey took the field as the organist noodled the homonym-inspired "Won't You Come Home, Bill Bailey?" Whether his success led to the playing of the song or vice versa, Dailey collected 21 saves that year, with a 1.99 ERA.

Naturally, it couldn't be considered a trend until New York decided it was cool. When reliever Sparky Lyle was traded to the Yankees in 1972, team PR director Marty Appel came up with the idea of playing "Pomp and Circumstance" when Lyle entered a game, suggesting that everyone in the ballpark was about to witness something special. But Lyle, who'd collect a league-high 35 saves that year, thought it put too much pressure on himself, rather than on his opponents, and quickly put a stop to it. The bar was lowered a bit over at Shea Stadium when the Mets started playing an Irish jig when goofball reliever Tug McGraw took the field in the late 1960s and early 1970s.

Fittingly, one of the templates for the Wild Thing character also had his own entrance music. Al Hrabosky—the "Mad Hungarian"—would take the mound as "Hungarian Rhapsody No. 2" played over the speakers, which served as a fitting prelude to his generally ominous, occasionally frenzied antics on the mound.

But that was pretty much it until *Major League* turned one of baseball's more mundane aspects into an adrenaline-pumping community experience. A new pitcher jogging to the mound—once a great reason to hit the men's room—now became the kind of thing you eagerly waited eight innings for. Post–"Wild Thing," theme songs became the norm, particularly for closers. Often fitting with the slightly unstable, there's-a-decent-chance-I-might-kill-you nature of their on-field personas, closers began coordinating with their clubs' PR departments to ensure that certain songs would be played when they took the field.

Within a few years, nearly every closer had a theme song, and while their entrances were never quite as dramatic as Rick Vaughn's, they served their purpose: to jack up the entering pitcher, rouse the home crowd, and give the opposing batters a little psychological static to try to tune out.

Few of the selections were memorable, but in a few cases, tune and talent merged and became hallmark, almost trademark moments. Most notably for baseball's top two all-time save leaders, both of whom wound up with harsh heavy-metal cacophonies as their intimidating anthems. In each case, the song was thrust upon the pitcher involuntarily. But each stuck.

In the middle of an incredible 53-save season in 1998, San Diego Padres closer Trevor Hoffman began coming out to AC/DC's ominous "Hell's Bells" and Padres fans quickly embraced it. Following Hoffman's lead, a year later the Yankee Stadium sound crew began playing "Enter Sandman" by Metallica whenever Mariano Rivera took the field for the ninth. Although Rivera didn't pick the song and didn't particularly care for it, it became his musical emblem, so much so that the Yankees announced that when Rivera eventually retired (which he finally did, at the end of the 2013 season), they'd retire the song as well, vowing never again to play it at Yankee Stadium.

It would be difficult to argue that Hoffman or Rivera or any of the countless other relievers who emulated Wild Thing were better pitchers because they had a theme song blaring over the sound system when they took the field. But not only was life imitating art (after art mildly imitated life), it added a bit of theatricality to baseball that it both needed and embraced as it fought to keep up with the ever-growing popularity of football, which had theatricality in its DNA.

Baseball needed a little Hollywood. And Hollywood provided it.

* * *

Just as *Major League* changed the scene for big-league closers, it turned Sister Mary Assumpta's world upside down.

Although she's on screen for less than 10 seconds, after the movie was released, she went from novelty to full-blown celebrity. She'd notice people staring at her with quizzical expressions in airports, on the street, even at Walt Disney World before they finally came up and asked, "Aren't you the nun from *Major League*?"

After the Indians reached the postseason in 1995, a Cleveland television station created a segment featuring her, called "Tribe Habit." She then got a call from CBS in New York asking her to be its national correspondent for the World Series, and the network sent her to spring training the following year for segments to be featured on *CBS This Morning*. *People* magazine and *Catholic Digest* published features about her, and Upper Deck issued a Sister Mary Assumpta baseball card.

In 2005, she was honored by the Indians when she threw out the first pitch at a Tribe game on her 60th birthday. To her surprise, in the third inning, she was led onto one of the dugouts and 20,000 fans sang "Happy Birthday" to her. Five years later, the Baseball Reliquary—a nonprofit organization dedicated to building an appreciation for baseball as part of American culture—presented her with their National Hilda Award, named after Brooklyn Dodgers superfan Hilda Chester, for her lifelong dedication to the game.

Along the way, Sister Mary parlayed all the attention into helping those in need and eventually created a modest dessert empire. Inspired by Paul Newman's "Newman's Own" line of salad dressings and popcorn, in 2002 she began sharing her baking prowess (which Indians ballplayers had known about for years) with the rest of the world when she started giving cookies to those who offered donations to the Jennings Center. The response was so big that she started a small business the following year, launching the "Nun Better" line of cookies. Customers could call in orders for pickup and eventually place orders online and have them shipped anywhere in the world. Of course, it was all done for charity, as volunteers baked up to two tons of cookies per year in the convent kitchen.

The hard work she put into the cookies actually put her on the disabled list in 2009, when she needed rotator cuff surgery after cranking out cookie dough from an industrial mixer through a busy Christmas season.

Sister Mary was back in the news in the spring of 2013 when she decided to leave the order to follow a calling to work full-time with the Sacred Art of Living, a ministry for the dying in Oregon. As word spread and she returned to Cleveland for the dispensation of her vows, Sister Mary—now returning to her given name, Maryhelen Zabas—was bombarded with phone calls and emails from well-wishers.

More than two decades after her theatrical debut, she remains the quintessential Tribe fan. Then and now, her cameo in *Major League* not only serves as a cute homage, but it sprinkled just the right amount of Cleveland flavor into the film—not unlike powdered sugar atop a Nun Better cookie.

* * *

Jobu, meanwhile, simply vanished.

After quick cameos in *Major League II* and *Back to the Minors* (he grudgingly appeared in the latter because, as the joke went, he initially refused to work in a minor-league film), nobody seemed to know what had happened to him.

All kinds of crazy rumors and urban myths spread over the years. He'd been stolen from the set. He had been broken and thrown away, or smuggled out of the country and into the possession of a third-world dictator who loved the movie.

JOBU SIMPLY VANISHED. NOBODY SEEMED TO KNOW WHAT HAD HAPPENED TO HIM.

For years, nobody knew exactly where he'd disappeared to, and he became the holy grail of sports relics and the subject of a nationwide manhunt, with fans patiently following leads for years in an attempt to track him down.

David Ward didn't have him, Dennis Haysbert didn't have him, and neither Paramount nor Morgan Creek had a record of him in their prop storage.

Meanwhile, Ward found himself answering all kinds of questions about the tiny voodoo icon. When people spoke with him about *Major League*, they'd invariably ask about Jobu—where he was and what he was doing, as if he were a real person. Even stranger, Ward would receive phone calls out of the blue from people offering to buy Jobu. One man offered $5,000 and would be doubly disappointed to find out that Ward not only didn't have him, but he had no idea who did. In the meantime, Jobu's legacy continued to grow, as he appeared on t-shirts and gained his own Facebook page and Twitter account.

As it turned out, Jobu's actual fate was far less interesting than the rumors. He had taken up residence on a staffer's desk at the Morgan Creek offices. Brian Robinson, son of company co-founder Jim Robinson, eventually inherited the figurine and has been the caretaker ever since. On the rare occasions when he takes Jobu out into the world for a special screening of the film, for example, Jobu becomes the center of attention, and Robinson has been offered as much as $35,000 for him.

Today, Jobu—a bit battered but decidedly unbowed—sits on a piano at Robinson's home, his cigar still planted firmly in his mouth and his bottle of rum resting beside him, daring anyone to take a drink.

•   •   •

For as much as they adore *Major League* and take pride in it, Clevelanders are forced to relive two painful memories each time they watch it. Perhaps without even realizing it, stomachs begin to cramp in the second scene of the film, when Rachel Phelps outlines her nefarious plan.

"It's hardly a whim," she snarls, cold and emotionless, to Charlie Donovan. "Miami's offered to build us a new stadium."

Six years later, another city would make an eerily similar offer to the owner of another Cleveland team, promising a tailor-made, $200 million stadium.

Phelps continues: "62,000 capacity, 45 VIP boxes . . ."

The real-life team was promised a 70,000-seat palace with 108 luxury boxes and 7,500 club seats capable of clearing an annual profit of $30 million.

In the shooting script, Phelps goes even further into detail: "No rent for the first million at the gate. Plus a $12 million media guarantee, 45 percent of the concession gross, all of the parking, and they pick up the stadium operations costs."

The actual stadium was promised rent-free, along with all proceeds from parking, concessions, and advertising signage, plus permission to charge $80 million in seat-license fees.

"No other franchise in baseball can match that deal."

The city of Baltimore not only matched it when wooing Art Modell and the Cleveland Browns six years after *Major League*, but exceeded it. In retrospect, it's as if Rachel Phelps were the Ghost of Christmas Yet To Come, warning Cleveland—and the entire sports world—of what lay ahead.

While the potential of the Indians moving had always loomed as a depressingly genuine possibility until Jacobs Field was built, the beloved Browns pulling up stakes had never seemed within the realm of reality.

But in November of 1995—a week after the Indians appeared in their first World Series in 41 years—Modell became a real-life version of Rachel Phelps, suddenly ripping the team away from Cleveland for a sweeter deal in Baltimore, darkly mirroring the offer Phelps received from Miami in *Major League*.

David Ward admits that the similarities crossed his mind at the time. To this day, most Cleveland fans still cringe when Phelps joyously rattles off the details of Miami's sweetheart deal, envisioning the golden parachute Modell was offered, then strapped on. It's a moment that—albeit unintentionally—still irritates perpetually tender scar tissue.

Major League is a double-edged sword in other ways. Online columnist Will Leitch conjectured that the film's success and endurance "might have secured the Indians' place in the public consciousness as a sadder franchise than it really is."

Even the franchise's wild success of the 1990s, which included an incredible 455-game sellout streak, takes a back seat to the durability of the film, which allows the Indians' reputation as a perpetual loser to persevere.

But to be fair, even in their glory years, the Indians kept kicking that can down the street. As if to rub salt in the wound, two years after the Browns moved, the Indians came within two outs of snapping their world-title drought after a magical postseason run. On the brink of both a cosmic balancing of the scales and a civic catharsis 50 years in the making, Cleveland saw it all thwarted by the obnoxiously undeserving Florida Marlins, who somehow had captured a championship in just their fifth year of existence. It was as though the Indians had been defeated by the team that Phelps had wanted to create in South Florida.

Nevertheless, *Major League* does more to heal the untreated wounds and ease the eternal suffering of Clevelanders than it does to open new sores.

·   ·   ·

Take the way the movie helped turn a spring snowstorm into a party.

An April baseball game in Cleveland getting cancelled because of wintery conditions isn't unusual. But what happened to the Indians' home opener in 2007—and more important, what happened next—was something else again.

After three days of snow wiped out their first two scheduled home games, the Indians were forced to play their home opener against the Los Angeles Angels in Milwaukee under the protective roof of Miller Park. Ticket prices were slashed to entice Wisconsin natives to witness the novelty, and, as was the case for one memorable weekend in the summer of 1988 at County Stadium, a larger-than-expected crowd of more than 19,000 showed up. In order to make it feel more like a Tribe home game—while simultaneously paying tribute to Milwaukee's role in *Major League*—X's "Wild Thing" was blared over the speakers as Cleveland closer Joe Borowski jogged onto the field in the ninth inning.

"I wasn't expecting to hear 'Wild Thing,'" Indians manager Eric Wedge said later after Borowski shakily closed out a Tribe victory. "But I should have expected it here."

Two weeks later—not long before a DirecTV commercial hit

the airwaves featuring Charlie Sheen reprising his role as Wild Thing—the Indians had their first official *Major League*–related giveaway. Each fan attending a Wednesday-night game at Jacobs Field received a pair of replica plastic "Wild Thing" glasses. Organized in partnership with Paramount, it was primarily designed to promote the "Wild Thing" special edition DVD of the movie that had been released that month. Copies of the DVD were given away as prizes to fans answering *Major League* trivia questions throughout the game as the evening became an unofficial tribute to the film—like the decision to subtly include Wild Thing–style glasses on one of the Indians' new racing hot dog mascots the following year.

The next year brought the team's first "official" tribute.

In June 2009, commemorating *Major League*'s 20th anniversary, the Indians wore 1988-replica uniforms for a mid-June game, the same style as in the original two *Major League* films. Afterward, fans were invited to stay in the park for a screening of an edited version of the film on the once-Jacobs-now-Progressive Field scoreboard. The evening was a undeniable hit at the gate. That year, the Indians averaged 21,000 fans per home game. That night, they drew just under 32,000—one of their best turnouts of the season.

Two nights later came "*Major League* Monday," coinciding with one of the most popular giveaways in team history. Negotiation and development began 11 months before, first with Paramount, then with Charlie Sheen, and the result was a well-crafted Rick Vaughn bobblehead figure in full windup, wearing cap and uniform with the trademark haircut and, of course, his thick black glasses.

"I couldn't believe it," Sheen says. "That was really an honor. I was so upset I couldn't be there."

The bobblehead drew a massive media buzz, not just in Cleveland, but across the nation, drawing mentions on MSNBC, CNN, and several other networks. Because of the excitement, ESPN picked up that night's Indians-Brewers game as its national-game telecast, which fittingly began with Bob Uecker, in town to broadcast the game for the Brewers, throwing out the first pitch. The location of that pitch came as no surprise. "If I hadn't thrown it way outside," Uecker says, "they probably would have gotten on my ass."

Just as had been the case the previous Saturday, the response was clear. Although the Indians were wallowing in last place in the middle of a 97-loss campaign, one of the largest weeknight crowds of the season filed through the turnstiles at Progressive Field. Many came from outside Cleveland, from as far away as New York, Chicago, and even Canada to get their hands on a Wild Thing bobblehead, which today generally sells for more than $100 on eBay. To cap it off, one of the Vaughn bobbleheads was donated to the Baseball Hall of Fame in Cooperstown, where it's proudly displayed alongside other artifacts from the game's rich history.

More tribute bobbleheads were produced and given away to commemorate the 25th anniversary of the film in 2014. Both the Indians' single- and double-A affiliates hosted *Major League*–themed nights and gave away, respectively, a Jobu bobblehead and a Jake Taylor "bobbleknees" figure, along with other gimmicks, such as randomly placing red tags under ballpark seats, "Hats for Bats" golf-head covers, and Willie Mays Hayes races.

These quirky soirees, combined with a bacchanalia of retrospective articles and videos over the years, demonstrated that even after a quarter-century through a dramatically changing baseball landscape, *Major League*'s effervescent influence was as potent as ever.

•   •   •

Rick Vaughn being enshrined in Cooperstown (sort of, anyway) wasn't the only occasion when the impact of *Major League* began to blur fantasy and reality.

To Charlie Sheen, at least, Vaughn was a real player. One of his most cherished possessions is the hat he wore in the movie, which he keeps in a glass case in his home, along with the baseball he used for the film's climactic strikeout. He has searched for years for the glove he used, which he gave to a young Milwaukee native who played a batboy after the filming was completed.

Sheen's shrine seems fitting for the character that personifies the essence of the film. "Wild Thing became the iconic character," David Ward says. "He's one of those characters who, for whatever reason, the public takes to their hearts, and they wind up signifying something in the culture. You can't always put your finger on it, but they live on and just seem to speak to generation after generation."

Another of those is Lou Brown. The day after the news broke that James Gammon, who'd portrayed Brown in *Major League* and its sequel, had died of cancer in 2010, the Indians put an image of Gammon on the Progressive Field scoreboard prior to a game, and the park paused for a moment of silence. Anyone who didn't know better would have assumed the Indians and their fans were paying respect for a beloved former manager, which, in a way, they were.

Just as Lou Brown is almost considered a real person, the *Major League* Indians team has achieved an almost mythic place in the team's history. Fictional though it might be, it holds the same status in the minds of many Cleveland fans as the Red Sox's "Impossible Dream" of 1967 and the "Miracle Mets" of 1969 do for their passionate fan bases. It was, as longtime beat writer Paul Hoynes wrote in 2003, "the movie that taught Cleveland it was all right to love the Indians again."

The line between fact and fable became even less distinct in 2014 when Topps produced a special line of baseball cards featuring the players from the film in the Topps 1989 card format. Beckett Publications, the voice of the sports collectibles industry, could barely contain its excitement when it announced the news, proclaiming: "Lou Brown would be proud."

As would have the man who brought Lou Brown to life.

Although Gammon had played dozens of roles in his four-decade acting career, his performance as Lou Brown was invariably mentioned in the first sentence of his obituaries. At his memorial service, his Lou Brown jersey was displayed prominently beside the podium. "It was his all-time favorite movie," Nancy Gammon says. "He loved the role of Lou Brown."

. . .

"IT WAS HIS ALL-TIME FAVORITE MOVIE. HE LOVED THE ROLE OF LOU BROWN."

Just as Charlie Sheen loved the role of the Wild Thing.

In the spring of 2011, Sheen drew a sellout crowd in downtown Cleveland during a 20-city tour for his one-man show, "My Violent Torpedo of Truth/Defeat is Not an Option."

Launched after he was fired from the popular television series *Two and a Half Men* following a public pissing match with creator Chuck Lorre, the tour started inauspiciously in Detroit, when Sheen was booed off the stage. But it was a completely different story in his adopted hometown three days later.

"Cleveland," Sheen remembers, "was a warm hug."

Appropriately, the show began (albeit 20 minutes late) with a solo electric guitar rendition of "Wild Thing," and Sheen took the stage at the State Theater (just across the street from the site of *Major League*'s premiere 22 years earlier) wearing a vintage Rick Vaughn Indians jersey and thick-rimmed black glasses. The crowd went bonkers, offering a roaring standing ovation that lasted several minutes. When it finally abated, Sheen was genuinely humbled. "People," he told the audience, "that was better than coming out of the bullpen in *Major League*."

Later that summer, both Sheen and *Major League* were again the talk of Cleveland when *Sports Illustrated* published a loving seven-page retrospective on the movie, which only seemed fitting because more and more often, references to the film were occurring outside Cleveland.

In 2011, Toronto pitcher Jo-Jo Reyes tried to turn around a rough start by chopping his hair into the zig-zag Rick Vaughn style. Two months later, Tampa Bay star slugger Evan Longoria—not even a pitcher, mind you—did the same.

That same year, the Vancouver Canadians—the Blue Jays' single-A affiliate—created a commercial mirroring the American Express ad in *Major League* in an attempt to get hockey fans to give their team a look. "Just because we don't eat, drink, and breathe hockey, nobody recognizes us," one of the players explains, "not even in our own hometown." The video became an Internet sensation and marked the beginning of a trend, as a handful of other minor-league and college teams filmed their own parodies of the commercial to increase ticket sales.

Major League was once again an ongoing topic of discussion throughout 2013, starting with another pair of film-related giveaways. In July, the Lake County Captains—the Indians' Class A farm team—handed out bobbleheads of the team mascot that paid tribute to songwriter Randy Newman, inducted into Cleveland's Rock and Roll Hall of Fame that year. At the press of a button, the bobblehead figure played "Burn On," Newman's Cleveland ballad inserted at the beginning of *Major League*. And Newman admitted that had the induction ceremony been held in Cleveland rather than Los Angeles, he would have played the song at his induction.

A week later, just down the road in Akron, the Tribe's double-A affiliate hosted a "Roger Dorn Night." Corbin Bernsen was in attendance, coinciding with the distribution of a Roger Dorn snow globe, which Bernsen designed. And finally, in the midst of a September drive to the playoffs, an improved Indians team stirred another *Major League* memory.

As a prank on relief pitcher Cody Allen, nicknamed "Chicken Al," his teammates somehow got a live chicken, dressed it in a cape adorned with the block C Indians logo, and brought it onto the field for batting practice. Instantly labeled the team's "Rally Chicken," the joke quickly spread through social media and national newscasts.

It didn't take long for somebody to connect the dots.

"More than two decades after fictional Indians outfielder Pedro Cerrano wanted to sacrifice a live chicken to get more power before a big game in the movie *Major League*, Cleveland finally got its live chicken," reporter Mark Emery wrote in his game story for MLB.com. "In the movie, of course, Cerrano's teammates made a compromise by bringing in a bucket of KFC. The real Indians went all out . . ."

Just as for Cerrano, the chicken paid off. The Indians scored four runs in the first inning that night and won a key game over Baltimore. But even if they hadn't, manager Terry Francona insisted the chicken wouldn't have wound up as dinner. Or, for that matter, a voodoo sacrifice.

As it turned out, the rally chicken sparked one of the greatest chapters in team history as the Indians, eerily mirroring the movie, caught fire down the stretch, winning 20 of their last 25 games—including their last 10—to capture a spot in the postseason. In a season defined by constant pontifications about poor attendance and fan support, the ballpark was packed on an October night for a one-game playoff. Naturally, it also didn't go unnoticed that the 2013 Tribe's 92-70 record was identical to the one posted by the team in *Major League*.

You just can't make this stuff up.

.   .   .

Despite the theory that *Bull Durham* was more attuned to a player's point of view, *Major League* has made as big an impact on players as it has fans. From the moment of its release, when it was praised by members of the Cleveland Indians at the world premiere, ballplayers—and certainly not just Cleveland ballplayers—have embraced the film and watched it time and again. It plays endlessly on clubhouse televisions, and DVDs are passed around and inserted into laptops on long flights.

"They know every line," Bob Uecker marvels. "When I walk into the clubhouse, they're watching it and they'll holler at me, 'Uke, you're on again!' I'll sit there with them and laugh, and they ask me to say the lines before they come up."

"What really resonated and spoke to people, not just with the public but with actual ballplayers themselves, was that they finally got to see what their experiences in spring training were like, what their first year in The Show was like. What a lot of the banter is like," Sheen reflects. "I think it gave everybody a sense of what it felt like, looked like, and sounded like in those private moments before you step between the lines."

"*Major League* exposed all the personal shit that these guys don't want you to see," Bernsen says. "I think that's why players like it. So many baseball players came up to me and said, 'Man, that's exactly what it's like. You're exactly right on.'"

> "SO MANY BASEBALL PLAYERS CAME UP TO ME AND SAID, 'MAN, THAT'S EXACTLY WHAT IT'S LIKE. YOU'RE EXACTLY RIGHT ON.'"

Chelcie Ross can testify to that, as well. Two years after the film's release, the Chicago White Sox invited him to a game at the new Comiskey Park. As he hung out in the clubhouse and dugout during batting practice, he was approached by multiple players, including Frank Thomas and Robin Ventura, who spouted lines from the movie and told him how much they'd enjoyed it. Although it was the jokes that lured them in, Ross felt it was the characters that really made the movie stick.

"I think they probably recognized every one of those characters and situations from some point in their careers," he says. "And they wish that's what they'd said or done."

There are several theories why the movie remains so appealing. Ward's careful casting strategy—ensuring that genuine-looking athletes were selected for the primary characters—played a big part. Steve Yeager's patient training and attention to detail was another vital component. "It really helps the movie that a number of the baseball scenes look really good," Bob DiBiasio says. "It wasn't like the fish out of water that you see in a lot of sports movies. So as a viewer, you don't get distracted by that. You can stay with the character and focus on what's happening."

"That's what I'm so proud of," Sheen says. "When you look at Tim Robbins in *Bull Durham*—he's an amazing actor and I'm a huge fan—they had to shoot him in close-up. And let's not even get into *Fear Strikes Out*. That was a disaster. Great story, great performance, but they had to hide the baseball."

"Major-league players have told me that it was the best baseball movie they'd seen," Yeager says of *Major League*. "They'd say the baseball looked great. I think they also liked the realism inside the clubhouse. The antics that are portrayed in the movie actually go on."

Players' appreciation of the film isn't evident only in the clubhouse and on their electronic tablets, but on their jerseys as well. Before *Major League*, only twice in the history of Major League Baseball had a player worn number 99 on his uniform, as Rick Vaughn did in the movie, and both occasions were less conscious choices than afterthoughts. In the 25 years after the debut of Rick "Wild Thing" Vaughn, 13 more players wore No. 99, seven of them pitchers. Clearly, not all of them chose the number as an homage to *Major League*, but it's safe to say the popularity of the film—and specifically of Charlie Sheen's Rick Vaughn character—opened the door for a jersey number that had heretofore been obscure.

Of this collection of pioneers, none better personified the spirit of Wild Thing better than the first, Mitch Williams.

With an intimidating six-foot-four frame and eventually sporting a mullet of wavy dark hair that spiraled out of the back of his cap, he put so much effort into each pitch he nearly tumbled off the mound after releasing the baseball. Once he did, no one quite knew what would happen. Walking nearly as many batters as he struck out, he set a club record with 36 saves for the Chicago Cubs in 1989, the same year *Major League* hit theaters, and it didn't take much imagination for fans to pin the nickname "Wild Thing" on him. A fan of the movie, Williams soon had the nickname tattooed on his right shoulder.

A year later, the Cubs traded Wild Thing Williams to Philadelphia, where he would etch his mark on baseball history. He became the centerpiece of a ragamuffin '93 Phillies team that stunned baseball by vaulting from a last-place finish in their division the year before into the World Series. Rarely dominant, statistically Williams was fantastic, racking up 43 saves, and further cemented his nickname by switching his uniform number from 28 to 99.

Although Williams said he made the switch in honor of former New York Jets star defensive lineman Mark Gastineau, who wore 99 during his NFL career, it appeared he'd essentially taken the final step toward becoming the real-life Rick Vaughn—and at the same time that *Major League II* was in production, to boot.

It didn't go unnoticed by Charlie Sheen. "I was pissed for years at Mitch Williams and said he never gave me credit," he says. "I finally met him, and he's a really good dude." Ward also found it interesting that Williams never credited the movie for the rise of his persona, but couldn't help but root for the guy and feel his pain when the real-life Wild Thing saga reached its dramatic conclusion.

Just as Sheen's Vaughn encountered continual on-field troubles in the sequel, Williams struggled in the '93 Fall Classic. The problems started in a wild Game Four that saw Philadelphia blow a five-run lead in the eighth inning, with Williams surrendering a pair of two-out, two-RBI hits.

But it was what happened three days later that Williams will always be remembered for, when he came into the ninth inning to attempt to close out a Phillies victory in Game Six that would have tied the series at three games apiece. Instead, he allowed a leadoff walk, then a one-out single before permitting a World Series–winning home run to former Indian Joe Carter in what instantly became one of the most memorable moments in baseball history.

"I have three words," Sheen says. "Karma's a bitch."

Not surprisingly, it symbolized the stark turning point of Williams's career. He was instantly traded and, after fighting through chronic knee problems, endured for another few years. Essentially, his career ended when Carter's bat hit the ball on that Saturday night in the SkyDome in October of 1993. He wound up becoming the only pitcher in the history of Major League Baseball who pitched more than 250 innings and allowed more walks than hits.

He got into broadcasting, eventually hosting a Philadelphia radio show called "Wild Pitch," then landed a spot as an analyst for MLB Network. He continued to embrace his given nickname, even parlaying it into a successful business venture when he launched "Wild Thing Southpaw Salsa." Yet he admits his projected persona might have hurt his reputation at times.

"Be careful of the nickname you might acquire," he warned readers in his 2010 book, cleverly titled *Straight Talk From Wild Thing*. "It can stay with you, and there might be a time you wish you didn't have it. I never minded being called Wild Thing when I played. I don't now. It's kind of how I've become known."

And just as Rick Vaughn's story fueled Mitch Williams's rise, Williams's fall helped sparked the revival of Vaughn's saga.

· · ·

For years, David Ward had been thinking that there might be another *Major League* story to tell. With countless movies from the 1970s and 1980s being rebooted and *Major League*'s popularity continuing to expand in the 21st century, he sensed there might be a window of opportunity to continue the series.

"I'd been thinking about these characters and where they'd be now and thought there'd be a good movie there," Ward explains. "There's also been a long, fallow period for the Indians where they'd sort of fallen back into the doldrums. So the time seemed right."

Morgan Creek agreed and in 2010 commissioned Ward to write a script. It focuses on the current Indians, led by manager Jake Taylor and coaches Pedro Cerrano and Willie Mays Hayes, trying to survive a tight pennant race. Nearing desperation because of key injuries, they bring in Rick Vaughn. He's been out of baseball for years after surrendering a Mitch Williams-esque walk-off home run to lose the World Series and discovers the Indians also have a young phenom pitcher who turns out to be the son Vaughn never knew he had.

With all of the creative elements in place and the principal actors all interested ("But if there's any sliding, they might have to do a rewrite," Snipes laughs), the only hurdle is acquiring the funding, which Ward and Chris Chesser have been attempting to do for years.

"We've sort of had to go out on our own looking for money," Ward says. "It's been very tough. We've been close a couple of times, but so far, we haven't found the *Major League* angel."

As the search continues, the fan base clamors with excitement. "I think they want to finish it off with their own touch," Bob DiBiasio says. "Not many people gave a thumbs-up to *II*, and nobody embraced *III*. They want to finish it the right way because it's their little baby. And I think people would really enjoy it, if they could bring all that together."

"A lot of people are asking, 'When's the next *Major League*?'" Corbin Bernsen says. "And it's the next generation. Kids who watched it with their dads now have their own kids asking, 'When's the next *Major League*?'"

Although it remains to be seen whether the new movie will ever come together, it appears to have karma on its side. After all, the magic from the original not only created a successful, classic film and wove itself into the fabric of baseball, it did something much more lasting and significant.

It saved the team it was based on.

•   •   •

Exactly one year, one month, and one day after *Major League* was released, Cleveland voters went to the polls to determine whether the team the movie championed was worth keeping.

Technically, Cuyahoga County voters would determine whether to approve the aptly named "Gateway" initiative, a 15-year tax on tobacco and alcohol to pay for a new stadium for the Indians, along with a new arena to serve primarily as the home of the National Basketball Association's Cavaliers.

Although building a new arena downtown was a selling point, it wasn't the centerpiece of the issue. The Cavs were currently playing in the barely-15-year-old Richfield Coliseum 20 miles south of Cleveland, which also hosted several major concerts every year, and the Browns weren't a part of the conversation. One way or the other, they would continue to play in Municipal Stadium.

Essentially, the issue put the Indians on trial, along with whatever economic benefits they brought or might bring to the city. Were the issue to pass, the Indians would get a sparkling new ballpark that would enable the team to compete financially and—presumably—finally field a championship-caliber team. Were the issue to fail, Cleveland would undoubtedly lose the Indians.

Baseball commissioner Fay Vincent came to town the week before the election and put it in simple, stark terms: Without a new ballpark, the Indians would be playing in a different city by the end of the 1990s.

Despite this very real, very clear message delivered directly from baseball's mountaintop, it was a close call. At one point on that fateful May evening, the Gateway issue was failing by 10 points. Thanks to a late surge, Gateway passed by a narrow margin: 51.7 percent to 48.3 percent, a difference of slightly more than 13,000 votes—or roughly the average attendance tally for an Indians home game.

The issue passed for many reasons. It had the support of much of the business community, including the mayor and the governor of Ohio. Supporters had also raised nearly $800,000 to promote it, causing opponents to grumble that victory had been bought, rather than won.

But somewhere in the background, never discussed, likely never even imagined, hovers another possibility.

Could *Major League* have made the difference?

"I think it got people on the bandwagon," explains Maryhelen Zabas, the former Sister Mary Assumpta. "It kindled that spark of enthusiasm that the fans needed."

Is it possible that the vision—however comical or unbelievable it might have been—that the popular film provided the year before might have entered the minds of some undecided voters? Could Clevelanders too young to have any firsthand visual imagery of the

Indians' glory years of the 1940s and 1950s have seen the fantasy inherent in *Major League* and more easily imagined what it would be like if Cleveland had a winning baseball team? Could the film—by now available on VHS and just beginning its long, successful run on cable television—have changed a few minds? Or, at the very least, inspired some to vote who otherwise wouldn't have?

"Call it movie magic," Margaret Whitton says. "Somehow the ethos made it possible. It made them perceive themselves differently."

"I would hate to sound egotistical or to take credit for that," Ward says, "but I do think it's plausible. Movies do sometimes function as more than just entertainment."

There's no way to know for sure. But the possibility is there, and the timing alone is intriguing. One spring brings the most exciting thing to happen to the Cleveland Indians in a generation. In the next, the Cleveland Indians are put on trial and found to be (just barely) worth saving.

But perhaps not. If *Major League* had never been made, maybe the outcome of that election wouldn't have been different. But as in any close election, it's always fascinating to examine how otherwise trivial, unanticipated factors make the difference. There are some who believe that the narrow 1976 presidential election between Jimmy Carter and Gerald Ford was affected—perhaps even decided—by the film version of *All the President's Men*. Released during the campaign, the movie dramatically outlined the width and breadth of the corruption of Richard Nixon, whom Ford replaced and then pardoned. If you believe a movie can affect a presidential race, then you must admit that the right movie at the right time could certainly alter a local election.

"*Major League* created a momentum shift," Bernsen says. "When a lot of people get together in a common direction, shit absolutely moves. I would stake my life on it that it was not just a factor [in saving the Indians], but an actual piece of the puzzle. I know it played a part. I guarantee it played a part."

Maybe—just maybe, mind you—*Major League* did more than just entertain long-suffering Indians fans. Perhaps it played a larger role in saving their woebegone franchise and helped pave the way toward the greatest era in franchise history.

"It's gratifying and surreal that after the movie the franchise became so much better and that people started rooting for them based on the movie," Charlie Sheen says. "I think the movie changed how that team was perceived and how they perceived themselves. And they didn't want to let their fans down because of *Major League*."

"IT'S GRATIFYING AND SURREAL THAT AFTER THE MOVIE THE FRANCHISE BECAME SO MUCH BETTER AND PEOPLE STARTED ROOTING FOR THEM."

•   •   •

Although undoubtedly star-crossed, the Cleveland Indians have several hallowed moments in their long history.

But today, the list includes a handful that are completely fictional, like the consequences of drinking Jobu's rum. Harry Doyle's menagerie of one-liners. Jake Taylor winning a division title with a bunt. And of course, Wild Thing walking out of the bullpen to his anthem before an adoring crowd.

A screwball comedy cooked up in the dream world of a long-suffering Indians fan has become part of the epos of the game. It energized viewers, revitalized a misbegotten franchise, and, most important, made us laugh.

"It's a sports classic," Tom Berenger says. "It's one of those movies that each generation comes along and knows it and watches it. It just keeps on living."

"It has something for everybody," agrees Rene Russo. "It was written beautifully and it had a great cast. You usually don't get all of that coming together. It's just one of those films that sort of had it all."

As a result, *Major League*'s popularity has continued to grow and now is a part of the game it portrays genuinely. There are many theories why, but no clear answer.

Corbin Bernsen offers a big-picture theory: "It speaks to the

American dream. The idea of the underdog story is huge. It keeps the flame of the dream alive."

Steve Yeager points to its shelf life. "It's a movie you never get tired of," he says. "It's a vision that never gets old. I think it'll be a hit for another 50 years."

And while many of the people who helped create the film have gone on to long and prosperous careers, there's just something magnetic that draws them back to *Major League*.

"I'm honored to have been a part of it," Charlie Sheen says. "I feel like I was a part of something historic. This is the shit my kids will be proud of."

Nevertheless, the enduring popularity of *Major League* is difficult to define, and the lasting power of its legacy is even harder to understand. Ultimately—relative to the framework of logic—the explanation resides in the same general vicinity of a Rick Vaughn fastball:

Juuuust a bit outside.

EXTRAS . . .

"It's nice that something you've done has become part of popular culture. Once it started, I thought it would go on for a couple of months and they'll move on. The fact that you still hear phrases from *Major League* now really surprises me."—David Ward

•

"You can have movies that have great depth and meaning, but at the end of the day, people like movies that somehow touch the human spirit. I think *Major League* works that way. It doesn't get all the respect of *Bull Durham* or *The Natural*. But when the fans talk about it—the real people, not the critics—it's always on their list."—Corbin Bernsen

•

"I'd been in a few films and TV shows before *Major League*, but I never thought this was going to be what it is. I absolutely never expected people to still associate me with it all these years later . . . People will see me on the street or at the ballpark and quote a Harry Doyle line from the movie. I'll go in the toilet and a guy will say, 'Juuuust a bit outside.' It's really something."—Bob Uecker

Epilogue

AFTER MAJOR LEAGUE...

DAVID WARD: Wrote and directed *King Ralph* (1991) and *The Program* (1993) before directing *Down Periscope* (1996) and writing the screenplay for *Flyboys* (2006). He remains one of the most esteemed "script doctors" in Hollywood, polishing screenplays just before or during production—most notably *The Mask of Zorro* (1998). He has also written pilots for television and a miniseries on the 1906 San Francisco earthquake. Since 2007, he has taught a screenwriting course and mentors graduate directorial students at Chapman University in Orange, California. As he has been since 1954, Ward is perpetually hopeful his Indians will someday deliver a world championship.

CHRIS CHESSER: Continues to work as an independent producer, shepherding such feature films as the animated version of *The Ten Commandments* and the direct-to-video psychological thriller *Bad Day on the Block* starring Charlie Sheen. One of his most notable successes was *The Rundown* in 2003, which starred Dwayne "The Rock" Johnson and was written by *Major League II* screenwriter R.J. Stewart. More recently, he produced the British comedy *Absolutely Anything*, directed by Terry Jones and starring Simon Pegg, Kate Beckinsale, the late Robin Williams, and members of the Monty Python troupe. Sadly, he still roots for the Yankees.

TOM BERENGER: Continued to expand his impressive film career into six decades with memorable roles in the 1990s *Sniper* film series and the Civil War epic *Gettysburg*, then a handful of other films in the following years, most notably *Inception* in 2010. He explored television through guest appearances on *Cheers*, *Law & Order*, and *Ally McBeal*, and recurring roles on *October Road* and *Peacemakers*. In 2012 he won an Emmy for Outstanding Supporting Actor for his work as Jim Vance on the History Channel's miniseries *Hatfields & McCoys*.

CHARLIE SHEEN: Where to begin? Finding his comedic sea legs after *Major League*, Sheen continued working in comedies, including *Hot Shots!*, *Navy Seals*, and the *Scary Movie* sequels. After a series of straight-to-video dramas, he broke into television as the replacement for Michael J. Fox in *Spin City*'s final two seasons, for which he won a Golden Globe. He then landed the starring role in *Two and a Half Men* on CBS in 2003, which quickly became one of the most-watched shows on television.

Fired after a public dispute with show creator Chuck Lorre in 2011, he began a memorable stretch in which he pontificated his thoughts on the world through Twitter and online videos, giving birth to his trademark "Winning!" catchphrase, and launched a one-man comedy tour. In 2012, Sheen landed another lucrative TV deal with the FX Network's *Anger Management*, which concluded its 100-episode run in 2014.

He has struggled with drug and alcohol addictions, broken marriages, accusations of domestic violence, and being named as a client of Hollywood madam Heidi Fleiss. Sheen remains the primary face of *Major League* and continues to emulate his "Wild Thing" persona.

CORBIN BERNSEN: One of the only three lead actors to appear in all three *Major League* films, Bernsen remained a regular cast member on *L.A. Law* until its conclusion in 1994. He has continued to work in films, such as *Kiss Kiss Bang Bang*, and has appeared in numerous television series, including a regular role on *Psych*, which ran for eight seasons. In a nod to *Major League*, Bernsen also appeared with Charlie Sheen in the final episode of *Anger Management* in 2014—playing a character named "Roger" who was the GM of a baseball team. Bernsen has also ventured into producing/directing, founding the production company Home Theater Films, which focuses on family-friendly, faith-based films.

WESLEY SNIPES: Became one of the biggest stars of the 1990s with starring roles in *White Men Can't Jump, Passenger 57, Rising Sun,* and *Demolition Man,* then brought the comic book vampire hunter Blade to life in a trio of successful films. In 2010 he was convicted of income-tax evasion and served a three-year prison sentence before his release in 2013. Snipes picked up where he left off, being cast alongside Sylvester Stallone and Jason Statham in *The Expendables 3.*

DENNIS HAYSBERT: Continued to expand his roles in film and television before landing a regular role on *Now and Again* in 1999, then another breakthrough role as President David Palmer on the highly popular FOX action series *24.* Another leading role on *The Unit* followed, but his impressive television work hasn't earned as much recognition as his stature as the face and voice of Allstate Insurance commercials since 2004. In addition to film and TV roles, he has also branched into voice work.

RENE RUSSO: Became one of the hottest actors of the 1990s, starring beside leading men Mel Gibson (*Lethal Weapon 3 & 4, Ransom*), Clint Eastwood (*In the Line of Fire*), Dustin Hoffman (*Outbreak*), John Travolta (*Get Shorty*), Kevin Costner (*Tin Cup*), Pierce Brosnan (*The Thomas Crown Affair*), and Al Pacino (*Two For the Money*). After a six-year respite from acting, she returned as the title character's mother in *Thor* and its 2013 sequel.

CHELCIE ROSS: After working on *Hoosiers* and *Major League,* he completed his checklist of roles in the trifecta of sports movies by appearing in *Rudy* in 1993, but also appeared in smaller roles in *Basic Instinct, Drag Me to Hell,* and *Trouble With the Curve.* He has also performed in the television series *Chicago Hope, Grey's Anatomy,* and *Mad Men.* Ross is active in the Chicago theater circuit and stays busy with commercial voice work.

MARGARET WHITTON: After several film and television roles in the 1990s, she remained active in the theater and started her own New York–based production company, Tashtego Films. She made her feature-film directing debut with *A Bird in the Air* in 2011 and was executive producer of the documentary *Casting By*, released in 2012.

JAMES GAMMON: His versatile career continued for 20 years following the release of *Major League*, cementing himself as one of the finest character actors in the business. He played dozens of roles in theater—he was nominated for a Tony Award for his work in Sam Shepard's *Buried Child* in 1996—and film (including *Cold Mountain* and *The Iron Giant*). Gammon also appeared on television, most notably as the father of Don Johnson's character in the CBS hit *Nash Bridges* and, ironically, as a Cleveland Indians coach on the World War II drama *Homefront*. He died in 2010 at age 70 of cancer of the adrenal glands and liver.

BOB UECKER: Despite heart surgery in 2010 and a hip replacement in 2013, Uecker remains the radio voice of the Milwaukee Brewers. He also served as color commentator for NBC's national television broadcasts during the 1990s. He was inducted into the National Radio Hall of Fame in 2001 and was presented with the Ford C. Frick Award from the Baseball Hall of Fame in 2003. In 2005, Uecker was added to the Brewers' Ring of Honor to commemorate his 50th year in baseball. A bronze statue of him was erected outside Miller Park in 2012, and another was erected inside the park in 2014.

CHARLES CYPHERS: Following his portrayal as tortured Tribe GM Charlie Donovan, he expanded his work in television, appearing on *Seinfeld*, *Murder One*, *Buffy the Vampire Slayer*, *ER*, *Murder, She Wrote*, and *JAG*. He's also active in the Los Angeles theater community.

STEVE YEAGER: After serving as technical consultant on *Major League II* and *Major League: Back to the Minors*, he became a minor-league coach for the Los Angeles Dodgers in 1999 and later spent three years managing independent-league teams in Long Beach. He then worked in sports radio, returning to the Dodgers in 2012 as catching coach.

PETE VUCKOVICH: Worked as a color commentator for Milwaukee Brewers TV broadcasts for three seasons, then joined the

Pittsburgh Pirates organization in 1992 as a minor-league pitching coordinator. He remained for nearly two decades, serving as the Pirates' pitching coach and in the front office in a variety of roles, including director of player personnel and assistant general manager. He joined the Seattle Mariners as special assistant to the general manager in 2011.

JULIA MILLER: Continued as David Ward's assistant until 1994, working with him on, and appearing in, *Major League II* and *The Program*, then served as an assistant to Bill Nye the Science Guy. After a handful of appearances in films and television series, she spent several years at EMC Corporation in Boston and is now the Director of Operations and New Business Development at Fay Ranches, Inc., in her home state of Montana.

NEIL FLYNN: Following his brief but memorable turn as the foul-mouthed construction worker in *Major League*, he continued to land a wide variety of television and film roles before his breakthrough as The Janitor on the NBC medical comedy *Scrubs* from 2001–2009. He followed that with a starring role in another hit comedy, ABC's *The Middle*.

MARYHELEN ZABAS (SISTER MARY ASSUMPTA): Continued to attend at least 10 Indians games per season while serving as the Mother Superior for the Sisters of the Holy Spirit and working at the Jennings Center for Older Adults. She left the order in 2013 to work at the Sacred Art of Living Center in Bend, Oregon, which is committed to transforming suffering by discovering the sacred in every aspect of living and dying.

JIM ROBINSON: Continued as the president of Morgan Creek Productions, overseeing a highly successful run in the 1990s when the company cranked out *Robin Hood*, *The Last of the Mohicans*, *True Romance*, and *Ace Ventura: Pet Detective*. The company's output has slowed in recent years, particularly after its critically successful, but financially troubled *The Good Shepherd* in 2006.

JOE ROTH: Shortly after the release of *Major League* in 1989, he became the chairman of 20th Century Fox, then served in the same role with Walt Disney Studios from 1994-2000 before founding Revolution Studios. Over that period, he became one of the most influential and powerful men in Hollywood. He has produced nearly 60 films and, in 2007, became part-owner of the Seattle Sounders of Major League Soccer.

SYDNEY POLLACK: Rounded out his career as one of the greatest filmmakers of his era with two more commercial successes as the director of *The Firm* and *The Interpreter* and a handful of hits as a producer, including *The Reader* and *Michael Clayton* (both nominated for Academy Awards for Best Picture). He died of cancer at age 73 in 2008.

JAMES NEWTON HOWARD: Went on to score more than 100 films and television series and become one of the most respected composers in the industry, providing the music for *The Fugitive*, *The Village*, *The Dark Knight*, and *The Hunger Games*, among other credits. He has earned eight Academy Award nominations and won an Emmy for Outstanding Main Title Theme Music for *Gideon's Crossing* in 2001.

MARK ROSENBERG: Following his role as executive producer with *Major League*, he formed his own production company, Spring Creek Productions, which produced *The Fabulous Baker Boys* and *Presumed Innocent*. He died of a heart attack at age 44 on the set of *Flesh and Bone* in 1992.

IRBY SMITH: Produced several other movies, including *City Slickers* and the reboot of *Angels in the Outfield*, and served as executive producer on *Rookie of the Year*. Also co-produced the Disney TV movie-spinoffs *Angels in the Endzone* and *Angels in the Infield* before retiring in 2000.

JULIE BERGMAN-SENDER: Produced several other feature films, including David Ward's *King Ralph*, and served as executive producer on *G.I. Jane* and *Six Days, Seven Nights*. She co-founded Balcony Films, which produces films and documentaries as well as public service and political campaign media, and co-directed the documentary *Harmony*, based on a book written by His Royal Highness Charles Philip Arthur George, Prince of Wales.

TEAM ROSTER

Major League focuses on six primary Indians players: Jake Taylor, Rick Vaughn, Roger Dorn, Pedro Cerrano, Willie Mays Hayes, and Eddie Harris, along with manager Lou Brown. However, several other players and coaches are not only shown, but are given jersey numbers and last names despite most not having any lines of dialogue. Sharp-eyed viewers can round out the fictional Tribe's roster by catching names, numbers, and in some cases, on-field positions sprinkled throughout the movie:

Name	No.	Position; other
Brown, Lou	34	Manager
Bushnell	33	-
Campi	27	-
Cerrano, Pedro	13	RF
Crespi	12	-
Dorn, Roger	24	3B
Friedman, Mitchell	-	Mentioned in fan conversation
Gentry	47	Cut during spring training
Graham	23	1B
Hayes, Willie Mays	00	CF
Harris, Eddie	10	P
Keltner	40	P
Kuntz	21	-
Larson	20	2B
Leach, Pepper	16	Pitching coach
Lindberg	26	-
Malina	-	SS; mentioned in play-by-play
Mosser	44	-
Pearson	28	-
Reaves	39	Bench coach
Reyna	15	SS
Rhoads	41	-
Schindler	45	-
Stocker	37	-
Taylor, Jake	7	C
Temple, Duke	8	Hitting coach
Tomlinson	38	LF
Van Dyke	14	-
Vaughn, Rick	99	P
Ward	30	1B; called "Metcalf" in play-by-play
Winter	49	-

BOX SCORE FOR THE FINAL
GAME OF THE FILM

	1	2	3	4	5	6	7	8	9	R	H	E
New York	0	0	0	0	0	0	2	0	0	2	9	0
Cleveland	0	0	0	0	0	0	2	0	1	3	10	0

New York	AB	R	H	BB	RBI	Cleveland	AB	R	H	BB	RBI
Warburg, rf	5	0	2	0	0	Mays, cf	5	1	1	0	0
Sazlo, cf	5	0	1	0	0	Taylor, c	4	0	2	1	1
Cheevers, 3b	3	0	0	2	0	Dorn, 3b	3	1	2	1	0
Haywood, 1b	3	0	1	2	0	Cerrano, rf	4	1	1	0	2
Williams, lf	4	0	0	0	0	Rhoads, dh	3	0	0	1	0
Springer, 2b	3	1	2	1	0	Metcalf, 1b	4	0	2	0	0
Dinello, ss	4	0	1	0	0	Larson, 2b	4	0	1	0	0
Parks, dh	4	0	0	0	0	Reyna, ss	4	0	1	0	0
Burton, c	4	1	2	0	2	Tomlinson, lf	4	0	0	0	0
Totals	35	2	9	5	2	Totals	35	3	10	3	3

New York	IP	H	R	ER	BB	SO	Cleveland	IP	H	R	ER	BB	SO
Jackson	8.1	8	2	2	3	8	Harris	8.2	9	2	2	5	6
Simpson, L	0*	2	1	1	0	0	Vaughn, W	0.1	0	0	0	0	1

*Pitched to two batters in ninth.

Game Winning RBI—Taylor
E - None. LOB - New York 10, Cleveland 9. HR - Burton, Cerrano. 2B - Sazlo. T - 2:20. A - 75,383.

SCRIPT EXCERPT: FINAL SCENE

It was a labor of love that took more than five years to go from a legal pad to the silver screen, but the results were worth the wait. Here's an excerpt from the final scene of David Ward's original script for *Major League*. We pick up the action with Willie Mays Hayes, the potential winning run, on second base and Jake Taylor coming to bat against Yankee closer Duke Simpson . . .

```
The stadium is really rockin' now. Duke prowls
the mound. Taylor steps out of the box and
flashes a sign to Brown.

                    PEPPER
          What's he doing?

                    BROWN
                 (to himself)
          That's a hell of an idea.

Brown flashes a sign out to Hayes. A hint of a
smile comes over Hayes' face as he dusts himself
off.

Taylor steps back in as Duke gets up on the
rubber. Taylor digs in his back foot, then
points to the left field bleachers ala Babe Ruth.
```

> DOYLE (V.O.)
> What's this? Taylor is pointing to
> the bleachers, calling his shot.

The crowd, electrified by Taylor's gesture,
remains on its feet. Duke stares in at Taylor,
comes to his stretch and then lets go a steaming
fast ball right at Taylor's head. Taylor goes
down in a swirl of dust, the ball missing him
by inches. The stadium explodes with boos, but
as soon as Taylor picks himself up, the crowd
begins to roar again.

Bobby, Vic and Johnny are pounding out a heavy
beat on the tom-toms. Everyone in the stadium
begins to clap in unison with the drums.

Taylor steps back in and once again points to
the bleachers.

> DOYLE (V.O.)
> Taylor points again. Unbelievable.
> They're on their feet here,
> stomping, clapping. C'mon, join in
> wherever you are out there. Let's
> hear you, Cleveland.

THE LONGSHOREMEN

and several of their friends at their bar,
huddled around the radio with the punks and
heavy metal kids we saw before. Slowly they
begin to clap in time with the tom-toms which
are audible on the T.V.

THE BUSINESS EXECUTIVE

at the opera with his wife, a radio earplug in
his ear. His hand taps on his leg in sync with
the tom-toms.

THE TWO KOREAN GROUNDSKEEPERS

beating on their shovels in the bullpen.

LARGE APARTMENT BUILDING

framed against the Cleveland skyline. In several
of the lit windows we see PEOPLE banging things
or clapping.

THE STADIUM AGAIN

Duke gets back on the hill. Getting the sign he
wants, he comes to his stretch, checking Hayes
at second.

As Duke starts his delivery to the plate, we
go to SLOW MOTION. The clapping in the stadium
stops as everyone hushes to watch the pitch.
We...

CUT TO:

THE LONGSHOREMEN, THE BUSINESS EXECUTIVE, THE
GROUNDSKEEPERS AND THE APARTMENT DWELLERS

They've all stopped too in anticipation of the
pitch.

THE STADIUM

Everything from here on will be in SLOW MOTION.
As Duke whips his arm toward the plate, Hayes
takes off for third. Taylor, instead of swinging
away, shortens up on the bat and BUNTS Duke's
pitch down the third base line.

The Yankee THIRD BASEMAN, caught completely
unaware, charges the ball frantically.

TAYLOR

barreling down the line toward first on his sore
legs, giving it everything he's got.

THE THIRD BASEMAN

scooping up the ball barehanded and firing on the
run to first.

TAYLOR

pounding down the line. He strains for the bag
as the Yankee first baseman stretches to his
limit for the throw. Taylor and the ball arrive
at almost the same time. Taylor hits the bag and
then sprawls in the dirt as his knees give out.

The umpire brings up his arms, and spreads them
wide. Safe. Taylor's beaten it.

The first baseman looks up to see something that
strikes fear into his heart across the field.
It's

HAYES

streaking for home, trying to score all the way
from second on a bunt.

The first baseman fires to the plate, as the
catcher positions himself for the throw. Hayes
launches into a flying feet-first slide. The
catcher brings the tag down. Hayes hooks to the
outside, his trailing foot reaching for the
plate.

                    DOYLE (V.O.)
          Hayes is gonna try to score! Here
          comes the throw. He slides. He is...

Hayes' foot catches the corner of the plate. The
umpire puts the palms down and whips them apart.
It's all over, folks.

                    DOYLE
          ...Safe. The Indians win it. The
          Indians win. Oh my God, the Indians
          win it!!

Pandemonium breaks loose in Municipal Stadium.
Everywhere people are hugging and kissing each
other. Bobby, Vic and Johnny are going berserk
in the bleachers. Thelma just sits quietly, a
broad smile on her face. We take

123.

QUICK CUTS

of our other fans. We see

A) THE BUSINESS EXECUTIVE stand up and yell "Yes!" in the middle of
the opera. Several other MEN stand up and express their
excitement as well.

B) THE LONGSHOREMEN whoop it up in their bar - exchanging fives and
hugs with the punkers and heavy metal kids.

C) THE VARIOUS APARTMENT DWELLERS dancing, clapping, yelling out the
windows.

D) THE TWO KOREAN GROUNDSKEEPERS just shaking their heads in
amazement.

E) Elsewhere in the stadium, the joyous exhultation continues
unabated. The crowd pours onto the field as Hayes runs toward
Taylor and literally leaps into his arms.

F) The two spin around throwing their fists in the air.

G) Marano and Harris embrace. Beck gives Vaughn a hug, then steps
back and decks him with a right hand.

H) Beck pulls him to his feet, and they hug again.

I) Up in the stands, Rachel watches all this with tears in her eyes.

J) Taylor starts off the field when he sees something that catches
his eye. Standing by the field rail is Lynn. She holds up her
left hand and smiles. There's no ring on it. Taylor races over to
her as she jumps down from the rail and hugs herself to him. We
hold on the celebration as it swirls all around them, and

ROLL CREDITS
                    THE END

SOURCES

INTERVIEWS

Lisa Beasley, Tom Berenger, Julie Bergman-Sender, Corbin Bernsen, Chris Chesser, Bob DiBiasio, Nancy Gammon, Dennis Haysbert, Julia Miller, Jim Robinson, Bill Rea, Chelcie Ross, Rene Russo, Charlie Sheen, Brian Sienko, Wesley Snipes, R.J. Stewart, David Ward, Margaret Whitton, Bob Uecker, Suzy Vanderbeek-Rea, Steve Yeager, Maryhelen Zabas.

BOOKS

Edelman, Rob. *Great Baseball Films*. New York: Citadel Press, 1994.

Jones, William B. *Classics Illustrated: A Cultural History, 2nd Edition*. Jefferson, NC: McFarland, 2011.

Markusen, Bruce. *The Orlando Cepeda Story*. Houston, TX: Arte Publico Press, 2001.

Pluto, Terry. *The Curse of Rocky Colavito*. NY: Simon & Schuster, 1994.

Silverman, Marty. *Swinging '73*. Guilford, CT: Lyons Press, 2013.

Torry, Jack. *Endless Summers*. South Bend, IN: Diamond Communications, Inc., 1995.

Uecker, Bob, and Mickey Herskowitz. *Catcher in the Wry*. New York: G.P. Putnam's Sons, 1982.

Vizquel, Omar, with Dyer, Bob. *Omar! My Life On and Off the Field*. Cleveland: Gray & Company, 2002.

Williams, Mitch with Darrell Berger. *Straight Talk From Wild Thing*. Chicago: Triumph Books, 2010.

VIDEOS

Charlie Sheen: Bad Boy on the Edge on FYI (The Biography Channel). Air date: 2011.

Charlie Sheen: Born to be Wild on A&E Networks. Air date: 2011.

PERIODICALS

American Cinematographer
Arizona Daily Star
The Atlantic
Classic Rock Magazine
Diversion
Los Angeles Times
Milwaukee Journal
Milwaukee Sentinel
National Post
New York Daily News
New York Magazine
The New York Times
The Pilot
The Plain Dealer
San Diego Union-Tribune

Seattle Times
Slate Magazine
Sports Illustrated
The Sporting News
Sun Newspapers
Sydney Morning Herald
Telegraph
Time
Tucson Citizen
Tucson Lifestyle
TV Guide
USA Today
Variety
Washington Post

WEBSITES

alhrabosky.com
ballparksofbaseball.com
baseballmovie.com
baseball-almanac.com
baseball-reference.com
beckett.com
biographychannel.com
boxoffice.com
boxofficemojo.com
ca.movies.yahoo.com
classicscentral.com
cnsblog.wordpress.com
crh.noaa.gov
didthetribewinlastnight.com
espn.com
filmbug.com
imdb.com
imsbd.com

jenningscenter.org
larrybrownsports.com
mlb.com
morgancreek.com
nesn.com
oldtucson.com
rogerebert.com
sabr.org
slpmode.com
sportsonearth.com
sports.yahoo.com
tcm.com
theclevelandfan.com
voices.yahoo.com
xtheband.com
yardbarker.com
youhitlikeshit.com